U0472455

Treasures for Scholars Worldwide

浙江省档案馆藏
中国旧海关瓯海关税务司与海关总税务司署往来机要函

Semi-official Correspondence Between Wenchow Commissioners and the Inspectorate General of Customs in Zhejiang Provincial Archives

主　　编 | 赵　伐　周彩英

本册编译 | 何习尧

4

GUANGXI NORMAL UNIVERSITY PRESS
广西师范大学出版社
·桂林·

提　要

本册收录了浙江省档案馆藏 1925 年至 1926 年瓯海关税务司与海关总税务司署总税务司及秘书科、总务科、铨叙科、造册处、秘书科等税务司的往来机要函（亦称半官函）。信函如包含有附件，则用符号（）将附件名称列在该信函标题之后。为简化每封信函的标题起见，信函的责任者与受文人只写人名的中文译名，其英文原名、职务、供职单位集中在以下表中列出。

姓名	职务
安格联（F. A. Aglen）	海关总税务司署总税务司
泽礼（J. W. Stephenson）	海关总税务司署代理总税务司
易纨士（A. H. F. Edwardes）	海关总税务司署秘书科税务司 海关总税务司署代理总税务司
福贝士（A. H. Forbes）	海关总税务司署襄办总务科副税务司
贺伦德（G. C. F. Holland）	海关总税务司署铨叙科税务司
卢立基（L. de Luca）	海关总税务司署造册处税务司
魏尔特（S. F. Wright）	海关总税务司署秘书科税务司
来安仕（F. W. Lyons）	海关总税务司署秘书科税务司
克赉乐（S. M. Carlisle）	海关总税务司署秘书科
威立师（C. A. S. Williams）	瓯海关署税务司

续表

姓名	职务
卜郎(I. S. Brown)	瓯海关暂代税务司
裴纳玑(E. Bernadsky)	瓯海关署税务司

Contents
目　录

1925 年

1 月 15 日，威立师致安格联：汇报前一年海关税收再创新高、常关税收减少的原因、监督从杭州返回、道尹变动、监督私留没收的劣等银元、建筑师抵达开始常关总关选址工作、将验货员宿舍续租给亚细亚火油公司、解释为引水员修建住处的必要性、钤子手就日本船只绑架孩童案出庭作证、烧毁鸦片等（S/O 315）（L060-001-0184-096） ………………………… 3

2 月 1 日，威立师致安格联：汇报中国炮舰到港运兵离开、桩标被民船撞坏需加固、已递交外班职员住宅的检查报告、已实施温州到瑞安航道管理暂行章程、已告知监督税务处可能取消对牡蛎壳免征常关税、若本关不再扣留会导致大量劣等银元输入等（S/O 316）（L060-001-0184-098） ………………………… 10

2 月 10 日，安格联致威立师：说明并未收到对华班钤子手的指控并要求公布对旅客货物征税的条例、认为暂时较难阻止监督对 50 里内常关税的截流（S/O）（L060-001-0184-097） …… 15

2 月 16 日，威立师致安格联：汇报当地部队司令官更换、设立与监督定期会晤并准备所议事宜备忘录的机制、认为引水员住处的使用年限将超过 10 年、表扬帮办卜郎撰写的文章、提醒朱金甫和 Coxall 申请调任等事宜（附瓯海关税务司致监督的备忘录、卜郎所撰关于温州的文章）（S/O 317）（L060-001-0184-099） ………………………… 16

3 月 2 日，威立师致安格联：汇报希望维持瓯海关现有引水制度、英领事抵达与当地官员协调亚细亚火油公司修建储油池及瓯海关所购英领事馆地产过户、当地官员更换后给海关工作带来的不便等（S/O 318）（L060-001-0184-101） ………………………… 41

3 月 9 日，安格联致威立师：说明不扣留劣等银元和允许运输劣等银元是两码事、已获悉朱金甫和 Coxall 申请调任、询问卜郎所撰关于温州的文章是否有参考文献（S/O）（L060-001-0184-100） ………………………… 45

3 月 16 日，威立师致安格联：汇报当地未于孙中山逝世后降半旗、认为孙传芳不会真正地臣服于政府、炮舰干扰港口和海关运行、新监督程希文到任、询问是否赞同对乘客行李征税试行章程的修订意见、说明卜郎独立撰写关于温州的文章等（S/O 319）（L060-001-0184-102） …………………………………………………………………………………………… 46

4 月 1 日，威立师致泽礼：汇报已为新任监督发放津贴、监督截流常关税收的情况、与盐务署和邮政局讨论出售关产、验货员 Finch 抵达瓯海关但尚未收到其任命通知（S/O 320）（L060-001-0184-104） …………………………………………………………………………… 50

4 月 13 日，威立师致泽礼：汇报已将职权暂时移交给帮办卜郎并将于次日赴宁波、供事刘谦兴申请调往闽海关、询问监督是否被革职、认为应建议邮政局在租约期满后另寻他处、钤子手 Coxall 将先赴上海完婚再赴岳州关就任等（S/O 321）（L060-001-0184-106） ………… 54

4 月 14 日，泽礼致卜郎：赞许其告知监督炮舰在港口内乱停放若引发事故责任不在海关、若军船不支付引水费后续可婉拒为其提供引水服务（S/O）（L060-001-0184-103） ………… 56

4 月 23 日，泽礼致卜郎：认同其在监督截流常关税收一事上的态度、说明当前无法批准常关总关的建造工程（S/O）（L060-001-0184-105） ………………………………………… 57

4 月 28 日，泽礼致卜郎：拒绝供事刘谦兴调回闽海关的申请、已获悉与邮政局终止房租契约的建议、已获悉钤子手 Coxall 赴沪完婚等（S/O）（L060-001-0184-107） …………………… 58

4 月 29 日，卜郎致泽礼：汇报威立师已离开、关员休假调任情况、痛惜安格联夫人去世、县丞对海关购置英领事馆房产的契据不予盖章并增添额外条款、已提交关于罚没、军火和官用物料的报表、意大利炮舰到港、监督继续截流常关税收、已向监督发放津贴等（S/O 322）（L060-001-0184-108） …………………………………………………………………………… 59

4 月 30 日，泽礼致卜郎：转达总税务司安格联的感谢并通知安格联夫人追悼会的情况（S/O）（L060-001-0184-111） ……………………………………………………………………… 65

5 月 13 日，魏尔特致卜郎：告知已收到其第 322 号半官函（S/O）（L060-001-0184-109） …………………………………………………………………………………………… 66

5 月 13 日，泽礼致裴纳玑：就供事柯呦苹被举报贪污受贿要求调查并汇报（附相关举报信）（S/O）（L060-001-0184-115） ……………………………………………………………… 67

5 月 20 日，裴纳玑致泽礼：汇报已到达瓯海关并拜访当地官员、其女儿患猩红热、中国炮舰“Chu Tai”到达温州、向军方和监督提供浙江沿岸海盗信息等（S/O 323）（L060-001-0184-113） ……………………………………………………………………………………… 69

5 月 26 日，裴纳玑致泽礼：汇报对柯呦苹的指控有名无实（S/O 324）（L060-001-0184-116） …………………………………………………………………………………………… 71

5 月 30 日，裴纳玑致泽礼：汇报应县丞要求更改英领事馆地产租约条款、可能需要请假赴沪看望生病的女儿（S/O 325）（L060-001-0184-118） …………………………………………… 74

6 月 2 日，泽礼致裴纳玑：希望其女尽快康复（S/O）（L060-001-0184-114） ……………… 76

6 月 4 日，裴纳玑致泽礼：汇报监督执意违反规定运出一批缴获的劣等银元（S/O 326）（L060-001-0184-121） ……………………………………………………………………… 77

6 月 5 日，魏尔特致裴纳玑：告知已收到其第 324 号半官函（S/O）（L060-001-0184-117） …… 79

6 月 17 日，泽礼致裴纳玑：指示就当地官员要求瓯海关更改其与英领事馆的租约一事以公文上报、希望裴纳玑女儿尽快康复（S/O）（L060-001-0184-119） …… 80

6 月 17 日，泽礼致裴纳玑：告知若监督执意运往上海的劣等银元是来自福建或广东则须先经得江海关的同意（S/O）（L060-001-0184-122） …… 81

6 月 18 日，裴纳玑致泽礼：汇报由于当地无外国银行可以汇款故将税款存于中国银行、永嘉县议会暂时休会、商会要求不再征收码头捐、劳工游街抗议高米价、监督经沪赴杭时并未携带劣质银币等（S/O 327）（L060-001-0184-124） …… 82

6 月 20 日，裴纳玑致泽礼：汇报当地学生和民众爱国运动详情、当地外国人群体情绪仍稳定（附游行标语和传单、《新瓯潮》刊登的相关电文）（S/O 328）（L060-001-0184-126） … 86

7 月 1 日，裴纳玑致泽礼：汇报已从上海接回病愈的女儿、监督欲运出的劣等银元来自福建和广东（S/O 329）（L060-001-0184-128） …… 93

7 月 6 日，魏尔特致裴纳玑：告知已收到其第 327 号半官函（S/O）（L060-001-0184-125） …… 94

7 月 7 日，泽礼致裴纳玑：告知已要求地方当局保护海关关产及职员的安全（S/O）（L060-001-0184-127） …… 95

7 月 9 日，裴纳玑致泽礼：汇报煽动者散播外国人在洋糖里下毒的谣言、华人传教士尤建人组建独立于外国传教士的教会、宪兵分遣队抵达温州维护治安等（S/O 330）（L060-001-0184-132） …… 96

7 月 10 日，魏尔特致裴纳玑：告知已收到其第 329 号半官函（S/O）（L060-001-0184-129） …… 99

7 月 20 日，裴纳玑致泽礼：汇报学生抵制日货和英货的情况、邮务长训斥私自拆开邮包的学生、得知国内反帝情绪高涨、就租约修改的措辞进行沟通、钤子手 Abramoff 从上海带其亲戚来温州但税务司认为此举不合适等（S/O 331）（L060-001-0184-134） …… 100

7 月 21 日，魏尔特致裴纳玑：告知已收到其第 330 号半官函（S/O）（L060-001-0184-133） …… 104

7 月 28 日，裴纳玑致泽礼：汇报协助安排一位被当地商人骗来但不甘当妾的德国女子登上广济号离开温州、圣道公会自立会成立并脱离外国传教士的控制（S/O 332）（L060-001-0184-136） …… 105

8 月 6 日，裴纳玑致泽礼：汇报收到反对海关虐遇华员会之宣言、请假送其女儿赴青岛上学、当地民众对月食的反应、因当地无外国银行故将税款暂存于中国银行（附中英文反对海关虐遇华员会之宣言）（S/O 333）（L060-001-0184-138） …… 108

8 月 14 日，裴纳玑致泽礼：汇报扣留进口含磷火柴、中国炮舰抵港带来抓获的海盗嫌犯、收到江海关税务司通知上海爆发霍乱及采取的措施、学生缴获并销毁日货和英货、《新瓯潮》刊登文章警告烟商不要贩卖英国和日本的香烟、当地抵制温州卫理公会学校、监督要求提供本港 1911 年至 1924 年的进出口数据等（S/O 334）（L060-001-0184-140） …………………… 128

8 月 17 日，魏尔特致裴纳玑：告知已收到其第 332 号半官函（S/O）（L060-001-0184-137） …………………… 133

8 月 19 日，魏尔特致裴纳玑：告知已收到其第 331 号半官函（S/O）（L060-001-0184-135） …………………… 134

8 月 24 日，泽礼致裴纳玑：要求尽快通过国内银行汇出税款（S/O）（L060-001-0184-139） …………………… 135

8 月 24 日，裴纳玑致泽礼：询问是否需要上报中药缉私的情况、因暂不打算送其女儿赴青岛读书故取消休假申请、就监督邀请其见证熔化没收的劣等银元认为应该拒绝（S/O 335）（L060-001-0184-142） …………………… 136

8 月 25 日，泽礼致裴纳玑：就是否向海关监督提供其索取的数据要求查阅第 2028 号通令（S/O）（L060-001-0184-141） …………………… 138

8 月 29 日，裴纳玑致泽礼：汇报缴获劣等银币详情及与监督沟通如何处理（S/O 336）（L060-001-0184-144） …………………… 139

9 月 7 日，裴纳玑致泽礼：汇报扣留美孚石油公司运往内地但无子口税票或常关文件的煤油及就此事的处理与公司负责人的沟通情况（S/O 337）（L060-001-0184-146） …………………… 142

9 月 8 日，泽礼致裴纳玑：说明中药缉私信息若无实际用处则不必汇报给伦敦办事处、要求就取消申请假期以公文汇报（S/O）（L060-001-0184-143） …………………… 145

9 月 12 日，魏尔特致裴纳玑：告知已收到其第 336 号半官函（S/O）（L060-001-0184-145） …………………… 146

9 月 14 日，裴纳玑致泽礼：汇报从监督处收到缉获劣等银元的奖金、收到信函举报监督占去大部分缉私银、得知宁波爆发霍乱及采取的措施、总巡赖登和帮办柯呦莘表现良好、江心屿上的房产可供高阶外班员工使用等（附对监督的举报信）（S/O 338）（L060-001-0184-148） …………………… 147

9 月 23 日，裴纳玑致泽礼：按照第 1345 号训令的要求汇报本关引水基金的运行情况并请示是否需作调整（S/O 339）（L060-001-0184-150） …………………… 175

9 月 24 日，泽礼致裴纳玑：要求以公文汇报美孚石油公司一案（S/O）（L060-001-0184-147） …………………… 176

10 月 1 日，泽礼致裴纳玑：告知已获悉江心屿上房产的情况（S/O）（L060-001-0184-149） …………………… 177

10 月 5 日，裴纳玑致泽礼：汇报当地电报局员工罢工、学生将疑似英日所产洋糖收缴并倒入河中、教会学校学生减少、美孚石油公司的代表将前来洽谈其煤油被扣一案、调任至滨江关的总巡赖登已离开等（S/O 340）（L060-001-0184-152） …………………… 178

1926 年

1 月 8 日至 1 月 21 日，裴纳玑与安格联、易纨士：就美孚石油公司在浙江开征煤油附加税后使用海关所签发之子口税票的意愿减弱、Li-tai 号轮船遭海盗袭击、部分本地学生南下广州参加黄埔军校作汇报及回复等（S/O 348）（S/O）（L060-001-0185-001） …… 217

1 月 21 日，易纨士致裴纳玑：告知已收到其第 347 号半官函（S/O）（L060-001-0184-173） …… 221

1 月 23 日至 2 月 17 日，裴纳玑与安格联、易纨士：就本地学生散发爱国传单、监督程希文从南京孙传芳处归来作汇报及回复（附相关传单及其译文）（S/O 349）（S/O）（L060-001-0185-002） …… 222

1 月 29 日，安格联致裴纳玑：告知可将空地出租并要求以公文汇报、感谢新年祝福（S/O）（L060-001-0184-171） …… 230

2 月 1 日，裴纳玑致安格联：汇报已将租用前英领事馆房产的年度租金交给监督、请示是否可向帮助海关员工脱险的厘金局员工发放奖金（S/O 350）（L060-001-0185-006） …… 231

2 月 11 日至 3 月 9 日，裴纳玑与安格联、易纨士：就监督关于海关租用前英领事馆房产的契约条款提出的新建议、向监督发放津贴、大公报在当地散发反对日本增兵东北的传单作汇报及回复等（附相关传单译文）（S/O 351）（S/O）（L060-001-0185-008） …… 233

2 月 22 日，泽礼致裴纳玑：要求就按年支付租金一事以公文请示、就可否向厘金局员工发放奖金一事要求参照第 2268 号通令执行（S/O）（L060-001-0185-007） …… 239

2 月 26 日至 3 月 16 日，裴纳玑与安格联、易纨士：就当地商会为防海盗申请警员搜查乘客及警员搜查敷衍了事、商办轮船招商局亦希望租用海关空地建货栈作汇报及回复（S/O 352）（S/O）（L060-001-0185-009） …… 240

3 月 9 日至 3 月 23 日，裴纳玑与安格联、易纨士：就将在与监督商讨后呈告其是否会在古鳌头设卡征税、因人手短缺调往滨江关的帮办柯呦苹暂时无法动身作汇报及回复（S/O 353）（S/O）（L060-001-0185-011） …… 244

3 月 23 日，裴纳玑致安格联：汇报引水新规的实施情况并建议将相关收入妥善支配以备来日所需、本地劳工因米价上涨而暴动示威（S/O 354）（L060-001-0185-012） …… 247

4 月 5 日至 4 月 28 日，裴纳玑与安格联、来安仕：就常关验货员试图阻止商办轮船招商局的轮船违规卸货而被殴打及后续处理作汇报及回复（S/O 355）（S/O）（L060-001-0185-014） …… 251

4 月 14 日，裴纳玑致安格联：汇报拒绝报关行关于在周日和节假日免除特别准单费验货的请愿、请示是否可向救援常关的厘局救火队发放奖励、汇报本地学生爱国运动的情况（附相关传单、标语译文）（S/O 356）（L060-001-0185-015） …… 257

4 月 28 日，裴纳玑致安格联：汇报平阳茶商请愿在瑞安开设海关分卡、就美孚石油公司所需缴罚款的起止日期作请示、《字林西报》所刊“英国进攻中国之计画”一文在当地广泛传播（附相关文章及译文）（S/O 357）（L060-001-0185-017） …… 270

5月5日，安格联致裴纳玑：就引水人薪金要求按新规执行并以公文形式汇报其建议（S/O）（L060-001-0185-013）…… 279

5月8日，裴纳玑致安格联：申请在其长假期间部分时间待在中国（S/O 358）（L060-001-0185-019）…… 280

5月12日至5月27日，裴纳玑与安格联、来安仕：就监督程希文回温州、Soothil一家到访温州情况、本地学生组织京案互援会并举办“五九”雪耻大会作汇报及回复（附学生运动相关传单、宣言书等）（S/O 359）（S/O）（L060-001-0185-021）…… 283

5月21日，安格联致裴纳玑：要求就美孚石油公司罚款案以公文汇报（S/O）（L060-001-0185-018）…… 302

5月21日，裴纳玑致安格联：汇报在Hua Feng号轮船查获走私火柴但经检验其不含磷故委托监督请示税务处是否不予销毁、与监督及其助手就在南门附近查获的铜币如何处置进行沟通（S/O 360）（L060-001-0185-022）…… 303

5月27日，安格联致裴纳玑：询问其休假的详细计划（S/O）（L060-001-0185-020）… 310

6月2日至6月19日，裴纳玑与安格联、来安仕：就为有效管理夹板船而做调查但尚无结果、本地学生无视当局禁止游行示威的规定举行五卅惨案一周年纪念活动作汇报及回复（附相关宣言及传单）（S/O 361）（S/O）（L060-001-0185-024）…… 311

6月9日，安格联致裴纳玑：询问所缴获火柴的最终处理情况、指示将没收的铜钱视为由常关缉获（S/O）（L060-001-0185-023）…… 321

6月11日，裴纳玑致安格联：汇报监督认为关于货物验货及装载的相关投诉短期内无法解决、将于15日开始实行双重报关制度、裴纳玑将申请1年假期、对罚没奖金体系调整的建议（附瓯海关总巡给税务司的备忘录）（S/O 362）（L060-001-0185-025）…… 322

6月15日至6月24日，裴纳玑与安格联、来安仕：就第51号机要通令所要求的信息作汇报及回复（附相关备忘录）（S/O 363）（S/O）（L060-001-0185-027）…… 326

6月21日，裴纳玑致安格联：请示可否向救火队发放奖励、就海关土地出租与商办轮船招商局的沟通情况、将对走私火柴的商人处以罚款（S/O 364）（L060-001-0185-028）…… 332

6月25日，安格联致裴纳玑：赞同其对缉私奖金体系的调整（S/O）（L060-001-0185-026）…… 334

7月2日，易纨士致裴纳玑：要求就可否向救火队发放奖励一事以公文请示（S/O）（L060-001-0185-016）…… 335

7月3日至7月20日，裴纳玑与安格联、来安仕：就裴纳玑请假1月送其女儿赴青岛上学、当地反帝反基督教宣传的情况作汇报及回复（附相关宣传册）（S/O 365）（S/O）（L060-001-0185-031）…… 337

7月12日至7月22日，裴纳玑与安格联、来安仕：就与亚细亚火油公司就对其现有货品暂不执行机制货物新规的沟通情况作汇报及回复（S/O 366）（S/O）（L060-001-0185-033）…… 386

7 月 19 日，贺伦德致裴纳玑：寄送《温州民报》对帮办陈孟礼的指控文章并要求调查后汇报（S/O） …… 390

7 月 15 日，易纨士致裴纳玑：表明无法批准其请假 1 个月（S/O）（L060-001-0185-032） …… 391

7 月 24 日，裴纳玑致易纨士：汇报美孚石油公司将缴纳罚款并随后提出申诉（S/O 367）（L060-001-0185-034） …… 392

8 月 2 日至 8 月 16 日，裴纳玑与易纨士、来安仕：就经调查发现《温州民报》对帮办陈孟礼的指控不实作汇报及回复（附相关报纸文章译文及函件）（S/O 368）（S/O）（L060-001-0185-036） …… 394

8 月 5 日，易纨士致裴纳玑：说明美孚石油公司罚款一案已通过公文处理（S/O）（L060-001-0185-035） …… 401

8 月 9 日至 8 月 19 日，裴纳玑与易纨士、来安仕：就上海和宁波出现霍乱及本港采取的应对措施、几位职员的工作情况和升职推荐、若任命已婚外班员工至瓯海关可收回江心屿上出租的房屋供其居住作汇报及回复（S/O 369）（S/O）（L060-001-0185-037） …… 402

8 月 20 日至 9 月 3 日，裴纳玑与易纨士、来安仕：就温州爆发霍乱已通知临近港口、本月 15 日台风过境并造成较大损失作汇报及回复（S/O 370）（S/O）（L060-001-0185-038） …… 407

9 月 2 日，裴纳玑致易纨士：汇报监督在与商人沟通后建议常关暂时仍沿用特别准单制度、本地霍乱已接近尾声本关一名船夫染病过世、《温州民报》报道本地学生抵制洋人学校等（附相关报道及译文）（S/O 371）（L060-001-0185-039） …… 410

9 月 15 日至 9 月 29 日，裴纳玑与易纨士、福贝士：就监督程希文前往杭州和南京、开始在古鳌头对运货的民船征税、霍乱结束、当地打击海盗的成果作汇报及回复（附当地为结束霍乱而采取的求神仪式记录）（S/O 372）（S/O）（L060-001-0185-041） …… 416

9 月 23 日，易纨士致裴纳玑：同意常关暂时仍沿用特别准单制度至年底（S/O）（L060-001-0185-040） …… 425

9 月 25 日，裴纳玑致易纨士：裴纳玑申请 1 年假期、认为当地夹板船愿意作为民船参与贸易但由于船只受台风破坏严重可能需要等到年底（S/O 373） …… 426

10 月 5 日，易纨士致裴纳玑：通知若其不愿意休假可提出申请（S/O） …… 428

10 月 7 日至 10 月 19 日，裴纳玑与易纨士、魏尔特：就拒绝向洋广局提供进出口数据、当地成立万县惨案后援会作汇报及回复（附《新瓯潮》的相关报道）（S/O 374）（S/O）（L060-001-0185-042） …… 430

10 月 11 日至 10 月 14 日，裴纳玑与卢立基：就密电码的具体条目作询问和回复（S/O）（L060-001-0185-043） …… 437

10 月 16 日至 10 月 28 日，裴纳玑与易纨士、魏尔特：就裴纳玑撤回 1 年休假申请作汇报及回复（S/O 375）（S/O）（L060-001-0185-044） …… 439

10 月 20 日至 10 月 29 日，裴纳玑与易纨士、魏尔特：就浙江政府令驻温警备队要求孙传芳在当地的军队缴械撤离、监督暂不打算返回温州作汇报及回复（S/O 376）（S/O）（L060-001-0185-045） …… 441

10 月 25 日至 11 月 8 日，裴纳玑与易纨士、魏尔特：就得知浙江省长夏超逃离及监督即将返回温州作汇报及回复（附温州道尹与驻温警备队司令的联合声明、当地教会给领事馆的建议信）（S/O 377）（S/O）（L060-001-0185-046） …… 445

11 月 8 日至 11 月 26 日，裴纳玑与易纨士、魏尔特：就驻温警备队司令更换、批准验货员 Finch 事假、调往津海关的钤子手 Abramoff 尚未出发、浙江省烟酒事务局开征洋酒税作汇报及回复（附洋酒税相关规定及译文）（S/O 378）（S/O）（L060-001-0185-047） …… 452

11 月 20 日至 12 月 9 日，裴纳玑与易纨士、魏尔特：就常关职员上交请愿书请求加薪但经劝说后撤回请愿作汇报及回复（S/O 379）（S/O）（L060-001-0185-048） …… 468

11 月 29 日，裴纳玑致安格联：汇报温州实施军管、被扣火柴的物主因未按期复出口导致货品损坏并请愿免征保结费（附相关凭单及请愿书）（S/O 380）（L060-001-0185-049） …… 472

12 月 11 日，裴纳玑致安格联：汇报商办轮船招局暂停上海至温州的航运服务、批准帮办陈孟礼 10 日假期赴沪看牙医（S/O 381）（L060-001-0185-051） …… 480

12 月 23 日至 1927 年 1 月 18 日，裴纳玑与安格联、魏尔特：就由福建撤离来的部队抵达温州引起社会各界恐慌及各方的反应作汇报及回复（S/O 382）（S/O）（L060-001-0185-053） …… 481

12 月 24 日，安格联致裴纳玑：就被扣火柴的物主请愿免征保结费一事表明尚未收到税务处的通知（S/O）（L060-001-0185-050） …… 489

12 月 31 日至 1927 年 1 月 12 日，裴纳玑与安格联、魏尔特：就各国炮舰抵港及军队动向作汇报及回复（S/O 383）（S/O）（L060-001-0185-054） …… 490

1925 年

INDEXED

390

S/O No. 315. Wenchow 15th January, 25.

Dear Sir Francis,

ease of
time Customs
nue.

Although a record Revenue Collection was recorded for Wenchow in 1923, the receipts for last year are higher still by Hk.Tls. 2,302.757, in the case of the Maritime Customs.

ons for
ease of
ve Customs
nue.

There is a decrease of Hk.Tls. 4,839.436 in the Native Customs revenue for last year, as compared with 1923, which is partly due to the preference for shipment in vessels of foreign type during the period of local disturbances. I feel sure, however, that a certain amount of intra 50-li duty is being wrongly diverted by the Superintendent's stations, and I hope some reorganisation of the local Native Customs system may gradually be effected as indicated in my Despatch No. 3833, N.C. No. 345. I have just heard

SIR FRANCIS AGLEN, K. B. E.,

Inspector General of Customs,

P E K I N G.

391

heard that another steam vessel, S.S. "Kuangchi" (光濟), has been put on the Shanghai-Juian run. If we can establish the fact that Juian is within our 50-li radius (vide my Despatch No. 3883, N.C. No. 365), we certainly ought to take it over from the Superintendent, as the Native Customs duty collection there must be rapidly increasing, though there is nothing to show for it, as it is farmed out and kept carefully at the same level in the Superintendent's official reports. The Superintendent has established one Examiner and one Watcher at Kuant'ou, two Watchers at Lilung, and one at Rocky Point, and instructed them to collect duty on everything coming to Wenchow, which is quite wrong and kills our collection at the Head Office. I had a case quite recently when the Superintendent's men at K'anmen had collected duty on goods from T'aichou - not being local products - consigned to Wenchow, i.e. goods

3

592

goods in transit, when this duty should be collected by us at Wenchow. A similar action was reported to you in my despatch No. 3886, N.C. No. 367, and I sincerely hope you will see your way to supporting me in taking a very firm stand against such abuses, which may lead to a general disintegration of the revenue if not speedily checked.

nts of
als.

The local Superintendent of Customs returned from Hangchow on the 21st ultimo. Taoyin Shên Chih-chien (沈致坚) left Wenchow on the 10th instant; it is announced that he has two months leave, but he is not expected back; we exchanged calls before he left; he is replaced by Chang Tsung-hsiang (張宗祥), formerly Chief of the Hangchow Educational Bureau, a young and energetic individual, who called on me on the 12th inst., and informed me that he was going to arrange for some restriction in the exportation of charcoal to Japan

4

393

Japan; he also stated that he had told the China Merchants S.N. Company to put another steamer on the Shanghai-Wenchow run. I returned his call on the following day.

ior Silver
.

In the last two cases of seizure of inferior silver coins the merchants concerned informed me that the Superintendent gave them back 3/10ths and kept the rest for himself without melting! We are not seizing any more, as instructed in your Despatch No. 1292.

rty
ions.

Mr. W.J. Leahy, Architect of the Works Department, arrived here on the 10th instant to study the plans and estimates of the proposed new Native Customs Head Office. As there is no good hotel accommodation I am putting him up, and he will probably remain about ten days. He is doing excellent work, and is most helpful, not only in the Native Custom House question, but also in other property matters I am working on.

I

5

394

I have rented the semi-detached portion of the Examiner's House to the Asiatic Petroleum Company for a further period of three months to the end of March on the same terms as before, viz. the Company agrees to move temporarily into half of the Constable's House, when the repairs and improvements I have recommended officially to you in my Despatch No. 3881 of the 4th ultimo are eventually granted. I should suggest that it would be best for you to withhold your decisions as to the various repairs and structural alterations to Wenchow property until Mr. Leahy has concluded his inspection work, when I will immediately report everything necessary for your final consideration.

Shelter. With reference to your Despatch No. 1294/101,470 (in reply to my Despatch No. 3871), instructing me to report in detail on the subject of Wenchow Pilotage Matters before you decide to sanction

6

345

sanction the expenditure of $250.00 for the construction of a shelter for our Boatmen-pilots at the entrance of the Wenchow river, you asked my predecessor to make a similar report, and he did so very comprehensively in his Despatch No. 3600 of 2nd August, 1921, but I am making you a précis of the rather voluminous correspondence on the matter and reporting again as requested.

I presume you are afraid that this expenditure is not in conformance with the General Pilotage Regulations, but we are quite safe in this respect, as we are not governed by or operating under these Regulations at Wenchow, and I am only asking you to expend a small part of the profits we derive from our own system of pilotage, which is not ordinary pilotage, but merely assistance rendered to shipping in the absence of properly constituted pilots.

...ing Case. With reference to the Kidnapping case referred to in my S/O Letters Nos. 312 and 313,

Mr.

7

Mr. Sia Liang (謝良), 3rd Class (Chinese) Tidewaiter, B, was called upon to give evidence in court, so I allowed him to do so.

-burning. We had a small public opium-burning on the 6th instant.

The Staff are all in excellent health, with the exception of three very aged Boatmen, who ought to be invalided very soon. The shooting is very good this year, and provides the foreign members of the Staff with a healthy recreation which they much enjoy.

Yours truly,

C. A. S. Williams

INDEXED

7988

S/O No. 316. Wenchow 1st February, 25.

Dear Sir Francis,

Movements. The Chinese Gunboat "Chao Wu" applied for a Pilot on the 24th ultimo (China New Year's Day) and arrived in port the following morning, when some 600 of the Fukien troops, who have been holding Wenchow, were taken away. I understand the remainder will also be removed and replaced by troops from Ningpo.

nt Rock On the 25th ultimo the Elephant Rock Beacon, maintained by this Port, was broken by the Junk "Chin Te Shun", which I am holding up as her Laodah declares he is unable to pay for the damage. If at any time the Coast Inspector sends a Surveyor - possibly Mr. T.H. Bülow-Ravens - to chart out the Wenchow 50-li radius, as suggested in my Despatch No. 3883, N.C. No. 365, he might

with

SIR FRANCIS AGLEN, K. B. E.,

Inspector General of Customs,

P E K I N G.

399 2

with advantage consider the advisability of strengthening this Beacon by means of a reinforced concrete foundation, which could not be damaged by vessels out of control or floating debris in the typhoon season. It has come down three times since I have been here, and I am sure we have spent more in repairs than the cost of a substantial foundation.

·s to
›r Staff
ers.

With reference to my last S/O Letter asking you to kindly defer your decision as to the various repairs and alterations to the different Outdoor Staff Quarters until Mr. W.J. Leahy has concluded his inspection work, I have now sent you, in my Despatches Nos. 3893 and 3896, final statements of all necessary work, supported by the Architect's reports, and I am now awaiting your authority so that I can get all the houses in order before certain Staff changes impending in April.

The

3

ow-Juian Launch ations.

The Provisional Regulations for the control of the Wenchow-Juian Canal Launch Traffic proposed in my Despatch No. 3868, and authorised by your Despatch No. 1281/100,962, have been duly issued by the Superintendent and myself after the necessary change in Article IX was effected in consultation with the Coast Inspector.

r-shells.

In accordance with the instructions of your Despatch No. 1221/97,530, I have suggested to the Superintendent that, in view of the decrease in the Native Customs duty collection, the Shui-wu Ch'u might be asked to discontinue the temporary exemption of Native Customs duty on oyster-shells from the 1st July.

or Silver

With reference to your Despatch No. 1292/101,344 instructing me to stop seizing inferior Kuangtung and Fukien silver subsidiary coins, I notice you have not sent a copy of this Despatch

to

451

to any other Ports, so if I allow the merchants to ship the coins as Treasure the Customs at destination will be doubtful as to what treatment to accord. At the same time I do not think that they should be shipped without reporting.

fer of Mr. oxall, 1st Tidewaiter, sted.

In my S/O Letter No. 306 of 1st September I informed you that Mr. P.W. Coxall, 1st Class Tidewaiter, wished to be transferred on account of his approaching marriage, and I was not in favour of moving him as I thought I would be able to provide him with married quarters. In your S/O Letter of 15th October you said that though Mr. Coxall cannot expect a transfer to suit his own tastes, yet his name will be noted for transfer this year if requirements permit. Mr. Coxall is going to be married in April, and I now find that, as the repairs of the Outdoor Quarters are still unattended to and may not be finished in time, the question of housing Mr. Coxall and his wife

wife will probably be more difficult than I anticipated. An unmarried man is preferable in many ways at the present time, so I think on the whole I should recommend Mr. Coxall's transfer in April, and I should be grateful if you can let me know if it can be arranged.

Yours truly,

C. A. S. Williams

INDEXED

INSPECTORATE GENERAL OF CUSTOMS.

/0

PEKING, 10th February 1925

Dear Mr. Williams,

I have duly received your S/O letters Nos.314 and 315 of the 27th December and 15th January. Charges against Chinese Tidewaiter withdrawn: anonymous writer says he has also communicated with I.G. Charges apparently due to strictness of examination of luggage.

He has not communicated with me again. Please see that the rules for payment of duty on goods carried by passengers, which are liable to duty, are given publicity.

Intra 50-li duty diverted by Superintendent's stations: Commissioner hopes that I.G. will support him in taking a very firm stand against such abuses.

I have more important matters on which to make a firm stand and firmer ground to stand on than this which is the old question of rival exchequers. I, of course, will support you in standing up for our rights, but Peking will not support me unless the case is flawless. There is some local spade work to be done, I think.

Yours truly,

F. A. Aglen

B. Williams, Esquire.

WENCHOW.

INDEXED

S/O No. 317. Wenchow 16th Feb., 25.

107

Dear Sir Francis,

ments of cials.

Commander P'êng Tê-ch'üan (彭德銓) left Wenchow for P'inghu (平湖) by the Chinese Gunboat "Chao Wu" on the 5th instant, and Hsia K'uei (夏楒), Chief of the Chuchow Gendarmerie, arrived here on the 8th, and was appointed Commander of the Wenchow and Chuchow forces. Kuo Shao-tsung (郭劭宗), Wenchow and Taichow Salt Inspector, has asked me to put up a French Salt Inspector expected here shortly. The British Consul from Ningpo is also intending to stay with me for a week or two before long.

ar Calls perintendent stoms.

In accordance with the instructions of your S/O Circular No. 45, I arranged to make regular fortnightly calls on the Superintendent every other Saturday at 11 a.m., and I have now initiated the practice of preparing a memorandum in English and

SIR FRANCIS AGLEN, K. B. E.,
Inspector General of Customs,
PEKING.

2

439

and Chinese, on the subjects I discuss with him, and I leave the Chinese version with the Superintendent for study and investigation. I also discuss other less important matters with him as well if necessary. I append, for your information, a copy of the English version of my last memorandum of this nature, which will give you a good idea of my outstanding cases. On the occasion of my visit on the 14th instant, I found the Superintendent very affable, and apparently willing to meet all my suggestions.

of
ner's
.

With reference to the Engineer-in-Chief's comments on my Despatch No. 3893, I think his estimate of 10 years life of the Examiner's House - to which some repairs and alterations are being recommended - is very low, and I feel sure that, if properly repaired, it will last considerably longer than that period.

Mr.

3

405

:iptive
; on
iow.

Mr. I. S. Brown, 4th Assistant, A, on the Staff of this Office, shows an intelligent interest in his work, and has an active mind. I gave him an essay to write recently on the subject of Wenchow, and he turned out a very readable article, a copy of which I append for your notice.

Transfers.

May I venture to remind you that in your S/O Letters of 31st July and 7th October, 1924, you informed me that you had noted the names of Mr. Chü Kam Po (朱金甫), 3rd (Chinese) Assistant, A, and Mr. P. W. Coxall, 1st Class Tidewaiter, for transfer. I mentioned in my last S/O Letter, No. 316, that as Mr. Coxall wants to get married in April, he is anxious to know whether he is likely to be moved this spring or not. Mr. Chü is Cantonese, and cannot get his children educated here, while the place does not suit his wife's health.

Yours truly,

C A S Williams

APPEND NO. 1.

in

Wenchow S/O Letter No. 317/I.G.

MEMO TO SUPERINTENDENT OF 14TH FEBRUARY 1925.

Case No. 1. - Native Customs Duty Collection.

According to the Peace Protocol of 1901 the duty collection of all Native Customs stations within the 50-li area was placed under the control of the Commissioner to be used as security for external loans, and in 1918 the extra 50-li collection was passed through the Commissioner and used as security for internal loans. It was not until 1913, however, that some of the intra 50-li stations were taken over by the Commissioner, viz: the Head Office, Passenger Station, North Gate Station, West Gate Station, South Gate Station, Puchow Station, Chuangyuanchiao Station, Ningtsun Station, North River Barrier, Huichiao Barrier, Shanghtoumen Barrier and Lungwan Barrier. The following places in the 50-li area should also be taken over by the Commissioner as their duty should be used for external loans, viz: Juian, Tungshan, Ch'angch'iao, Tashut'ai, Ch'ili, P'anshih and Kuant'ou. At present, however, it is difficult for many reasons for these stations to be taken over, though perhaps in the future, when a motor launch is supplied and the

47

the staff is enlarged, these stations may be taken over and some of the other 50-li stations closed as they are of little use. It is very important however that all goods consigned to the Wenchow Head Office should pay duty at the Head Office and not at other stations along the river through which they pass. It has been clearly laid down and agreed to by the Shui-wu Ch'u and former Superintendents and Commissioners and notified to the public that no change is to be made in this practice, and duty should only be collected on native products shipped direct from Superintendent's stations to the Head Office, and not on goods in transit; otherwise confusion will be caused and two charges of duty levied on the same cargo. The merchants always pay duty at Wenchow and object to paying in transit. Goods coming to Wenchow by canal should pay duty at Wenchow (vide Letter from Superintendent of the 5th May 1913). As the same time when receipts of duty on passengers' luggage are issued by the Head Office they should be honoured by the Superintendent's stations; these receipts are in English and Chinese and a sample has been sent to Superintendent.

The above matters cannot be quite clearly

understood

understood by the Superintendent as several cases have occurred recently which are evidently due to misunderstanding. It is necessary to come to a definite agreement on these matters, or the duty collection will be very difficult to arrange. In the recent Kuant'ou case the goods were not local products, but were in transit and should have paid at Wenchow. Even the duty was a wrong amount and the goods were wrongly declared. In fact the whole case was wrong and the duty should be refunded by the Kuant'ou Station to the merchant. If goods come through a station in transit to Wenchow it is not practical to send them back to their place of provenance to pay duty. This hinders trade and they should proceed to Wenchow to pay duty. Can the Kuant'ou duty be refunded? The matter has been referred to the I.G. and he prefers me to settle it locally. If it cannot be settled locally it will be taken up by the I.G. with the Shui-wu Ch'u. The same argument applies to the K'anmen case, and the duty should be refunded. Moreover in the K'anmen case the document was issued afterwards and did not accompany the goods. This is very wrong. The duty on the cloth should be refunded. In any case I propose to bring

bring the duty to account. Has the duty on the passengers' luggage been refunded by the Chianghsia Station?

<u>Case No. 2. - Improvement of bunding and communications.</u>

Funds to be supplied by levy of wharfage Dues. The question of the wharfage dues tariff should not be left to the Chamber of Commerce, as this body will never take any action in the matter as it objects to all tariffs on principle. The tariff should be drawn up by the Customs, and I have supplied the Superintendent with all the necessary information so the Superintendent can make the tariff and arrange matters with the Chamber of Commerce.

<u>Case No. 3. - Ground rent of former Consular property.</u>

Has the Magistrate sealed the lease? Everything is all fixed, and the District Assembly has nothing more to do with it. The I.G. wants the lease at once.

<u>Case No. 4. - Asiatic Petroleum Co.'s Oil Tank Installation site.</u>

Some time ago the former Superintendent wrote to

917

to me and said that the Company's site was approved. If this is the case the Regulations ought to be signed by this time and a copy should be sent to me. The question of the pontoon concerns navigation and can be settled later.

Case No. 5. - Seizure of Japanese Torpedo.

In the Superintendent's last letter on this case he said the Shanghai Japanese Consul had been applied to for further funds to cover the Customs usual reward of 4/10ths value. Can this reward now be issued?

Case No. 6. - Temporary exemption of Duty on Oyster-shells.

Oyster-shells are a regular article of trade being required to make lime for building purposes. There is no reason why the exemption should continue indefinitely. The merchants wrote a very cleverly worded petition which excited the pity of the Shui-wu Ch'u which allowed temporary exemption over a year ago.

Case No. 7. - Wenchow-Juian Canal Launch Regulations.

These regulations are working well and I hope there will be less complaints about the mis-management of the launches to the danger of navigation.

141

R E F E R E N C E S .

Case No.	Subject.	To No.	To Date.	From No.	From Date.
1	Native Customs Duty Collection:				
	Hemp Cloth from Kuant'ou.	198	5.Dec. 1924	269	11.Dec. 1924
		210	24. " "	277	20 " "
				283	29 " "
	Native Cloth from K'anmen.	7	9.Jan. 1925	2	5.Jan. 1925
	Duty on Passengers' Luggage.	14	16.Jan. 1925		
2	Improvement of bunding and communications.	8	8.Jan. 1924	302	24.Dec. 1923
		74	15.May "	193	11.Sep. 1924
		153	19.Sep. "		
		165	6.Oct. "		
3	Ground rent of former Consular Property.	122	18.Aug. 1923	223	8.Oct. 1923
		143	27.Sep. "	240	26. " "
		66	26.Apr. 1924	149	26.Jul. 1924
		94	29.June "	282	29.Dec. "
		111	25.July "	14	21.Jan. 1925
		177	28.Oct. "	20	4.Feb. "
		211	24.Dec. "		
		21	5.Feb. 1925		
4	Asiatic Petroleum Co.'s Oil Tank Installation site.	86	23.June 1924	96	20.May 1924
5	Seizure of Japanese Torpedo.	123	11.Aug. 1924	160	11.Aug. 1924
		146	10.Sep. "	197	15.Sep. "
6	Temporary exemption of Duty on Oyster-shells.	202	14.Dec. 1923	300	21.Dec. 1923
		21	17.Jan. 1924	24	19.Jan. 1924
		22	21. " "		
		11	14.Jan. 1925		
7	Wenchow-Juian Canal Launch Regulations.	8	8.Jan. 1925	12	19.Jan. 1925

APPEND NO. 2.

in

Wenchow S/O Letter No. 317/I.G.

412

NOTES ON WENCHOW.

(Prepared by Mr. I.S. Brown, 4th Assistant A)

Geography and History. - Wenchow, properly called Luch'êng (鹿 城), is the chief city of Wenchowfu, in the south-eastern corner of Chekiang. It is situated on the south side of the Ou river, about 20 miles from the mouth; the Custom House is located in latitude 28 deg. 1 min. 30 sec. N., longitude 120 deg. 38 min. 45 sec. E. The city was founded in the fourth century A.D., the exact date being variously given. The name Luch'êng is said to be derived from the fact that soon after the wall was built, deer were in the habit of resorting to its vicinity.

This wall, about 4 miles around, and from 15 to 50 feet high, is built of squared slabs of granite; it has a parapet, a watch tower, and 7 gates, two on each side but the east. It is in good preservation, and a few breaks were recently repaired. Over almost the whole of its circuit, it surmounts low hills, being in some places 200 or 300 feet above the level of the surrounding plain.

Tradition

413

Tradition has it that the founders had the choice of building the wall farther out, down on the plain, permitting expansion, or of building on the circle of hills, with a view to making the city impregnable at the cost of future growth; and chose the latter course. Impregnable the city seems to have been, for its history records no disturbances worth mentioning. From this course of the wall or from the topography of the country - a broad valley surrounded completely by mountains - comes the classical name for the district and river, Ou (甌), a bowl. The highest of the surrounding mountains is the Remarkable Peak of the charts, locally known as Hart Peak, about five miles below the city and across the river; it is about 1,800 feet. Some distance up river is a mountain of 4,000 feet.

From the sea, the Ou is navigable to Wenchow for steamers of draft up to 20 feet, which must, however, make the crossings with the tide well up, and under the direction of pilot. The lower anchorage, just above Hart Peak, is not good, being without shelter and of uncertain depth. That opposite the city proper is good and shows no tendency to fill up. The maximum rise and fall of spring tides is

47

is 18 feet; speed, 3 to 5 knots per hour.

Up stream, the Ou is navigable for small boats for at least 150 miles. From the upper reaches, the portage across to the headwaters of the Ch'ientang river is not long; in this manner Hangchow can be reached. The Nöe Ch'i, or as foreign residents call it, North river, which joins the Ou across from Wenchow, is navigable for small boats 20 miles or so. But perhaps the most important means of transportation is the canals. These form a maze through the city and the whole district, and all traffic is carried on them; there are no pack animals or wheelbarrows. The largest canal runs from Wenchow to Juian (瑞安), 30 miles south, with steam launch service twice daily. From Juian, P'ingyanghsien (平陽縣) on the Fukien border, is easy of access.

Conquest Island (a foreign corruption of the native name Qua Sang (江心), or Heart of the River), is located opposite the city, and has on each end an ancient pagoda, one in good preservation, the other fast going to ruin. According to the Encyclopedia Sinica, the "Island of the two pagodas" was a place of refuge for the Emperor Ti Ping during the time of Kublai Khan, about 1,258. The large Buddhist

temple

45

temple which is the main feature of the island is said to have among its archives original works of Ti Ping and of the celebrated caligrapher, Wang Yu-chün. The quarters of the Customs Tidesurveyor and Examiner (the former British Consulate) are also on the island.

At the mouth of the North River, opposite the city, are two more pagodas, in decayed condition; and outside the South Gate, another which might vie with the Tower of Pisa, for it leans toward the southeast a distance more than half its own diameter, and withstands typhoons in this condition as well. The city is said to contain about thirty temples, besides a large number in and on the surrounding hills.

Up the river about 50 miles is a waterfall known as the Szee Mun Dong, or Rocky Gate, about two hundred and fifty feet high, which is a remarkable sight soon after a heavy rain. About half way to Juian, near the canal, is another fall, perhaps 50 or 60 feet high.

About 30 or 40 miles north of the mouth of the Ou, in Lotsinghsien, is a famous scenic spot called the Yen Tang Shan, or Wild Goose Hills. The

feature

46

feature of the place is the peculiar formation of the rocks, and American visitors have likened it to the Garden of the Gods in Colorado. Two small steam launches which recently have come into operation have made it easier of access than heretofore.

General Considerations. - The population of Wenchow city is estimated at from 80,000 to 100,000, and of the whole hsien at about 200,000. The people are quiet, industrious, peaceful, and courteous to foreigners, although in the early days trouble was several times experienced. The language is a distinct dialect not spoken elsewhere and not intelligible to other Chinese. As with the Ningpo and Shanghai dialect, it is a transition tongue between the Mandarin and the extreme southern dialects, as those of Foochow and Canton. It has eight tones, arranged in two series, an upper and a lower, each having four tones. In many respects the similarity to Mandarin can be traced, but a large part of the colloquial is a patois for which no characters exist. The pronunciation is peculiar among Chinese dialects in that every word ends in a vowel, there being no final consonants, although there are some final liquids. This feature makes the pronunciation of English

extremely

1117

extremely difficult for natives of Wenchow.

There are about 45 white foreign residents, and about 30 true Japanese, with about 25 Formosans. The Japanese are all engaged in trade; the white foreigners are missionaries and members of the Customs. The missions operating in the district are the China Inland Mission, the United Methodist Mission (English), the Seventh Day Adventist Mission (American), and Catholic Fathers and Sisters, of French nationality in the main. Activities extend pretty well over the whole fu.

Schools are maintained by the government and by the missionary societies. Government schools are of primary, and secondary grades, with special normal, commercial, and technical schools. Attendance at the technical school is very small, and the commercial school suffers from indefiniteness of purpose, but does some good work. Perhaps the most promising branch is the normal school. Teachers, in so far as possible, are educated in the English language as well as Chinese, and some are excellent men. The government schools are a great credit for the time they have been at work.

The largest mission school is the Methodist

College

College for boys, with an enrollment of approximately 200, well housed and well taught. The China Inland Mission maintains a school for boys and one for girls, both under foreign supervision, which cover grammar school and a few secondary subjects. The Seventh Day Adventist Mission has a school in which girls spend part of their time making their way by turning out embroidery, cross stitch, etc.

Wenchow people seem to be supporters of education, and literacy is becoming more diffused; also, English and Mandarin, more particularly the latter, are spreading.

Wildfowl shooting at Wenchow is good, as the district is not visited by outside hunters. There are a few snipe and quail; pheasants are not numerous in the vicinity of the city itself, but are said to be more plentiful up river a short distance. Pigeons are numerous. There is no other game.

Health. - Winter temperature seldom gets to the freezing point; summer temperature reaches 95 to 100 Fahrenheit. There is no ice obtainable. Cholera occurs every few years, and is very fatal to natives, but since the early days has not attacked foreigners, although it formerly was very fatal to them. Malaria seems

419

seems prevalent in the district among natives, but foreigners do not suffer from it. Plague has never been known. Dysentery is very widespread in the season, and foreigners suffer from it more or less, but usually not seriously. All the other usual Chinese diseases are found among the native population. Leprosy is rare.

Sanitary conditions are better than in most Chinese cities; the streets are straighter and wider than the average, mostly well paved, and fairly well drained by the canals which parallel many of them.

The United Methodist Mission maintains Blyth Hospital, under the charge of a regularly qualified foreign physician and nurses. The French Sisters have a dispensary, and the Wenchow Hospital is under the charge of foreign-educated Chinese. There are also other smaller dispensaries and hospitals of little standing.

Typhoons visit the port comparatively often, there rarely being a summer without two or three, and do damage in varying amounts; in fact, Wenchow is often regarded as the typhoon center of the Chinese coast.

During the spring months there are variable rains,

4 80

rains, which merge into a marked rainy season in the latter part of May, all of June, and the first part of July. From this time until the end of September, the rains are intermittent, with long stretches of fine weather inclined to predominate. October to December, inclusive, with a kind of hazy Indian summer, is regarded as the best part of the year, while January and February are the "cold" months, with an overcast sky most of the time. While the weather at this time does not get particularly cold, the humidity, lack of sunshine, and piercing northwest wind which prevails, combine to make it a chilly climate when one is not moving about.

One pleasant feature of the Wenchow summers is the unfailing regularity of the sea breeze, which blows daily from the southeast from soon after noon until sundown, but usually falls at night.

On account of the hilly or mountainous nature of the up-river country, and practical absence of any broad valleys, an unusual amount of rainfall in the spring often produces floods, which have terrible consequences. Historic ones are those of 1887 and 1912. An eyewitness* gives the following brief account of the latter:

"The

*J.W. Heywood, Methodist Mission.

421

"The level of the town of Chingdi 40 miles above Wenchow is perhaps forty-five feet above the average level of the river, and the water eventually rose to a height of some forty feet above the city. At first all the people moved into their upper stories, and as the water rose to that point, moved to the roofs. Most of the houses being of brick, the inhabitants were forced to float away on bedsteads or other wooden objects, and those who had no buoyant material at hand were drowned, unless their houses happened to be of wood, in which case they floated away bodily.

"This mass of water full of floating houses and property came down to Wenchow, filling the whole valley, on the north, which is three or four miles wide, and sweeping across it in a wave as high as a one-storey house. One minute one could see a village in the plain; the next minute the houses crumpling up; and the following, an expanse of water full of floating humans and debris. Houses from up river would come floating by with the inhabitants on the roofs, and we would shout encouragement, but were powerless to help them. In fact, one girl from Chingdi was picked up among the islands of the

estuary,

422

estuary, about 30 miles below Wenchow, and about 70 from her home.

"When the water had subsided a bit, a fund was made up for relief, and administered by a committee of Chinese and foreigners."

<u>Trade and Industry</u>. - Wenchow was opened as a treaty port in 1877 under the Chefoo Convention, although there had certainly been clandestine trading by foreign ships for some years before. Trade development, however, has not been up to expectations. In 1882 the total valuation was 468,000 Hk.Tls., which forty years later had become 6,650,000 Hk.Tls. Within the past two years, a remarkable development has been made, as is indicated by the comparative revenue collection, as follows:

Average,	1912-1921,	Hk.Tls.	58,000,
	1922,	"	69,000,
	1923,	"	101,000,
	1924,	"	103,500.

It should be noted that the 1924 figure was attained in spite of military disturbances which practically paralyzed trade during September and October.

This increase seems not to be predominantly due to any one item, but to be spread over the whole

whole list of imports and exports.

The Wenchow district is under intensive cultivation, even to the hilltops, terrace upon terrace, where sweet potatoes and yams are grown, while rice is raised on the plains. Consequently imports of staple foodstuffs are confined to flour and sugar, although the list of food luxuries is a respectable one. Nor is food exported; the Wenchow territory seems to have reached an equilibrium of self-sufficiency. Fish are plentiful, but are all consumed locally.

Imports cover the whole list pretty thoroughly, the principal items being piece goods, kerosene, and dyes. The chief inland towns supplied from Wenchow are Juian and Pingyang, to the south; Chingdi, Chuchow, and Songyang, up the river; Lungchuan and Chingyuen, across the mountains from the above, over in the south-estern part of the province; and Yotsing (乐清), just north of the mouth of the Ou. The inward transit trade, however, is not large, and the outward transit trade is nil.

The following minerals are said to be found in the Wenchow district: coal, at Lingken (岭根); soapstone at Chingdi (青田); alum at Chihch'i (赤溪), near

429

near Pingyang; manganese, quartzite, gypsum, mica, antimony, graphite, molybdenum, and a superior grade of iron pyrites. Attempts at working the coal, molybdenum, and iron have been made and abandoned; soapstone and alum are being worked in quantities at present.

The seven principal exports of Wenchow are kittysols, tea, oranges, charcoal, softwood timber, alum, and eggs. Other important items are lard, tobacco, medicine, mats of straw and coir, and soapstoneware.

The kittysols are locally made on the Japanese pattern, which was adopted some years ago, and a large part of the market is found in Japan. The export in 1924 was $1\frac{1}{3}$ million. Wenchow tea is of fair, but not high, quality; it is mostly exported "unfired", for further treatment in Shanghai; export in 1924, 32,838 piculs. Three kinds of oranges are grown in Wenchow, the important one exported being the Kan-tzu (柑子) or Wenchow bitter orange, a mediumsized orange with a tart and slightly bitter flavor, and a most excellent keeper, as it can be preserved from December to June. Markets, Shanghai and Tientsin. Charcoal and softwood timber come from the

425

the vicinity of Chuchow, 100 miles away, and their export is to be deprecated, as the wood supply is already very slender. The timber goes to Shanghai, the charcoal to Japan. Alum comes by junk from Juian as a shipping point, and is sent to Shanghai for distribution; eggs, both salt and fresh, are said to be transhipped from Shanghai in considerable amounts.

Lard exports originate in the immediate neighborhood of Wenchow; medicinal roots and barks, in the surrounding mountains; mats are woven in the city, largely from tough and pliable grass grown in the swampy sections along the river bank. Soapstone work is done at both Chingdi and Wenchow, and consists of carvings out of stone only, or of the stone of various colors laid into various kinds of wood. There was formerly a large market for this kind of work in Central and South America, and some residents of Chingdi have been all over the world selling it; but the business seems now to be falling off.

Wenchow has at present two regular Shanghai steamers, averaging about four days apart, and three small ones a week, regularly, to Ningpo via Haimen. About fifteen lorchas are regularly engaged in the Wenchow-Shanghai trade. Occasionally ships call from the

426

the south on their way to Shanghai, but very rarely do so going the other way. There are no lorchas running to the south, and aside from one or two small motor vessels, the trade there may be said to be in the hands of junks. The Japanese charcoal trade is taken care of by Japanese steamers coming from Shanghai and returning direct. Practically speaking, the coastwise treaty port trade may be said to be a monopoly of the China Merchants S.N. Co.; other lines have tried to compete and been squeezed out because too small, while the more powerful lines stay away by agreement.

Wenchow has three Chinese newspapers, of which one is soon to be moved to Hangchow; none has a very large number of subscribers. The telephone company has about 230 subscribers. The old electric light plant, for years badly overloaded, has just been replaced with a modern and well-installed plant of German make (A.E.G.). The present number of subscribers is about 5,000, but it is predicted by engineers that the capacity of the plant, 20,000, will all be taken up within five or six years. The current now supplied is 220 volts, alternating.

The principal foreign companies, mostly

represented

477

represented by Chinese Agents, are the Standard Oil Co. of New York, the Texas Company, and the Singer Sewing Machine Co. (American), the Taikoo Sugar Refining Co., the British-American Tobacco Co., and the Asiatic Petroleum Co. (British), the latter now constructing an installation on North River; and the Mitsui Bussan Kaisha and I-wai & Co. (Japanese).

429

S/O No. 318. Wenchow 2nd March, 25.

)

Dear Sir Francis,

.ge. The Coast Inspector, in his Comments on my Despatch No. 3898, is arguing under a fallacy, as he is evidently under the mistaken impression that, judging by present pilotage income, the Wenchow pilots will always have enough to live on. He evidently does not realise that in Wenchow pilots are not required by regular steamers, but only by occasional gunboats and irregular vessels chiefly engaged in the charcoal trade - a trade which will soon fall away, as it is becoming increasingly difficult to obtain supplies of charcoal owing to the wholesale destruction of timber in this district. I foresee, moreover, that, owing to strong local opposition to the exportation of charcoal, the enforcement of prohibition of shipment of this article will eventually be carried through. I strongly advocate the continuation of the present

procedure

SIR FRANCIS AGLEN, K. B. E.,

Inspector General of Customs,

P E K I N G.

2

420

procedure, which has run smoothly for 40 years with no complaints at all. It is neither practical nor just to turn our two best Boatmen adrift and force them to take up an occupation which will not pay them a living wage except under the present abnormal conditions.

nts of
als and
Local

Mr. H.F. Handley-Derry, H.B.M. Consul for Hangchow, Ningpo and Wenchow, arrived on the 26th ultimo, and intends to stay with me for some considerable time, or until he can arrive at a satisfactory settlement of the Asiatic Petroleum Company's Installation Site Agreement, which I gather the Wai-chiao Pu has sanctioned but the local officials still oppose. The Consul is also trying to persuade the Magistrate to seal the lease I have drawn up for the ground rent of the former Consular property, and has told him that i: this cannot be done he is quite willing to rent the ground as before and the Customs can simply pay the rent to the Consul. These two matters

are

are being held up purely and simply because the local authorities hope to be able to squeeze money out of them in some roundabout way. As we have again a complete change of local officials, the old arguments have to be all taken up afresh. I invited the new Taoyin, Commander, and Magistrate to tiffin on the 28th ultimo, and the Consul and Ningpo A.P.C. Agent were also present. I am hoping that we may now be able to do something definite, but unfortunately at this juncture Superintendent Yang Ch'êng-hsiao (楊承孝) - a protegè of the former Commander - was impeached to the provincial authorities by the local gentry, who were very much annoyed because he did not provide the usual number (about 60) of sinecure appointments as his "Advisers" (vide my S/O Letter No. 306 of 1st September, 1924), and he had to clear out on the 27th ultimo in a great hurry. The new Superintendent Ch'êng Hsi-wên (程希文), formerly Secretary of the Civil Governor, has not yet arrived.

4

432

arrived. A new Chief of Police Ma Chên-chung (馬振中) has just been appointed, and his first official action was to force the rickshaw owners to spend $2,000 on additional rickshaw licences, which they did not require, as there are far too many rickshaws already. The new Magistrate also carried out a lucrative arrangement by selling the monopoly of the cargo-boat business, and cargo-boats licenced by the Customs cannot ply without his permission, which is refused unless they belong to the highest bidder for the monopoly. The River Police are also searching passengers' luggage on the steamers and interfering with our work, while the same thing is being done by the Likin people. I have naturally complained about this, but with local administration as it is I see little hope of obtaining any redress at the present time.

Yours truly,

C. A. S. Williams.

INDEXED

INSPECTORATE GENERAL OF CUSTOMS,

S/O

PEKING, 9th March 1925

Dear Mr.Williams,

I have duly received your S/O letters Nos.316 and 317 of the 1st and 16th of February.

Inferior Silver Coins: Commissioner instructed to stop seizing. As copy of despatch has not been sent to other ports, they will be doubtful how to treat on arrival, if Commissioner allows merchants to ship as Treasure.

It is one thing not to seize and confiscate and quite another thing to allow shipment. I can't make instructions of this kind general for very good reasons !

Transfers of Messrs. Coxall and Chü Kam Po recommended.

Noted !

Descriptive Notes on Wenchow, by Mr.Assistant Brown.

Did he write the essay without reference to authorities ? It is quite good but looks to me as if it had been compiled by drawing freely on books of reference !

Yours truly,

F. A. Aglen

[illegible]. Williams, Esquire.

WENCHOW.

INDEXED

473

0 No. 319. Wenchow 16th March, 25.

)

Dear Sir Francis,

f Sun
.

Your telegram instructing me to half-mast the flag from the 12th to 14th instant on account of the death of Sun Yat Sen arrived too late at 12 p.m. on the 14th, and the Superintendent did not transmit any Ch'u instructions in the matter. The Military Governor Sun Chuan-fang will probably not submit entirely to effective government control as long as his arch-enemy Lu Yung-hsiang has any say in political affairs. The flag was not half-masted here.

treatment
ustoms by
.

The Chinese Gunboats are not treating the Customs properly at this port. The Maritime Police Gunboat "Hsin Pao Shun" refused to take up the berth assigned to her, and anchored in the middle of the fairway, thus obstructing the traffic and endangering navigation.

IR FRANCIS AGLEN, K. B. E.,
Inspector General of Customs,
P E K I N G.

2

134

navigation. I informed the Superintendent that gunboats usually conform to the port harbour regulations which are approved by the Chinese and foreign governments, and that if Chinese vessels ignored them the Customs could not be blamed if any accidents to shipping occurred.

The Sloop "Chao Wu" owes us a good deal of pilotage money, and has gone away twice without paying. Query: Shall we continue to accord free pilotage to Chinese Men-of-war ? The foreign Gunboats always pay.

…erintendent.

The new Superintendent Ch'êng Hsi-wên - the <u>fifth</u> in the last couple of years - arrived on the 12th instant. I have exchanged calls with him, and I found him very pleasant. He said he was going to Hangchow in a few days ! I told him I had many matters to discuss with him, and therefore hoped to see him on his return in the near future. Has his appointment by the

Provincial

3

425

Provincial Authorities been approved by the Ch'u ? I have reported his arrival officially, and asked for your telegraphic instructions as regards the issue of his Allowance.

…ion of duty …age.

With reference to my Despatch No. 3899, N.C. No. 370, of 11th ultimo, reporting, by your instructions, on the experimental procedure for collection of duty on passengers' luggage, I should be interested to know whether you approve of the continuation of the procedure with the suggested modification as regards luggage on vessels in the stream; I consider that these vessels should not come under the procedure, which should be strictly confined to luggage on the wharves, or on ships which berth at the wharves.

…tive Notes …how.

In your S/O Letter of the 9th instant, you ask if Mr. Assistant I.S. Brown wrote his descriptive essay on Wenchow (copy sent in my

S/O

4

136

S/O No. 317) without the aid of authorities. I gave him permission to consult the Customs returns, but there are no other books of reference from which he could have obtained much information about this port. He quotes from the Encyclopaedia Sinica on Wenchow, but this authority only has an article of a few lines, and, moreover, contains certain errors which he has corrected. The essay is original for the most part and the details are accurate. I should recommend sending it to the North China Daily News as it would attract attention in mercantile circles and might perhaps be some good to the local trade. May I suggest this to Mr. Brown ?

Yours truly,

C. A. S. Williams

INDEXED

S/O No. 320.　　Wenchow　　1st April, 25.

)

intendent's
uctive
e Customs
y.

Dear Mr. Stephenson,

In accordance with the instructions of your telegram of 25th ult., I issued the Allowance to the new Superintendent from 2 B: Special Appropriations, pending confirmation of his appointment by the Central Government. He went to Hangchow on the 21st to take part in Sun Chuan-fang's birthday celebrations and has not yet returned. He is exerting every effort to increase his Native Customs duty receipts at the expense of mine, and has instructed his offices to intercept all goods on their way to Wenchow. He also insists on having a duty collecting branch office at Kuant'ou (just on the other side of the river) in spite of my protests to the former Superintendent, who tried the same trick. I have informed him that I cannot agree to these unauthorised divergences from the orthodox

procedure

. W. STEPHENSON, ESQUIRE,

Officiating Inspector General of Customs, ad interim,

P E K I N G.

2

439

and will continue to charge duty at Wenchow as before unless I receive definite Inspectorate instructions to the contrary. His Kuant'ou Office, which is a checking station under his Ch'ili Office (both well within the 50-li area), is collecting duty on our imports, and issuing Chili documents. None of the goods even originate from Kuant'ou, but are merely passing through on their way to Wenchow. The merchants quite naturally object to the double charge and would be glad to have the Kuant'ou Office abolished. If I agree to the Superintendent's new arrangements (which he claims are not new but in accordance with the rules) I might as well hand him over the intra 50-li control altogether, as our duty collection would be effectively killed for good. Moreover the merchants arrange to pay a lower duty at the Superintendent's Stations to avoid the proper charge at Wenchow.

I

3

440

I doubt if this matter will trouble you officially as I feel confident that my attitude is entirely logical and cannot be objected to by the Shui-wu Ch'u.

rty.

Mr. R.L.P. Baude, Salt Inspector, and Mr. R.A. de Jaurias, Hangchow Postmaster, have been staying with me since the 27th ultimo. They both want to buy property for Office use, and I have been advising them to the best of my ability. I do not think the Salt Administration can do better than to buy our old Native Customs Head Office, which we shall not require when we move to the bund. As regards the Postal requirements we could sell the quarters now rented to the Post Office, when the new N.C. Office (with Tidewaiter's quarters) is built. I shall place these matters before you officially as soon as the Superintendent has obtained a grant from the

Revenue

4

141

Revenue to purchase the required site for the new N.C. Head Office, as approved in your Despatch No. 1306/102,354, N.C. No. 223.

Mr. C. Finch, Assistant Examiner, A, arrived here on the 23rd ult., but I have not yet received your official despatch appointing him to this port. Mr. Finch's wife is coming out from England in a few months' time, which suits me very well as the Outdoor Quarters are under repair at present.

Yours truly,

C. A. S. Williams

S/O No. 321. Wenchow 13th April, 25.

Dear Mr. Stephenson,

ing over
...s.

I am handing over charge to Mr. Brown today in accordance with your telegraphic instructions, and I leave for Ningpo tomorrow by a direct steamer. My family will follow later via Shanghai, as there is no suitable accommodation for ladies and children and no food provided on the direct boats.

...ted Transfer
...r. Lau Kieng
..., 1st Clerk C.

Mr. Lau Kieng Hing (劉謙興), 1st Clerk, C. has just asked me to recommend him for transfer to Foochow in order to attend to his children's education. He is Fukienese and has been here about three years. I recommend his application to your favourable consideration.

...of
...ge of
...tendent.

I hear that the Superintendent has been discharged, but do not know whether my information

J. W. STEPHENSON ESQUIRE,

Officiating Inspector General of Customs, ad interim,

PEKING.

2

644

information is correct or not ! Mr. Baude, of the Salt Administration, told me.

enewal of
of Premises
d to Post
e advisable.

I omitted to mention in my handing over charge memorandum that it is becoming difficult for us to handle our increasing volume of exports while the Post Office continues to occupy our premises in the Custom House compound, and it is now time for us to suggest to the Postal Administration that the Post Office should find accommodation elsewhere when their lease expires at the end of this year, and the lease should not be renewed.

ge of Mr.
xall, 1st
dewaiter,
te while on
er.

Mr. P.W. Coxall, 1st Class Tidewaiter, whose intended marriage was reported in my Despatch No. 3906, and who is now transferred to Yochow by your Despatch No. 1311, is going to get married at Shanghai on the 25th instant en route for Yochow, with the permission of the Yochow Commissioner duly accorded.

Yours truly,

C. A. S. Williams

INSPECTORATE GENERAL OF CUSTOMS.

S/O

PEKING, 14th April 1925.

427

Dear Mr. Brown,

I have duly received Wenchow S/O letters Nos. 318 and 319 of the 2nd and 16th March.

Chinese gunboats anchor in fairway: Superintendent warned by Commissioner that Customs will not be responsible for accidents.

This was correct. You should point out to the Superintendent that, if accidents occur, there will be claims for damages and that the observance of the rules is best for everyone in the long run.

Chinese Sloop will not pay Pilotage fees: shall Customs continue to accord free pilotage to Chinese Men-of-War ?

You might find it "inconvenient" to supply a pilot next time - but don't raise any ill feeling.

Yours truly,

J. W. Stephenson.

S. Brown, Esquire.

WENCHOW.

INSPECTORATE GENERAL OF CUSTOMS,

S/O PEKING, 23rd April 1925.

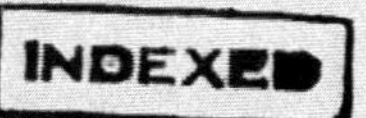

4/12

Dear Mr. Brown,

I have duly received Wenchow S/O letter No.320 of the 1st April:

Superintendent's Obstructive Native Customs policy: Commissioner's attitude.

The attitude adopted was correct.

Property: New Native Customs Offices.

It is to be remembered that a building programme cannot be sanctioned at the present time, as has been officially notified.

Yours truly,

J. W. Stephenson.

Brown, Esquire,

WENCHOW.

INSPECTORATE GENERAL OF CUSTOMS,

S/O

PEKING, 28th April 1925

045

INDEXED

Dear Mr. Brown,

I have duly received Wenchow S/O letter No.321 of the 13th April:

Suggested transfer of Mr. Lau Kieng Hing, 1st Clerk C., to Foochow.

All Fukienese want to be appointed to Foochow. He was stationed at the latter port for 8 years before going to Wenchow !

Non-renewal of Lease of Premises rented to Post Office advisable.

Noted.

Marriage of Mr. P.W.Coxall, 1st Class Tidewaiter, at Shanghai en route for Yochow.

Noted.

Yours truly,

J.W.Stephenson

Brown, Esquire,

WENCHOW.

S/O No. 322. Wenchow 29th April, 25.

406

Dear Mr. Stephenson,

Mr. C. A. S. Williams, after handing over charge here, left for Ningpo by direct steamer on the morning of the 14th instant. The following morning, Mr. G. E. Cammiade, Assistant Examiner, A, proceeding on long leave, departed for Shanghai. Although his leave really was granted from the 16th, I allowed him to go one day early, as this was the last direct boat, and the last one with foreign accommodations, by which he could make his home steamer, sailing on the 23rd; and as his successor had been here for more than three weeks, there seemed no necessity for keeping him. Mr. Williams' family left for Ningpo via Shanghai on the 22nd, and Mr. P. W. Coxall, 1st Class Tidewaiter, departed on the same date for Shanghai, en route to Yochow.

Mr. B. S.

J W. STEPHENSON, ESQUIRE,

Officiating Inspector General of Customs, ad interim,

PEKING.

447

Mr. B. S. Abramoff, 3rd Class Tidewaiter, arrived from Shanghai on the 27th, having been detained a few days by sickness. I have detailed him to the Native Customs, the post formerly occupied by Mr. Coxall.

...Feeling ...ing Mr. ...ns.

Mr. Williams' departure was helped on by a youthful brass band and, I am told, 170,000 firecrackers. The entire Maritime, and most of the Native Customs staff, went to the wharf -- some distance -- to see him off; and one of the clerks told me it was the most enthusiastic send-off he had ever seen accorded to a Commissioner. The general sentiment of the city was certainly one of regret in seeing him leave -- not, I think, because he bore any reputation for leniency in administration, but because the merchants all felt he had their interests at heart. Attached hereto is a clipping from the "North China Herald"; it was written by Mr. J. W. Heywood, superintendent of the United Methodist Mission, and the oldest foreign resident of Wenchow.

I trust

3

I trust the above comments from me may not be thought out of place; surely cordial relations such as these may well be a source of pride to the Service, and the high admiration for Mr. Williams entertained by myself and other members of the staff here make it a pleasure to set down the foregoing for your notice.

.len.

The members of the staff were grieved to learn of the death of Lady Aglen. To date we have had no details beyond the short notices published in the Shanghai papers.

te
y; Deeds
d With
For
ion;
ed.

The deeds of the British Consulate property, recently bought by the Customs, have been returned by the Magistrate, unstamped, with requests for two additional provisions, as follows:

1. No change to be made in the rent agreement without the consent of both parties (present wording specifies Customs only).
2. Purchaser, or lessee, to be designated the Wenchow Customs, instead of the Wenchow Commissioner, as agent for the Inspector General.

This may

4

449

This may be merely a continuation of the policy of delay and obstruction that has been pursued in this matter by the officials for some time. I am leaving this for the attention of Mr. Bernadsky, and not touching it myself. It will doubtless be reported officially in due course.

Repairs to the Constable's house in this property have now been completed, and as soon as the varnish dries, the premises will be ready for occupancy by Mr. Finch.

t[illegible]ly r a[illegible]hed.

I sent off over my own signature on the 23rd instant, the Confiscation, Arms, and Government Stores Reports, as I feared inconvenience might be caused by holding them until they could be signed by some one of higher rank. The English version of the Confiscation Report had the verbal approval of Mr. Williams before he left, and the Chinese versions of all the reports were carefully checked by Mr. Lau Kieng Hing, 1st Clerk, C.

[illegible] Italian

The Italian Gunboat "Sebastiano Caboto" (Capt. di Corvetta Angelo Iachino) arrived here

from

5

450

from Amoy on April 27th. I called that afternoon, and my call was returned the same day. I invited the officers to tennis on the courts at the Commissioner's house, but they were unable to accept. Mr. and Mrs. Ryden had them to tea and tennis on the 28th, and the ship left for Ningpo today, the 29th. The professed purpose of the visit was merely to see what Wenchow looks like.

ied
il
tion By
s N. C.
cs.

Cases of unauthorized collection of duty by the Superintendent's Native Customs stations, in an apparent effort to "steal" the intra-50-li revenue, as reported in previous S/O letters, continue to occur. Mr. Chü Kam Po, 3rd Assistant, A, in charge of Native Customs, has prepared me a memo on each of the cases. These combined form an accurate history of the whole transaction, which I shall hand over to Mr. Bernadsky; I am not touching it myself.

ndent's
e Issued
cted.

I have just received your telegram of today, instructing me to issue the Superintendent's allowance as directed in your telegram of March 25th, and I have done so at once. Probably

I

6

I bothered you needlessly about this; however, the telegram of March 25th contains the words, "until appointment is confirmed by Central Government." Since that time Ch'eng has definitely failed of confirmation through the appointment of Kao, and as I could find no previous instructions from you on a case fully in point, I thought it safer to telegraph. The Superintendent was not aware that I did so, and issue of the allowance was not delayed thereby.

From what I heard some time ago, I am expecting Mr. Bernadsky to arrive in a week or ten days.

Very truly yours,

Irving S. Brown

INSPECTORATE GENERAL OF CUSTOMS. 457

S/O

PEKING, 30 April 1925

INDEXED

Dear Mr. Brown,

With reference to my telegram of the 19th April, I am now writing to inform you that I sent the following telegram by wireless to Sir Francis:

"Whole Staff at Inspectorate and all ports native and foreign and numerous official and private friends grieve with you and unite in heartfelt sympathy. Memorial Service twenty-second",

and that I have to-day received from him a telegram dated Port Said 29th April, requesting me to convey to all, his thanks for the sympathy which they have expressed. Will you kindly communicate this message to your Staff.

I also wish to let you know that a Memorial Service for Lady Aglen, conducted by Bishops Scott and Norris, was held at the British Legation Chapel on Wednesday, April the 22nd at 12.30 p.m.

Yours truly,

J.W. Stephenson

B wn, Esquire,

W CHOW.

—42]

452

INSPECTORATE GENERAL OF CUSTOMS,

PEKING, 13th May 1925.

ar Sir,

I am directed by the Inspector General

form you that your S/O letter No. 322,

29th April, has been duly

ed.

Yours truly,

Stanley F Wright

Personal Secretary.

~~Private Secretary.~~

own, Esquire,

WENCHOW.

MAY 1925

INSPECTORATE GENERAL OF CUSTOMS,

PEKING, 15 May, 1925.

INDEXED

Rgl. 26. 5. 25. R.

Dear Bernadsky,

I am directed by the O.I.G. to send you, enclosed herewith, a petition accusing K'o Yu-p'ing, 2nd Clerk B on your Staff, of bribery and corruption, and to request you to return this document S/O with a report.

Yours truly,

Monsieur Bernadsky,

W E N C H O W.

敬禀者竊緣甌海關關員柯吻革久任關務弊竇叢生所有商
民貨物充公招買非賄渠多金不能購成一切商家往來禀呈經伊
謡譯是非倒置賄賂公行且甌海關建築工程均由伊一人承辦
與工匠合股坐分盈餘之利若不沐更調在商民不堪其苦在
鈞關多一弊政為此仰乞
稅務司大人鑒核

新順興

浙江永嘉商民 興昌書東 林永豐 謹叩

五月四號

CUSTOM HOUSE, 456

No. 323. Wenchow, 20th May, 1925.

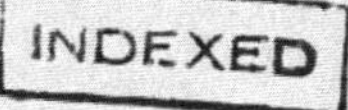
INDEXED

Dear Mr. Stephenson,

I arrived on the 14th instant, accompanied by my family, i. e., wife, five children, and nursery governess. I am sorry to state that my third daughter was stricken with scarlet fever at Shanghai. She was put at once into the Isolation Hospital there, but now I must keep a special watch on the other children, who played with the sick girl during our stay in the hotel at Shanghai.

Since taking over charge on the 15th, I have been chiefly occupied in studying the local regulations and situation.

To ...ls. The official visits to the Superintendent, Taoyin, Commander of the Gendarmerie, and Magistrate, have been made, and my calls duly returned.

. STEPHENSON, ESQUIRE,

Officiating Inspector General of Customs, ad interim,

PEKING.

The Chinese gunboat "Chu Tai" arrived at Wenchow on the 16th instant, and I provided the Commander with information in regard to piracies which have occurred recently along the Chekiang coast. This information was derived from petitions of the owners of the pirated vessels, and from Customs examination of the cargo which remained on these vessels when they arrived in port. The Commander asked me to forward all possible information about piracy to Admiral Hsü, of the Coast Guard Administration, at Woosung, reporting particulars of all new cases without delay. The same question was raised during my conversation with the Superintendent, and the latter asked me to forward to him all required information, so that he could take the necessary steps at once; i. e., in urgent cases, send telegrams to the Coast Guard Administration, etc. This I promised him to do.

My sincere thanks for your selecting me for this responsible position and pleasant port!

Yours truly,

E. Bernadsky

CUSTOM HOUSE,

461

No. 324. Wenchow, 26th May, 1925.

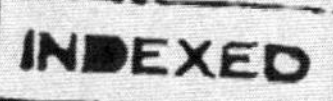

Dear Mr. Stephenson,

tion
t K'o
ng,
lerk,

In reply to your S/O letter of the 13th instant,

forwarding a petition accusing K'o Yü-p'ing, 2nd Clerk, B, on the Wenchow staff, of bribery and corruption, and requesting me to return this document S/O with a report, ---

I beg to state that my investigation proved the letter of accusation anonymous and ungrounded. The accusers do not give any concrete facts, and try to hide themselves under false tzu-hao's.

1. The managers of the shops bearing the characters 生昌號 and 新順興 stated

(a) that though the characters given in the

W. STEPHENSON, ESQUIRE,
Officiating Inspector General of Customs, ad interim,
PEKING.

2

462

in the letter are their respective tzu-hao's, the chops are not theirs;

(b) that they never wrote any letter to Peking; and

(c) that they respectively do not know each other, and that they do not know the other signers.

2. The other two firms, tzu-hao of which are 興昌 and 林永豐, cannot be found here.

3. Mr. J. W. Ryden, Tidesurveyor, B, states that all auctions of confiscated goods are conducted under his personal supervision, and that K'o Yü-p'ing has no connection with them except in helping Mr. Ryden to prepare notifications in Chinese.

4. All contracts for repairs are personally made by Mr. Ryden with the contractors, and K'o Yü-p'ing helps only in interpreting when Mr. Ryden asks him to do so.

5. Mr. C. A. S. Williams, Acting Commissioner, in his handing-over-charge memorandum, gives to K'o Yü-p'ing a very high recommendation, such as is rarely accorded to clerks; and my impression from this

3

46

this short period of stay at Wenchow is also quite favorable; i. e., he is quiet, intelligent, and a hard worker.

6. The petition accusing K'o Yü-p'ing, 2nd Clerk, B, is returned herewith.

Yours truly,

E. Bernadsky.

CUSTOM HOUSE,

No. 325. INDEXED Wenchow, 30th May 1925.

Dear Mr. Stephenson,

Lease Of British .

In my interview today with the Superintendent, I showed to him a draft of a lease made for the piece of land on the island, on which our newly purchased buildings (the former British Consulate) are located. Mr. Williams, my predecessor, during his tenure here prepared a draft of a lease for the above land, but it was returned to him through the Superintendent with a request made by the Magistrate

(a). To make the lease in the name of the Customs, and

(b). To specify that no change may be made in the rent agreement without the consen of both parties. (Vide S/O to I.G. No. 322 of 29th ult.)

As we

W. STEPHENSON, ESQUIRE,

Officiating Inspector General of Customs, ad interim,

PEKING.

2

As we cannot change the attitude of the Magistrate in this question, the required alterations have been made, and the Superintendent expects no more objection to signature by the authorities. Appended herewith are copies of

1) leases prepared by Mr. Williams and me, respectively, for the property in question, and
2) the Superintendent's letter requesting the alterations.

After receiving your approval, I shall officially forward the new lease to the Superintendent.

As mentioned in my S/O No. 323 of the 20th instant, I left a sick daughter in Shanghai. Up to now, news of her is not favorable, and I fear I shall be obliged to go to Shanghai at the doctor's request. In such case, I shall inform you by telegram of my departure. If, on the other hand, she progresses satisfactorily, then in about a month's time I shall need to go to bring her home. The entire trip both ways will take about five to seven days. I am sorry that circumstances compel me to leave my post so early in my period of charge.

Yours truly,

E. Bernadsky

INSPECTORATE GENERAL OF CUSTOMS,

S/O

PEKING, 2nd June 1925

Dear Mr. Bernadsky,

I have duly received your S/O letter No.323 of the 20th May:

Commissioner's daughter developes Scarlet Fever at Shanghai on the way to Wenchow.

I am very sorry to hear this and hope the others will have escaped infection.

Yours truly,

J.W. Stephenson

...rdsky, Esquire,

WENCHOW.

CUSTOM HOUSE,

No. 326. Wenchow, 4th June 1925.

INDEXED

Dear Mr. Stephenson,

nt Of
or
Coins
nchow
ntend-

From the enclosed copy of a letter to Mr. Lyall, you will see that a shipment of inferior silver coins is going to be made by the Wenchow Superintendent.

After this office had put into effect your instructions of last December, that such coins are not to be seized here until further notice, a despatch was received from the Superintendent in April last (copy forwarded to you in April Non-urgent Chinese Correspondence) requesting us to seize inferior silver coins in accordance with Shui Wu Ch'u instructions. This morning when the Superintendent applied for a document permitting him to ship such coins, I pointed out that such procedure was contrary to his previous official request, and not permitted by the regulations; and I advised him to apply to the Central Government for permission, if these funds must be transported

to

STEPHENSON, ESQUIRE,

Officiating Inspector General of Customs, ad interim,

P E K I N G.

2

471

to Hangchow. He definitely stated that it is impossible for him to obtain such permission from the Central Government, but he expects that he will be able to settle the matter with the Shanghai Customs, as the case is a special one.

Some explanation of his eagerness to transport the coins to Hangchow may be found in the fact that the exchange value of such coins at that place is about ten per cent. greater than here; at least, so I am told.

Yours truly,

E. Bernadsky.

2]

15 JUNE 1925

4614

INSPECTORATE GENERAL OF CUSTOMS,

PEKING, 5th June 1925.

Dear Sir,

I am directed by the Inspector General to inform you that your S/O letter No. 324, dated 26th May, has been duly received.

Yours truly,

Stanley F. Wright

Personal Secretary.

...radsky, Esquire,

WENCHOW.

INSPECTORATE GENERAL OF CUSTOMS, 467

S/O

PEKING, 17th June 1925

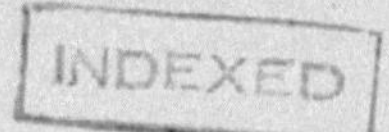

Dear Mr. Bernadsky,

I have duly received your S/O letter No.325 of the 30th May:

Alteration in Lease of British Consulate Property.

Please refer this officially giving a summary of all correspondence with the Local Officials on the subject, and forwarding a copy of the indenture covering the purchase of the property in question from H. B. M. Government.

Probability of Commissioner having to visit his daughter in Shanghai.

I am extremely sorry to hear that the news about your daughter is so unfavourable. I hope that by this time she is really better.

Yours truly,

J. W. Stephenson

...sky, Esquire,

...CHOW.

INSPECTORATE GENERAL OF CUSTOMS,

S/O

PEKING, 17th June 1925

472

Dear Mr. Bernadsky,

I have duly received your S/O letter No. 326 of the 4th June:

Shipment of Inferior Silver Coins to Shanghai by Wenchow Superintendent: Latter states he will be able to settle the matter with the Shanghai Customs.

Are these coins from the Fukien or Kwangtung Mints? If so, you should tell the Superintendent that if, as he says, he can arrange with the Shanghai Customs for their landing there he ought to do so before he asks you to allow them to be shipped - that you can't permit shipment of coins which the Shanghai Commissioner has instructions to seize!

Yours truly,

J. W. Stephenson.

N Bernadsky, Esquire,

WENCHOW.

CUSTOM HOUSE,

No. 327. Wenchow, 18th June, 1925.

INDEXED

279

Dear Mr. Stephenson,

ice Foreign

With reference to your telegram of the 5th instant, instructing me to remit revenue through a foreign bank or agency: there are no foreign banks or agencies through which we can remit our revenue, therefore all collection will be deposited here in the Bank of China.

ent rict

The 1925 session of the Wenchow District Assembly (永嘉縣縣議會) adjourned on the 15th instant; this body will re-convene in April next.

ent Of Roads.

This office received yesterday a letter from the Superintendent of Customs transmitting to us the decision of the Chamber of Commerce that as merchants at Wenchow have been overburdened with different forms of taxation, no proposed Wharfage

Dues

STEPHENSON, ESQUIRE,

fficiating Inspector General of Customs, ad interim,

P E K I N G.

2
475

Dues can be introduced at this port for the development of the Bund and adjoining roads. The case will be reported by the Chamber of Commerce to the Shui Wu Ch'u. The interesting fact in this question is that while the proposal was approved by the higher authority of the district, i. e., the District Assembly, it could not be put into force because of the veto of the lower semi-administrative unit, i. e., the Chamber of Commerce ---- both bodies being under the chairmanship of the same person, Mr. Yeh Wei-chou (葉維周). If I find a practical way by which the question of introducing wharfage dues for development of the Bund, etc., can be pushed forward, I shall try to speak or communicate with the Superintendent again, and I shall inform you.

On the 15th instant, all rice shops raised the price of rice about 1 cent per catty. The labourers of the city strongly objected to this, and organized a demonstration requesting all shops to close until the price be brought down. Last night some labourers began to make a noise on the street with empty kerosene tins, as a sign of protest against the high price. Four of them were arrested

by

476

by the police. This morning a crowd of labourers went to the police requesting release of their men, but were pushed out with rifles and four of them were wounded with bayonets. On the 16th instant, some students went to a rice shop which was under suspicion of smuggling rice abroad, looted it, and took the owner of it for punishment.

Up to now all shops in Wenchow are semi-closed.

Of Coins ...ow ...n-

The Superintendent left Wenchow for Hangchow on the 5th instant. Our Chinese tidewaiter who cleared the ship at 5 A. M. reported that no silver coins were shipped on board the s.s. "Kwangchi". At the same time he stated that the ship was not working at night, and thus was not under immediate Customs supervision from about 10 P. M. to 4 A.M.; hence this shipment might have been made at night. The usual search before clearance gave no result. In view of the possibility of shipment having been made, I asked the Shanghai Customs to search the ship. The reply received reads as follows:

"The Superintendent had left the vessel before the news of your telegram reached the Chief Tidesurveyor. Our

4

Our men were told that the Superintendent did not bring the coins."

Yours truly,

E. Bernatzky.

CUSTOM HOUSE,

INDEXED

No. 328.

Wenchow, 20th June, 1925.

Dear Mr. Stephenson,

Of The In on With Trouble.

Since arrival of the news about the incidents in Shanghai, the local students have begun to work to "Save Their Country", as they say; i. e., to organize demonstrations; issue pamphlets, pictures, and theatrical plays on the subject of the day; and to collect funds from merchants for supporting the labourers in their strike at Shanghai. Student demonstrations took place every day during the first week after the news was received, but the biggest one occurred on the 6th instant. Boys and girls of the different middle and normal schools, in number about 2,000, paraded the main streets of the city, and passed the Custom House. They carried flags and banners, and shouted the inscriptions given on the latter, as per Append No. 1; and distributed handbills, vide Append No. 2. The Chinese Christian community has

STEPHENSON, ESQUIRE,

fficiating Inspector General of Customs, ad interim,

P E K I N G.

has organized a body, styled the Wenchow Christian Nation Salvation Corps (温州基督救国团), with a view to backing up the Shanghai matter.

The local newspaper 新瓯潮 of course gives daily news on the subject. Two telegrams printed in it which seem worthy of notice are appended herewith (List No. 3).

Two articles of agitative character appeared in this paper, stating that Mr. Chapman, principal of the Wenchow Methodist College, and Mr. Worley, principal of the China Inland Mission Middle School for Boys (both men of British nationality) threatened their students with pistols when the latter desired to march out for a demonstration. But on the next day there appeared in the same paper an article prepared by the faculty of the Methodist College, stating that Mr. Chapman had been in the college for more than 20 years, during which time they stated he had bought no pistol; and the newspaper authority was therefore requested to amend the article in the issue of the previous day.

There was also a note in the paper stating that the local authorities have received

instructions

481 3

instructions from the Tupan and Sheng Chang stating that all foreign residents and tourists are to be effectively protected.

At Wenchow there are 102 foreign residents; i. e., Americans, 11, British, 20, French, 7, Japanese, 53, Russian, 9, and Swedish, 2. Up to now there is no great anxiety in the foreign community, but if events should take a wrong course and the community ask me to secure protection, then I shall send a telegram to you.

Samples of pictures distributed and posted on walls are enclosed herewith.

Yours truly,

C. Bernadsky.

482

APPEND NO. 1.

The inscriptions on the flags carried by Wenchow students, merch nts, etc. on demonstration of 6th June 1925 were:

1. (收回租界) Claim back settlements.
2. (收回裁判權) " " extraterritoriality.
3. (援助被難工人) Back up labour-sufferers.
4. (援助上海學生) " " Shanghai students.
5. (捐款救濟上海被難工人) Contribute to help Shanghai labo r-sufferers.
6. (誓雪國恥) Revenge for National disgrace.
7. (要求英日懲兇賠償) Ask Great Britain and Japan to punish offenders and compensate sufferers.
8. (抵制仇貨) Boycott enemies' goods.
9. (打倒帝國主義) Overthrow monarchy.
10. (收回海關) Claim back Customs.

62

APPEND NO. 2.

Students' Handbill distributed on demonstration of 6th June 1925.

The Japanese without reason killed the Chinese labourer, Ku Cheng Hung. (日人無故殺死華工顧正紅).

The British Police shot the Chinese students, labourers and merchants. (英捕槍殺學生和工商). (23 of them are dead; numerous wounded; many girls arrested. (死者二十三人，傷者無數，女生被捕多人).

All of us should come up to have the revenge done! (大家急速起來雪恥).

Boycott the enemies' goods to the utmost! (絕對抵制仇貨).

Contribute to help the labour-sufferers! (募款援助被難工人).

APPEND NO. 3.

(a) <u>Telegram sent to Wenchow on 5th June 1925 by Chekiang Provincial Assembly, Educational Association, Newspaper Offices, etc.</u>

As the Shanghai British Police and Japanese killed Chinese without reason, a League of Association should be formed with a view to sever economic relations with Great Britain and Japan.

(b) <u>Telegram sent on 5th June 1925 by Wenchow Nation Salavation Association (温州救国团) to Shanghai.</u>

Fund will be raised to back up the labour-sufferers in order to make a stand to the last.

Chinese version of Telegrams of Append No. 3.

録新甌潮日報六月六日公電二則

a.

杭州来電　各縣各法團均鑒上海英捕日前慘殺同胞多人蹂躪我民族侮辱我團体在省各法團及其他公團同深憤懣已將聯合會組織成立决先與英日兩國經濟絕交務請各屬即日召集聯席會議一致團結合力對付無任盼切杭州浙江省議會浙江省自治法會議浙江縣議會聯合會杭州總商會省農會省教育會律師公會省垣中等以上學校職教員聯合會杭縣議會參事會覔橋商界聯合會江干教育會江干鄉農會杭州青年幹事團杭州工人協會皋塘鄉教育會臨平鄉農會東陽工界協會省會商會聯合會商報之江日報大浙江報浙江民報全浙公報支〔五日下午一時十分到〕

b.

温州去電　上海民國日報轉雪恥會鑒敝會募欵援助工人望堅持到底温州救國會微　五日上午十時五十五分發

087

CUSTOM HOUSE,

No. 329. Wenchow, 1st July, 1925.

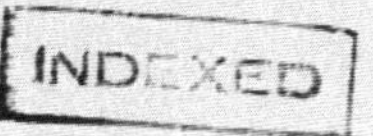
INDEXED

Dear Mr. Stephenson,

From i. On the 21st of June I received a letter from the Isolation Hospital at Shanghai, requesting me to take my daughter home. I had no friends whom I felt I could ask to keep even for a few days a girl just recovered from scarlet fever; and being assured that I could be back on the 28th or 29th, I decided to myself at once, and notified you by telegram. I left port on the ~~24th~~ 23rd, and returned on the 29th. Mr. I. S. Brown, 4th Assistant, A, who was left temporarily in charge, reported that nothing unusual occurred during my absence. Thank you very much for your sympathy regarding my family trouble, expressed in your S/O of the 17th ult.

Of In reply to your S/O of the 17th ult., I beg to state that the proposed shipment consisted, so I was told, of coins from the Fukien and Kwangtung mints.

Yours truly,

E. Bernadsky.

. STEPHENSON, ESQUIRE,

Oficiating Inspector General Of Customs, ad interim,

PEKING.

[-42]

478

INSPECTORATE GENERAL OF CUSTOMS,

S/C

PEKING, 6th July 1925.

Dear Sir,

I am directed by the Inspector General to inform you that your S/O letter No. 327, dated 18th June, has been duly received.

Yours truly,

Stanley F. Wright

Personal Secretary.
~~Private Secretary.~~

Bernadsky, Esquire,

Wenchow.

the Custom House

INSPECTORATE GENERAL OF CUSTOMS, 486

S/O

PEKING, 7th July 1925.

Rec. 13.7.25.

Dear Mr. Bernadsky,

I have duly received your S/O letter No.328 of the 20th June:

Local situation.

I hope you will have no trouble. The Local Authorities have been especially instructed to provide adequate protection for all Custom Houses and Staffs; and I trust that they will do so.

Yours truly,

J. W. Stephenson

Bernadsky, Esquire,

WENCHOW.

CUSTOM HOUSE,

No. 330. INDEXED Wenchow, 9th July, 1925.

Dear Mr. Stephenson,

In
ion
hanghai
.

a. Anti-foreign propaganda.

On the 6th instant, in my last interview with Mr. Chang, temporarily in charge of the Superintendent's office, the latter asked me to advise the staff not to go into the country, on account of anti-foreign propaganda. The beginning of the propaganda was a sad accident on the 14th and 15th of June, when about 150 Chinese people living near the south gate of Wenchow died suddenly after eating some Chinese cakes. What kind of poison was used in them is up to now uncertain, although a few of the patients were put into the hospital, under the care of a foreign doctor. Agitators used the case in their interests, and succeeded in spreading a rumor that foreigners had added drugs to foreign sugar imported for sale; and that

. '. STEPHENSON, ESQUIRE,

Officiating Inspector General Of Customs, ad interim,

P E K I N G.

that they intended to poison wells. The latter propaganda has been vigorously spread in the Juian district, about 70 li from Wenchow. Mr. J. W. Heywood, head of the United Methodist Mission in the Wenchow and Juian districts, fearing that the rumor might have a bad effect with regard to foreign missionaries living in that vicinity, called on a member of the Provincial Assembly here and asked him to write to the Juian magistrate requesting the latter to take steps to stop this kind of propaganda. The request was met willingly. I informed the staff of the Superintendent's request, and I also told Mr. Heywood of the interview.

b. Movement of Chinese Christians to form a church independent of foreign missionaries.

Mr. Yu Chien-jen (尤建人), a Chinese minister in the Methodist church at Wenchow, who is recognized by missionaries as one of the most energetic and able men among the local Christians, knowing the present anti-foreign feeling among Chinese, has started to organize a church independent of foreign missionaries. The missionary property at Wenchow is quite valuable,

and

3

415

and if Mr. Yu thinks that he will be in charge of it in case of expulsion of foreigners, then he no doubt will spend all of his energy to make his propaganda successful.

c. Arrival of detachment of hsien-ping (憲兵).

A detachment of about 20 military police sent here by the Occupation Commissioner at Ningpo for the maintenance of peace, arrived on the 4th instant.

Yours truly,

E. Bernatzky.

−42]

418

INSPECTORATE GENERAL OF CUSTOMS.

PEKING. 10th July 1925

r Sir,

I am directed by the Inspector General
orm you that your S/O letter No. 329 ,
1st July , has been duly
d.

Yours truly,

Stanley F. Wright
Personal Secretary.
~~Private Secretary.~~

adsky, Esquire,
WENCHOW.

CUSTOM HOUSE,

409

Wenchow, 2nd July, 1925.

received a letter from the
Customs, asking me to instruct
ass a shipment of 32,750
gtung twenty-cent pieces, to
s.s. "Pingyang". The
military escort, and is covered
the Occupation Commissioner
transported from Ningpo to

this office was instructed
that Fukien and Kwangtung
e not to be seized here in
ice, as they are by proclamation
of the local authorities legal currency in Wenchow.
I informed the Superintendent that no covering documents could be issued by the Native Customs, as this shipment may be subject to confiscation at Ningpo; and
I

A. S. WILLIAMS, ESQUIRE,
Commissioner Of Customs,
N I N G P O.

INDEXED

CUSTOM HOUSE, 497

No. 331. Wenchow, 20th July, 1925.

Dear Mr. Stephenson,

a. Boycott of British and Japanese goods.

At one of the student meetings held in June last it was decided to boycott British and Japanese goods. This decision was approved by the local Chamber of Commerce, and up to the present only a very small amount of the cargo in question has been imported under shipping orders. The merchants, however, tried to bring it through the post-office. This fact was observed by the students, and on the 14th instant some of them dressed as rickshaw coolies stationed themselves just outside the gate of the post-office. Some of the merchants after receiving their parcels used the rickshaws, but the latter took them to the schools, where the cargo was confiscated. At present there remain in the post-office some parcels of which the merchants do not want to take delivery, preferring to send them back to Shanghai.

There

. STEPHENSON, ESQUIRE,

ciating Inspector General Of Customs, ad interim,

PEKING.

498 2

There was another case in connection with the post-office on the same day, when a mail bag being sent to the interior was opened by students in the streets of Wenchow. The postal courier immediately came back and reported the case to the Postmaster. The latter at once went to the place of the occurrence, recovered the mail matter, brought the leader of the students to the post-office, and gave him a lecture on the sanctity of the mail and on the grave consequences of tampering with it. It seems the students agree to abstain, as no more cases happened afterwards.

b. Anti-foreign propaganda.

Mr. Benjamin F. Gregory, an American in the S.D.A. Mission at Wenchow, who travels a good deal in the interior, told me a few days ago, that at present there is really a strong anti-foreign feeling in the country. At the beginning of July, during his last trip, he was detained several times by countrymen who accused him of poisoning wells. After investigation by the officials at the various places, he was released, but at the same time he was advised to refrain from further travelling in the country. Mr. Gregory added that

that at present adherents of the mission prefer to remain at a certain distance from their foreign teachers when the latter walk along the streets of the villages and towns.

In a draft of lease referred to you for approval under Wenchow Despatch No. 3926 of 17th July, 1925, it is stated, "if any change is to be made, it should be agreed to by both parties", while your instructions contained in I.G. Despatch No. 1267/100,079 of the 23rd August, 1924, are to obtain a lease of the land "renewable on the same terms on the expiry of a certain number of years." It seems either of these expressions would safeguard Service interests, but as the wording is different, I think it advisable to mention it here.

On the 9th instant, Mr. B. S. Abramoff, 3rd Class Tidewaiter, applied for two weeks' leave from the 10th instant, with the intention of going to Shanghai to meet some relatives -- Russian refugees -- and to arrange board and lodging for them there. On recommendation of the Tidesurveyor, this leave was granted.

500 4

granted. He came back to-day, and to my great surprise he brought his relatives here -- a lady and her son of about 10 years. Mr. Abramoff explained to me that the cost of life in Shanghai is such that he cannot afford to keep them there, but he hopes that he can manage to keep them here in a Chinese house.
I pointed out to him that under the present circumstances it is quite inadvisable to bring foreigners here and that it would be much more reasonable to keep them in Shanghai.

Yours truly,

E. Bernadsky

-42]

INSPECTORATE GENERAL OF CUSTOMS.

PEKING, 21st July 1925.

) r Sir,

I am directed by the Inspector General
ı rm you that your S/O letter No. 330,
9th July, has been duly
1.

Yours truly,

Stanley F. Wright
Personal Secretary.
~~Private Secretary.~~

isky, Esquire,

WENCHOW.

]

CUSTOM HOUSE,

497

Wenchow, 20th July, 1925.

of British and Japanese goods.
the student meetings held in
to boycott British and Japanese
s approved by the local Chamber
the present only a very small
question has been imported under
rchants, however, tried to bring
e. This fact was observed by
14th instant some of them
es stationed themselves just
post-office. Some of the
their parcels used the rickshaws,
to the schools, where the
cargo was confiscated. At present there remain in the post-office some parcels of which the merchants do not want to take delivery, preferring to send them back to Shanghai.

There

, STEPHENSON, ESQUIRE,

ciating Inspector General Of Customs, ad interim,

P E K I N G.

CUSTOM HOUSE,

492

No. 332. INDEXED Wenchow, 28th July, 1925.

Dear Mr. Stephenson,

Mrs. ... formerly ...nzel.

On the 27th instant, at about 5:30 P. M., a sister from the local French Charity Hospital and a German woman in a distressful state visited me in my office, and asked me to help the latter to leave the port for Shanghai. According to her statement, she, then Miss Menzel, was married in Berlin several years ago to a Chinese soapstone merchant named Ming, who three years ago brought her to his home in an interior place about forty miles up from Wenchow. Here she found that her husband was already married to a Chinese woman, and that she must take her place in the home as a second wife. Being dissatisfied with her position, she tried to return to Germany, but was not allowed by her husband to do so. Several times she tried to run away from the place, but she was found, returned to her Chinese home, and badly treated. The sister added that in view of the present

J. . STEPHENSON, ESQUIRE,

Officiating Inspector General Of Customs, ad interim,

P E K I N G.

present anti-foreign feeling, their establishment feared to take her, as it might cause trouble. I told them that I could make arrangements to put her on board the s.s. "Kwangchi", then in port, but that as she was under Chinese jurisdiction, the Commissioner for Foreign Affairs must deal with the case. At their request, I promised them to inform the Commissioner for Foreign Affairs privately, and to ask him to protect this German woman.

Today her husband found her on board ship, but when it was explained to him there that the case was already known to the Commissioner for Foreign Affairs, and that he could take her home only with the permission of the latter, he preferred to leave her alone, and left the ship.

n
n
nghai

Movement of Chinese Christians to form a church independent of foreign missionaries. (Continuation of S/O No. 330, b).

Establishment of a church independent of foreign missionaries (聖道公會自立會) took place in Wenchow on the 26th instant at 9 A. M. There were about seven or eight speakers, and all of them

tried

3

504

tried to prove that separation from the British and other foreigners is absolutely necessary, as such are Christians only in words. Christianity is love, but where have British or other foreigners shown any love for people? The government of India, unequal treaties, the Opium War, the oppression of Indians in America to such an extent that this nation will soon disappear, etc., etc., were brought up as examples showing that we who want to be Christians should keep as far from the foreigners as possible.

Yours truly,

P. Bernadotz.

CUSTOM HOUSE, 56

No. 333. Wenchow, 6th August, 1925.

INDEXED

Dear Mr. Stephenson,

...ation ... Ill-...ent Of ...s Chinese ...

A few days ago the Chinese Staff at Wenchow received from Canton a Promulgation issued by the Association Against Ill-treatment of Customs Chinese Staff, an original copy of which is enclosed herewith with its translation.

... Vernadsky's ...e...

To-day I have forwarded to you my application for 20 days' leave of absence from the end of August to the middle of September to proceed to Tsingtao to put my two or three girls into a girls' school. In view of the uncertainty of steamer traffic between Wenchow and Shanghai, I cannot state from what date to what date I want to have this leave of absence. I applied for 20 days as the maximum number, but if I can arrange to put my children into a girls' school at Shanghai, or if I can make this trip to Tsingtao and back in a

shorter

... STEPHENSON, ESQUIRE,

Officiating Inspector General Of Customs, ad interim,

P E K I N G.

2

537

shorter period of time, I shall certainly do it. Of course I shall have to stay in Shanghai or Tsingtao a few days during the children's examination. I shall be much obliged if you can grant me this leave of absence.

On the 4th instant, between 7:00 and 8:30 P. M., an eclipse of the moon was seen here. During this hour Wenchow appeared to be one of the noisiest spots on the globe. Practically every house, every member of every Chinese family tried to save the moon from being swallowed by the dragon or dog (天狗) -- the latter is the belief of the lower classes -- by beating on drums, tins, planks, etc., with brass spoons and sticks. Thousands and thousands of crackers were fired and children shouted at the tops of their voices, "Huan Kuang Fo (還光佛)!"

At present there is the sum of Hk. Tls. 20,000 that could be remitted to Shanghai, but in view of the absence of foreign banks or agencies we cannot do it, and the amount is being held on deposit here in the Bank of China.

Yours truly,

E. Bernadsky

508

S/O No. 333 of 1925.
ENCLOSURE.
Copy of
PROMULGATION ISSUED BY THE ASSOCIATION AGAINST ILL-TREATMENT OF CUSTOMS CHINESE STAFF.

反對海關虐遇華員會之宣言

全國各機關各學校及各報館鈞鑒邇者廢除不平等條約及推翻帝國主義之口號遍於全國然帝國主義之澎湃莫海關若洋員喧賓奪主趾高氣揚卑視華人儼同牛馬盤踞海關視若外府狐埋狐搰莫之敢攖既養尊而處優復薪俸之加厚華員則疲於奔命而其所入曾不足以供饘粥之資嗚呼海關者中國之機關也而洋人竟以之為殖民地供其揮霍凡西方諸無賴胥舉而納諸海關中帝國主義之鷹揚寧過於此此而可忍孰不可忍故將其種種不平之處為我邦人君子一詳陳之華員之初入關供職也其在內班月薪祇四十餘兩若由稅務學校分發入關者月薪祇五十兩其在外班月薪則三十餘兩以視洋員之初供職於海關內班則幾及二百兩外班則幾至百兩者相去不啻天壤藉曰洋

人遠適異國諸多不便故不得不優其薪金俾資挹注然吾華員之遠調他省與去國奚殊又何以不聞若何之加薪此薪金之不平一也洋員在關每歲一加薪或數月一加薪更有一擢而躐數級者然華員則四五載而不遷其號為升遷最速者須適三載一級遂使積資三十餘年之華員其薪金之優曾不若洋員之積資二稔而華員固維日孜孜勞形案牘也洋員祇解游手好閒簽押畫諾暇則鬥雞走狗沉湎酗酒而已然彼等竟能享厚薪而蟬聯直上不平之事寧過於此（前數載海關有所謂重訂華員薪金之舉然祇給微利以市恩并非真有覺悟以示愛好於華員彼其心未嘗不知專欲難成故稍予河潤以息衆怒觀乎近日壓置所有應遷之華員而不遷司馬氏之心路人可見然則前此之所謂改訂實取法於狙公夫已氏直狙視華員耳謀亦狡矣）此升遷之不

平二也且海關之對待洋員更為優異有房舍供其住宿有傢具供其使用有侍僕為其服役有疾病則供其醫藥即其顧傭亦得此異數而皆取償於海關然而關中諸華員則絲毫不能膺此擢利雖曰海關有醫生不過徒具形式於事無補邇來生計日高費用浩繁華員有請求其稍予優待藉資彌補者竟至十上書而不報此待遇之不平三也華員雖有才智之士位不過幫辦從未得有稅務司之缺以本國之征收機關而華員獨不得為之長可痛孰甚不寧惟是華員積資雖老仍伈伈俔俔以聽命於資格最淺之洋員之下其尤甚者則九龍拱北陳村等關竟以內班人員若供士等歸諸外班水手洋員轄制一若以吾國人為無道德無教育即以彼國一最下賤之傖夫亦足以駕吾華有識人士之上其蔑視我國民人格為何如耶夫吾人供職於外人政府之下受此

種種待遇固無足論其是非獨惜服務於本國機關而竟有此等現象國未亡而先受亡國之慘苛虐奚如此位置之不平四也然而夫巳氏之陰謀尤復層出不窮彼見大歐戰之後彼邦人士失業者衆乃欲遂其殖民地主義藉口海關收入日增於是續招洋員亂行安插又恐經費之輸出過甚於是將服務既久而薪金稍厚之華員偶有小疵藉故剔除(若天津某案是其明証)而又於初入關之華員加以種種摧殘若覔店户之担保也一歲經醫生數次之驗身也折扣薪金而美其名曰儲金也(當立儲金制之時曾言明每半歲利息最少六釐并不得以為他項作用乃竟以吾人之儲金作收買內國公債之投機事業而利息祇付四厘半慢令致期謂之賊誰謂外人多顧信用哉)務使其視海關為畏途以達其位置同類之私心其錄用華員則以無骨氣乏抵抗之能力者

512

為上觀於巴羅氏（Bowra）之演説謂海關不必用才智之華員祇求其能脅肩諂笑就我馳驅於斯已足愚民政策其肺腑昭然若揭矣夫海關之聘用洋員豈不以其學識優長康隅砥礪足資楚材晉用乎球顧海關洋員中受有高等教育而得學位者幾人其外班不由苦力廚子水手及燒火出身者有幾人內班之中有文法不通者矣外班之中有並自己姓名而不識繕者矣乃一則身進海關即享厚薪一則朝方丐食夕作總巡固無所謂學識也更進言其道德則酗酒滋事是其所長至若使其嬌妻橫陳甲帳籍徼恩寵雞姦侍僕恣其獸慾位置私生子俾作偵探其尤著者則中江有毆打報關商人之幫辦粵西有買物不給值之副司粵海則某副司藉學漁色哈埠則某稅司迷窰是好更有身生花柳吸食鴉片種種臭穢罄竹難書此僅就其個人私德而言其餘則有

513

盜賣煤斤擅放私鹽私販鴉片監守自盜若某關之巡船船主足資明証此不過舉一以例其餘非謂祇此已也更有串通商人走漏古玩匿報花紗收受陋規擅走軍火影響於國家之稅收與治安莫此為甚吾人苟一讀戴洛爾(Mr. Tailor)所著安格林對中國海關一文(Aglen Russ Against Chinese Maritime Customs)則覺此中黑幕不堪言喻嗚呼吾中國誠富庶何必歲糜鉅款以豢養此一班西方無賴剝國人中多日謀升斗而不暇給者哉故吾人苟不欲濟其國於保護國(Chientota)之列即不能安於緘默而任其宰割不得不努力奮鬥而為收回海關之運動其濟則國之大幸即不然亦應有下列之表示一曰海關中須華員為稅司也洋員雖有債權關係不應視海關若禁臠任意調劑祇可立於稽核地位其稅司一缺應返諸華人免至太阿

514

倒持國不成國即最低限度或設華洋稅司各一使無偏頗二曰限制僱用洋員也洋員中流品太雜前已論之詳矣故於其資格應嚴密審查對於名額尤應限定免至有虛糜國帑之弊三曰對於華員應須優遇也華員在關事務多而待遇殊屬不平以後應對於華員其薪金升遷及各種權利應重行釐定與洋員平等以昭大公凡此種種深望執政諸公有與夫巳氏厲行交涉而尤望邦人君子為之聲援此豈海關華員好為鷄鶩之爭實國家之榮辱繫之也倘他日華員有行要求必須之手段各華華學子勿應海關若何之召募以維國民之人格嗟乎見被髮於伊川知百年之將戎我國人其鑒諸

575

TRANSLATION OF

PROMULGATION ISSUED BY THE ASSOCIATION AGAINST ILL-TREATMENT OF CUSTOMS CHINESE STAFF.

"To the National Governmental Organs, Schools and Newspaper Offices:

Recently action for the cancellation of unequal treaties together with the watchword that imperialism be overthrown have been spread throughout the whole nation. But imperialism holds its highest supremacy in the Chinese Customs. Foreigners in the Service make themselves masters in all respects whereas Chinese are deprived of their own rights. The former look proud and despise the latter, who are treated as cattle and horses. Foreigners take possession of the Customs and regard it as a foreign governmental institution. They have done what they like; nobody dares to disturb them. They make themselves dignified and occupy the best positions. they draw high salaries. The Chinese staff are tired of their work, and their pay is insufficient to buy congee. Alas! The Customs is a Chinese organ but foreigners take it as a colony to do with as they like. All the western vagabonds are employed in the Service. There is no imperialism

more

516

more clearly shown than this. It is impossible to be patient now and therefore it is necessary to announce the various points of unequal treatment of Chinese Staff in the Customs to all our fellow countrymen. When a Chinese joins the In-door Staff, he draws as pay only some Tls. 40.00 a month. If he is a graduate of the Customs College, he will get Tls. 50.00 a month. If he joins the Out-door Staff, he will earn only some Tls. 30.00 a month. Compare this with the case of a foreigner who, on joining the In-door Staff, draws a salary of nearly Tls. 200.00; if he joins the Out-door Staff, he will draw a pay of about Tls. 100.00. The difference is too vast. The pretext is that foreigners leave their own countries, hence everything to them is inconvenient. Their salaries should therefore be liberal in order to compensate them. But when a member of the Chinese staff is transferred from one province to another remote province, his condition is not far different from that of a member of the foreign staff, but an increase of pay in such a case has never been heard of. The difference of pay is the first unfairness. Foreigners in the Service have their pay increased every year. Sometimes, their

511

their salaries are increased every few months. Furthermore, it often happens that they jump several steps of promotion at a time. Chinese for four or five years do not get a promotion. The quickest promotion they get is in three years. Therefore the pay of a Chinese who has been in the Service for more than 30 years would not be so large as that of a foreigner who has only been in the Service for 2 years. Chinese staff have to work very hard for the whole day whereas foreign staff are idling all the time. To sign and initial only are their duties. They enjoy cock-fighting and play with dogs whenever they have time. They become intoxicated. However they draw high salaries and are successively promoted. Nothing is more unfair than this. A few years ago a revised scale of pay took place, but this was merely a show of grace with very slight real benefit. In reality, it was not a show of sympathy towards the Chinese Staff. It was evident that it was impossible to succeed with selfishness; therefore a slight benefit was accorded with a view to calming the anger of the public. In view of the recent suppressive arrangements, members of the Chinese staff who are entitled to be promoted are

518

are not promoted. The wicked mind (like that of Shih-ma-shih, a traitor in the Han Dynasty) is known by everybody. The reorganisation of Chinese staff hitherto effected is based on the system of Chü Kung (who in order to quiet the monkeys promised to give 3 meals in the morning and 4 meals in the evening instead of 4 meals in the morning and 3 meals in the evening previously given). The way of promotion is the 2nd unfairness. The foreign staff in the Customs are well treated. They are furnished with houses, furniture and servants. When they are sick, they are attended to by Customs doctors and supplied with medicine. Even their employees, when sick, are treated the same as their masters. All these are paid for by the Customs. But Chinese staff are not entitled to enjoy even a little bit of the abovementioned. Although the Customs is provided with a doctor, Chinese staff are not benefitted. As the cost of living has at present gone up day by day, and more money is required to meet expenditure, Chinese staff in view of this have requested a better treatment to make up losses. More than 10 petitions have been submitted but no reply has been given. This kind of treatment is the 3rd unfairness.

Chinese

549

Chinese staff who are capable and well-educated occupy only the position of assistants; none of them has been a Commissioner. It is painful that Chinese staff are not allowed to head the Revenue-collecting Department of their own country. A Chinese staff of good seniority has to be submissive under the direction of a junior foreign staff. The worst can be seen from the Kung Pei (拱北), Ch'ên Ts'un (陳村), etc. Customs in Kowloon where Chinese In-door staff, i.e. Clerks, have to be under the control of a foreign Tidewaiter. Chinese staff are regarded as men of no morality and without education, who have therefore to be under the control of foreigners of the lowest class. The personality of Chinese has been disregarded. Is not this true? If we were working under a foreign government, there could of course be no complaint over this sort of treatment, but it is a pity that when we are working in a department of our own government, we have to submit to such a condition. Our country still exists, yet we have to suffer as men whose nation has lost its independence. How do you think of this ill-treatment? The positions in the Service are the 4th unfairness. The intrigues have been without ends. Since

520

Since the European war, many foreigners have been thrown out of work. The ideal of colonisation has therefore to be realised. The increase of daily Customs revenue is used as a pretext for indiscriminate admission of more foreigners into the Service. But in order to meet the excessive expenditure, senior Chinese staff drawing high pay are discharged whenever found guilty of petty faults (Vide the case of the Tientsin Customs as a proof). Again, newly-enlisted Chinese staff are ill-treated by all means as in the case of securing bonds and physical examinations many times during the year. The scheme of contribution is merely another good term for curtailment of salary. (At the time of the inauguration of the Contribution Scheme it was stated that the lowest rate of interest would not be less than 6 % per semi-annum and that the contribibtion would not be used for any other purpose. But it is now utilised to purchase National Loan Bonds, which is a kind of speculation, bearing an interest of 4.5 % only. "To delay orders at first and to hasten the execution of them at the last moment is injurious to the people." Does any one say that foreigners never break a promise?) All these are intended

521

intended to make Chinese afraid of joining the Customs so that the selfish policy of enlisting more foreigners may be realised. The Customs wants to employ Chinese who have no personalities and who are lacking power of resistance. Just refer to Mr. Bowra's speech. "It is no use for the Customs to employ Chinese possessing ability and knowledge but all that is required is willingness to flatter and to submit to control". The policy of making Chinese fools is clearly shown. The object of the Customs in employing foreigners is that they should be well educated and experienced so that they will do excellent work. How many foreigners are there in the Customs who have received high education or degrees? How many are there of the foreign Out-door staff who were not once coolies, cooks, sailors or firemen? Some of the foreign In-door staff make grammatical errors while others among the Out-door staff do not know how to write their own names. But as soon as they enter the Customs they enjoy high pay. In the morning they are beggars, but in the evening they become Chief Tidesurveyors. It is needless to speak of knowledge and experience. With regard to their moral charactor, to abuse themselves in wine

and

522

and to create trouble are their specialities. In order to be favourites with their superiors, some have released their wives to the amours of their chiefs. Some of them have indulged their animal passions by performing sodomy with their boys; others have found positions for their illegitimate sons in order to use them as private spies. The most notorious cases are those in which one of the Shanghai foreign Assistants beat a Customs broker, one of the Deputy Commissioners in a certain Western Kwangtung Customs refused to pay for what he bought, one of the Deputy Commissioners in the Canton Customs seduced certain ladies under the pretext of teaching and a Commissioner of the Harbin Customs abused himself in brothels. Again some are infected with venereal ulcers. Others smoke opium. There are various sorts of disreputable things which can hardly be described. The above descriptions concern only the moral charactor of individuals. Besides, some of them have stolen coal for sale, released salt at will and sold opium secretly. They have abused their power. This can be proved as in the case of the captain of a certain revenue cruiser of a certain port. This

is

523

is only intended to show a part of their vices to prove many others. In addition, some received bribes, and smuggled arms and ammunition, which affected Customs revenue and also maintenance of peace very much. If one will read the book "Aglan Ruas against Chinese Maritime Customs" written by Mr. Tailor, he will realize that the disclosures made there are unspeakable. Alas! Our China is indeed a rich country. Why should she spend so much money a year to feed those Western vagabonds? Moreover Chinese always find it difficult to earn means of subsistence. If we do not want to see China a protectorate, we can not keep silence to let foreigners do as they like. We must struggle hard to claim back the Customs. This will, if it succeeds, be a great good fortune to the country. If not, the following should be obtained:-

1. The Customs should employ Chinese as Commissioners. Although China owes debt obligations to foreign countries, foreigners have no right to regard the Customs as private property to do with as they like. They are only entitled to supervise the Customs. The position of Commissioner should be given back to

Chinese

529

Chinese with a view to avoiding contradiction and to saving China from ruin. Or, at least, to be fair, one Chinese and one foreign Commissioner should be appointed.

2. The employment of foreigners should be restricted. Among the foreigners, there are too many bad characters; this has already been mentioned as above. Therefore it is necessary to study their qualifications carefully. The number of foreign employees should more particularly be readjusted with a view to saving unnecessary expense to the country.

3. The Chinese staff should be well treated. Their duties have been too many and their treatment bad. This is unfair. Hereafter, in order to sho fairness, their salaries, promotions and other privileges should be readjusted on the same footing as those of foreign employees.

On all the above points, it is sincerely hoped that the Chief Executive and others will pursue a strict course with the man responsible. It is hoped that our fellow countrymen will assist. It is not a mere bickering of the Customs Chinese staff,

but

but a matter of national honour. Later on, if the Chinese staff want to carry out necessary measures in securing their demands, students must not respond to calls for enlistment in the Customs to maintain the quota of Chinese. Alas! If one sees the omens of trouble, he must conclude that fighting is inevitable. Fellow countrymen, you have to wake up."

(527)

CUSTOM HOUSE,

No. 334. Wenchow, 14th Aug., 1925.

INDEXED

Dear Mr. Stephenson,

rtation Phosphorus nes.

During July last there arrived here from Shanghai three shipments of white or yellow phosphorus matches, a total of 960 packages, valued at Hk. Tls. 1,600.00. According to I. G. Circular 3475, the importation and sale of this article is prohibited from the 1st July. When the importation of the first lot took place, the Superintendent was notified of the case and destruction was proposed. (Vide non-urgent Chinese correspondence for July). But after receiving a reply from the Superintendent, I informed the applicant that the cargo might be re-exported to Shanghai, and a permit to land the cargo temporarily was granted under bond. Then the importation of the other two lots took place. The importers pointed out to me that the cargo passed the Shanghai Customs before the 1st July, and on the strength of this asked me to release it. I explained to them that

their

'. STEPHENSON, ESQUIRE,

'fficiating Inspector General Of Customs, ad interim,

P E K I N G.

526 2

their request might have been satisfied if only importation had been restricted, but that in this case sale is prohibited, and therefore I could not help them. Still, I promised to release the cargo if they could produce a letter from the Superintendent guaranteeing that the goods would not be sold. It seems they are unable to obtain such a letter, and up to now the cargo is lying in a godown under bond. The match merchants tell me that they have sent a petition to the Nung Shang Pu, requesting prolongation of the period of coastwise trade for this article, but that no reply has been received yet. If their petition does not produce a favourable outcome, I shall allow the cargo to be re-exported to Shanghai.

..ure Of Men ..ected Piracy.

On the 7th instant, the Chinese Maritime Police gunboat "Haip'ing" brought to Wenchow four small junks with arms on board, together with fourteen men -- crew of the junks -- suspected of piracy. The preliminary investigation was made by the commander of the "Haip'ing", and the captives were publicly tortured for three days at his private residence; but this treatment was productive of very little result; i.e. only

3

539

only a few of the prisoners acknowledged their piratical connection, saying they were unable to stand more torture.

ɪra. On the 11th instant I received a telegram from Mr. Lyall, "Cholera epidemic at Shanghai". The Superintendent of Customs and the Medical Officer were notified at once, and sanitary regulations are being applied to steamers arriving from Shanghai. There have already been four or five cases of cholera here this month, and I have asked our doctor to keep me informed of the course of the disease. I am going to send a similar request to the Superintendent.

ts In ɪection ghai ble. a. The following British and Japanese goods which had been clandestinely imported into Wenchow against the wishes of the patriotic students, and had been discovered and seized by them, were publicly destroyed in the compound of the 10th Middle School to-day at 10 A. M.:

Cotton thread in balls,	4	cases
Mustard	1	pkg.
Buttons	10	gross
Collar-buttons	4	cards

Medicine

4

Medicine 37 pkg.

Hats 1 piece.

A notification of the proposed destruction was issued by the students on the 13th instant.

b. There was published to-day in the local paper (新甌潮日報), in the advertising columns, A Warning to Cigarette Traders, issued by the Wenchow Revenge Association (溫州五卅雪恥會). A summary of it reads:

"On account of the Shanghai tragedy, to sever financial relations with Japanese and British is the only way for the salvation of the nation. The cigarette traders selling Hatamen, Chienmen, etc. cigarettes, should return the above-mentioned cigarettes to the original companies and should not buy them any more; otherwise there may be destruction of cargo and imposition of fines."

c. There is a movement here to boycott the Wenchow Methodist College, directed by the British teacher, Mr. T. W. Chapman. With this purpose in view, the students and their supporters have opened a new school with the same curriculum as the Methodist College, and have issued a proclamation urging all students who love their country to join this school. The missionaries here do not seem optimistic over the situation.

Incidentally,

5

Incidentally, the senior students of the Methodist College who went on strike say that the local Board of Education has granted them all diplomas without examination.

ain
tistics
uested
Super-
ndent.

The Temporary Acting Superintendent called on me to-day and asked me to help him to supply the Board of Finance with figures of direct foreign imports and exports from 1911 to 1924. I told him that in such cases, when special tables, not published in our returns, are to be prepared, I must ask the Inspector General's instructions. If he sends me an official letter about these statistics, I shall write to him that the desired figures cannot be supplied without instructions transmitted through you.

Yours truly,

C. Bernatzky.

—42]   5505

INSPECTORATE GENERAL OF CUSTOMS,

PEKING, 17th August 1925.

ar Sir,

I am directed by the Inspector General orm you that your S/O letter No. 332, 28th July, has been duly ed.

Yours truly,

Stanley F. Wright

Personal Secretary.

adsky, Esquire,

WENCHOW.

CUSTOM HOUSE,   506

Wenchow, 6th August, 1925.

few days ago the Chinese Staff om Canton a Promulgation issued inst Ill-treatment of Customs inal copy of which is enclosed slation.

ay I have forwarded to you my s' leave of absence from the middle of September to proceed two or three girls into a ew of the uncertainty of Wenchow and Shanghai, I cannot to what date I want to have this leave of absence. I applied for 20 days as the maximum number, but if I can arrange to put my children into a girls' school at Shanghai, or if I can make this trip to Tsingtao and back in a

shorter

TEPHENSON, ESQUIRE,

Officiating Inspector General Of Customs, ad interim,

PEKING.

—42]

501

INSPECTORATE GENERAL OF CUSTOMS,

PEKING, 19th August 1925.

ar Sir,

I am directed by the Inspector General orm you that your S/O letter No. 331, 20th July, has been duly ged.

Yours truly,

Stanley F. Wright

Personal Secretary.
~~Private Secretary.~~

qedsky, Esquire,

WENCHOW.

CUSTOM HOUSE,

502

Wenchow, 28th July, 1925.

'th instant, at about 5:30 P. M.,
l French Charity Hospital and
listressful state visited me in
ne to help the latter to leave
According to her statement,
was married in Berlin several
soapstone merchant named Ming,
rought her to his home in an
rty miles up from Wenchow.
er husband was already married
d that she must take her place
ond wife. Being dissatisfied
tried to return to Germany, but
was not allowed by her husband to do so. Several times she tried to run away from the place, but she was found, returned to her Chinese home, and badly treated. The sister added that in view of the

present

. I. STEPHENSON, ESQUIRE,

Officiating Inspector General Of Customs, ad interim,

PEKING.

INSPECTORATE GENERAL OF CUSTOMS, 526

S/O

PEKING, 24th August 1925

INDEXED

Dear Mr. Bernadsky,

I have duly received your S/O letter No.333 of the 6th August:

Revenue Collection in hand.

You should remit this balance as soon as possible. The Native banks having re-opened at Shanghai, there is no longer any objection to the employment of Chinese Banks or Agencies.

Yours truly,

J. A. Stephenson

Bernadsky, Esquire,

WENCHOW.

CUSTOM HOUSE,

No. 335.

Wenchow, 24th Aug., 1925.

INDEXED

335

Dear Mr. Stephenson,

In
ction
S/O
49.

At Wenchow we make seizures mostly if not exclusively of Chinese drugs from Chinese vessels or Chinese passengers arrived from Shanghai, Ningpo, or inland places. If such information is not required by your S/O Circ. 49, please let me know, otherwise it will be forwarded to the London office in due time.

Bernadsky
Jnable To
Leave
Absence
ed.

My sincere thanks for your granting me 20 days' leave of absence, but I am sorry to state that I am unable to take it at present. From the letters of the Shanghai and Tsingtao schools for girls, just to hand, I have learned that the first school does not provide board, while the second one does not provide any facilities for the transportation of children to their homes for the Christmas and summer vacations. Therefore if I put

my

W. STEPHENSON, ESQUIRE,

Officiating Inspector General Of Customs, ad interim,

PEKING.

2

534

my girls there, I should be obliged to apply for leave of absence four times a year to bring them to and from the school, which -- from the Service point of view as well as my own -- is very inconvenient or even impossible. And though I am at present in some difficulty in the matter of schooling for my children, still it is probably better to avoid at the very beginning such steps as would have to be corrected later on. I am very sorry for having troubled you with my application for leave of absence.

...nce Of ...issioner ...ested At ...ing Of ...rior Silver ...s.

On the 7th July we confiscated 8,000 inferior twenty-cent silver coins, and on the 8th instant they were handed over to the Superintendent. The latter in his reply of the 11th instant addressed to me, says that he will invite me in due time to be present at the melting of these coins.

I.G. Circular 3481 mentions that the meltage of coins will be arranged by the Superintendent independently of the Commissioner. Therefore I think I must decline his invitation when sent me, although previous practice is for the Commissioner to attend.

Yours truly,

E. Bernadsky.

INSPECTORATE GENERAL OF CUSTOMS,

S/O

PEKING, 25th August 1925

Dear Mr. Bernadsky,

I have duly received your S/O letter No.334 of the 14th August:

May the Commissioner supply certain statistics to the Superintendent?

The instructions in this matter are contained in Circular No.2028.

Yours truly,

J.W. Stephenson.

. Bernadsky, Esquire,

WENCHOW.

536

CUSTOM HOUSE,

/O No. 336. INDEXED Wenchow 29th August, 1925.

Dear Mr. Stephenson,

ure Of
en Inferior
er Coins.

On the 24th instant, three applications for export of 29 packages of silver cakes to Shanghai were produced to this office. Information was given us that these cakes made of melted Fukien 20-cent pieces contained unmelted silver coins, and Customs examination proved that they were mere shells of silver with coins inside, some being imbedded in the upper crust, which had been poured on in a molten condition. All the cakes were broken open and the components separated into three classes, as follows:

Fukien 20-cent inferior silver coins,
pieces 70,971, value $ 12,260.00

Ingots with Fukien inferior silver
20-cent pieces imbedded, piculs
18.40, value " 20,606.00

Ingots without coins, piculs 12.80,
value " 14,327.00

The seizure

. W. STEPHENSON, ESQUIRE,
Officiating Inspector General Of Customs, ad interim,
P E K I N G.

2

537

The seizure was handed over to the Superintendent on the 27th instant. On the same day, at the latter's request, his secretary, Mr. Chang, called on me and asked me to have pity on the owners of the goods. The seizure, said he, is exceptionally big, and the loss of the owners will be too great if they have to pay us 2-10ths of the value as seizure reward. He added that the intention of the applicants was to send this cargo to Shanghai for melting; therefore the Superintendent was very sorry for them and asked me to claim seizure rewards only for the silver coins, but not for the ingots. I told him that my investigation of the case proved that the merchants are local banking firms, and that they instructed their employees to make these cakes with the special purpose of cheating the Customs and smuggling the coins to Shanghai. They knew quite well how to melt the coins properly, and if they had really wanted to melt them they could have done it locally. For these reasons I did not see how I could apply to them a different treatment than to other smugglers; therefore I should be obliged to protest officially if the Superintendent should insist on issuing rewards for coins only.

Then

3
538

Then Mr. Chang raised the question of separate treatment of ingots with coins imbedded, and of ingots without coins, and asked me, for settling the question smoothly without reference to the higher authorities, to be satisfied with a reward issued for coins and for ingots with coins imbedded, without insisting on reward for ingots without coins. Not being sure that in this case the higher Chinese authorities would agree with the Customs procedure of confiscating both contents and containers, I told him that if the Superintendent should take the course indicated, I should not send a protest against it.

In my interview yesterday with the Superintendent, the latter mentioned to me that the Customs value of Fukien inferior silver coins is too high. I told him that we are ready to accept his valuation if he is able to find out the real value of the seizure.

Privately he told me that he intends to return the coins and ingots to the owners without melting, as it takes too much time and expense to melt such a big seizure. I replied that I never interfere with the Superintendent's arrangements on melting or non-melting of seizures.

Yours truly,

C. Bernadsky.

CUSTOM HOUSE, 54

0 No. 337. INDEXED Wenchow, 7th Sept. 1925.

Dear Mr. Stephenson,

ard Oil
ny Case.

On the 22nd of August, the Standard Oil Co.'s installation shipped for Yotsing via Kuant'ou, 1495 gallons of kerosene oil in 99 tins and 27 drums. The value of this oil is estimated at Hk. Tls. 397.670, and that of the containers at Hk. Tls. 200.000. As the cargo was not covered by either a Transit Pass or a Native Customs document, it was detained by the Native Customs Examiner. Mr. J. E. Brackett, the travelling inspector of the Standard Oil Co., called on me and stated that their agent had intended to pay duty on the cargo in question, but that the company's employe arrived at the Native Customs at 4:30 P. M., when the office was closed. When the employe returned to the installation, about 15 li distant from the Native Customs, to report to the manager his failure to obtain the required documents, the junk had already finished loading and left the place for

W. STEPHENSON, ESQUIRE,

Officiating Inspector General Of Customs, ad interim,

P E K I N G.

2

544

for Kuant'ou. I told Mr. Brackett that if my investigation of the case proved his statement correct, then we must change the present system of control over the company's installation, and introduce a new one which would make impossible in future the shipment of their cargo without the Customs documents. I also asked him to send me their Delivery Order Book for this year. To my great surprise I have found by checking this book that a great majority of the shipments for inland places have taken place without covering Maritime Customs or Native Customs documents. This discovery was quite sufficient proof of a system for avoiding payment of Transit Dues or Native Customs duty. In addition I have found that the Native Customs was closed on the day of the shipment in question at 6 P. M. Evidently the statement of the company's employe about his arrival at the Native Customs was not correct, and Mr. Brackett had been misinformed.

Therefore 1) the detained cargo was confiscated and resold to owner for Hk. Tls. 250.00, and 2) there was drawn up and proposed to the company a new set of regulations making it impossible

for the

3

142

for the company to ship any cargo without Customs permit. The check of the installation book proved that over a million catties (200,000 gallons) of kerosene oil has been shipped already this year without Customs documents. The Native Customs duty on this quantity is about Tls. 750.00; or if Transit Passes had been taken, the dues would amount to about twice this sum. I have asked the company to produce for me the installation books since 4th September, 1922, the date of issue of the installation license.

Mr. Brackett again called on me and asked what I intend to do. I told him that the company would have to pay at least the whole amount of duty of which the Native Customs had been defrauded since 1922. I am inclined to insist on payment of Native Customs duty only, because there has been lack of supervision on our part, inasmuch as the books have not been checked since the installation was licensed, and also because it seems evident that the company has been defrauded by its agents, who billed it for duty which they did not pay.

Yours truly,

E. Bernadsky.

INSPECTORATE GENERAL OF CUSTOMS,

S/O

PEKING, 8th September 1925.

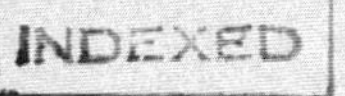

Dear Mr. Bernadsky,

I have duly received your S/O letter No.335 of the 24th August:

Query in connection with S/O Circular No.49.

If the information is clearly not useful to the purpose in view, viz., providing information which may help in the detention of the "smugglers" who are sending out the stuff, it need not be sent to London Office.

Commissioner unable to take short leave.

As leave was granted officially, you should report officially that you do not intend to avail yourself of it.

Yours truly,

J. W. Stephenson

Bernadsky, Esquire,

WENCHOW.

[A.—42]

S/O

INSPECTORATE GENERAL OF CUSTOMS,

PEKING, 12th Sept. 1925.

Dear Sir,

I am directed by the Inspector General to inform you that your S/O letter No. 336, dated 29th August, has been duly received.

Yours truly,

Stanley F. Wright

Personal Secretary.

~~Private Secretary.~~

Bernadsky, Esquire,

WENCHOW.

CUSTOM HOUSE,

Wenchow, 7th Sept. 1925.

n the 22nd of August, the
nstallation shipped for Yotsing
allons of kerosene oil in 99
The value of this oil is
. *397.670, and that of the
s. 200.000. As the cargo was
r a Transit Pass or a Native
was detained by the Native
r. J. E. Brackett, the
of the Standard Oil Co., called
at their agent had intended to
go in question, but that the
ived at the Native Customs at
4:30 P. M., when the office was closed. When the employe returned to the installation, about 15 li distant from the Native Customs, to report to the manager his failure to obtain the required documents, the junk had already finished loading and left the place for

W. STEPHENSON, ESQUIRE,

Officiating Inspector General Of Customs, ad interim,

P E K I N G.

CUSTOM HOUSE,

/O No. 338. Wenchow, 14th Sept., 1925.

INDEXED

Dear Mr. Stephenson,

re Of n ior r Coins.

Continuation Of S/O No. 336 of 29th August, 1925.

On the 29th of August I received from the Superintendent a cheque for $4000.00 as reward for the seizure of Fukien 20-cent inferior silver coins, pieces 70,971, and of ingots with Fukien inferior silver 20-cent pieces imbedded, pcls. 18.40 -- value of both of which items were estimated by the Superintendent at $20,000.00. The value of the third item of the seizure he did not alter, as no reward was issued for it. When I saw the Superintendent, I asked how he arrived at this figure of $20,000.00. He explained to me that in Fukien Province 220-230 cents of this money is the equal of $1.00 big money. Therefore, according to this calculation, the value given is fairly accurate. I am sorry to say I have no basis except the market value on which I can object to his calculations; but as I understand that the

W. STEPHENSON, ESQUIRE,

Officiating Inspector General Of Customs, ad interim,

P E K I N G.

2

54

that the reward for this kind of seizure is calculated according to the actual value of the silver, and not according to the market value of the coins, I have accepted his valuation and duly entered it on the Seizure Report. As to the non-issuance of reward for the ingots without coins, pcls. 12.80, I told the Superintendent that although I shall not send a protest against this procedure, still I must inform the Peking authorities.

In connection with the receipt by the Customs of $4,000.00 as reward, and with the Superintendent's handing back the coins to the owners unmelted, I have received several letters, copies of which, together with their translations, are attached herewith, from a person named Mei Tso-kong. He is a citizen of Wenchow who makes his living by writing petitions, letters to courts, officials, etc.; that is, he is a kind of shyster. After receiving his first letter in which he stated that the banks were fined $10,000.00, while the Customs received only $4,000.00, I invited him to my office by notice (批). He did not come, but sent me a second

3

546

second letter. I then sent a coolie-messenger informing him that I wanted to see him. My idea was to find out whether the letters were anonymous, and if not, to ask him if he had sufficient proof that the Superintendent obtained an amount larger than was handed over to us. If he could certify that his statement was correct, then I intended to report the case to you officially. But the writer, instead of seeing me, sent me a third letter stating that he had reported the case to the Shui Wu Ch'u. I am glad that owing to his last action I am not forced to become an accuser of the Superintendent, but if the Shui Wu Ch'u finds it advisable to investigate the case, it may possibly be of some advantage in clearing the situation.

<u>N.B.</u> a) The writer in his letters mentioned another seizure of silver coins which was simultaneously released without melting. This is probably the seizure of 8,000 coins reported to you in S/O No. 335 of 24th August. I received from the Superintendent $150.00 as reward for this seizure, and he mentioned

mentioned in his letter accompanying the remittance, that the seizure had been melted.

b) Messrs. Lü and Yang mentioned in the letters as mediators are respectively Chief of the Gentry and Member of the Provincial Assembly; thus they are prominent persons in the city.

lera.

On the 26th of August I received a despatch from Mr. C. A. S. Williams, informing me that there is an epidemic of cholera at Ningpo. The Superintendent of Customs and the Medical Officer were notified, and sanitary regulations are being applied to steamers arriving from that port. The Superintendent informed me that there were 6 cases of cholera at Wenchow during August, and that there have been three cases so far in September; but according to the doctor's verbal statement, there were about 30 cases during August and the beginning of September.

f And
ters.

In view of the approach of the season for movements and promotions, I beg to bring to your notice

598

notice a few words about certain members of the Wenchow staff, and about the Customs quarters.

1. Mr. J. W. Ryden, Tidesurveyor, B, is a very capable and energetic Tidesurveyor and Harbour Master. During the last three months, in addition to his ordinary work, he has

    a) re-sounded the river from west of the city to Ch'itutu Island, and prepared two charts based on these soundings;

    b) erected two additional beacons to mark the channel; these have proved of considerable use to shipping.

   He deserves to be promoted to higher rank and to be appointed to a larger port.

2. Mr. K'o Yü-p'ing, 2nd Clerk, B, is a thoroughly competent and desirable type of Chinese employe -- intelligent and hardworking. I entirely agree with the opinion of him expressed by my predecessor, Mr. C. A. S. Williams, in his handing-over-charge memorandum -- that Mr. K'o is fully qualified for promotion to Assistant's rank; and I hereby recommend him to be transferred to this rank.

There

6

749

There is at present vacant on Conquest Island a very comfortable house, just repaired, and suitable for a Senior Tidewaiter or even for an employe of higher rank.
If a married employe should be appointed to Wenchow, he would have no trouble in settling down comfortably.

Very truly yours,

E. Bernadsky.

1st letter from Mr. Mei Tso-kêng.

550

税務司先生鈞鑒敬啟者日前海關查獲甌裕源等莊夾運劣毫並銀餅多件聞已由呂文起楊雨農經手罰洋壹萬元准將原獲之銀餅劣毫照數發還並將前獲之潤源莊私運新角一併給還此等辦法究係援照何項關章迄今數日並未見關署詳晰宣示且外間紛紛議傳均稱關中僅收罰金四千元案關該莊等收受減輕分量之銀幣用夾帶方法轉行交付于人本干刑律制裁地方人民異常注目用特肅函質問敬乞即日　批覆以釋羣疑是所盼切祇候

台綏

梅佐賡謹上

十四年八月三十一日

551

TRANSLATION OF 1ST LETTER FROM MR. MEI TSO-KÊNG.

To the Commissioner of Customs.

A few days ago, the Customs seized a large quantity of inferior silver coins in silver cakes smuggled by the local banks Yü Yüan (裕源), etc. It is reported that the case was settled through the mediation of Messrs Lü Wên-ch'i (吕文起) and Yang Yü-nung (杨雨農) by fining the said banks $10,000, and both the silver cakes and inferior silver coins were consequently released. Besides, the inferior silver coins clandestinely shipped by the local bank, Jun Yüan (润源), and seized by the Customs were also simultaneously released. On what Customs authority are the above treatments based? Many days having passed, there has been no clear announcement regarding the matter from the Customs. A rumour is circulated to the effect that the Customs actually received only $4,000 as fines. The action of the above mentioned banks in collecting light silver coins and sending them to others by smuggling is a violation of the penal code. The public is extraordinarily taken up with this question. The undersigned therefore

542

therefore writes to you and ask you to kindly reply immediately in order to allay the people's doubt. It is anxiously hoped for.

(Signed) 梅佐賡 (Mei Tso-kêng).

31st August 1925.

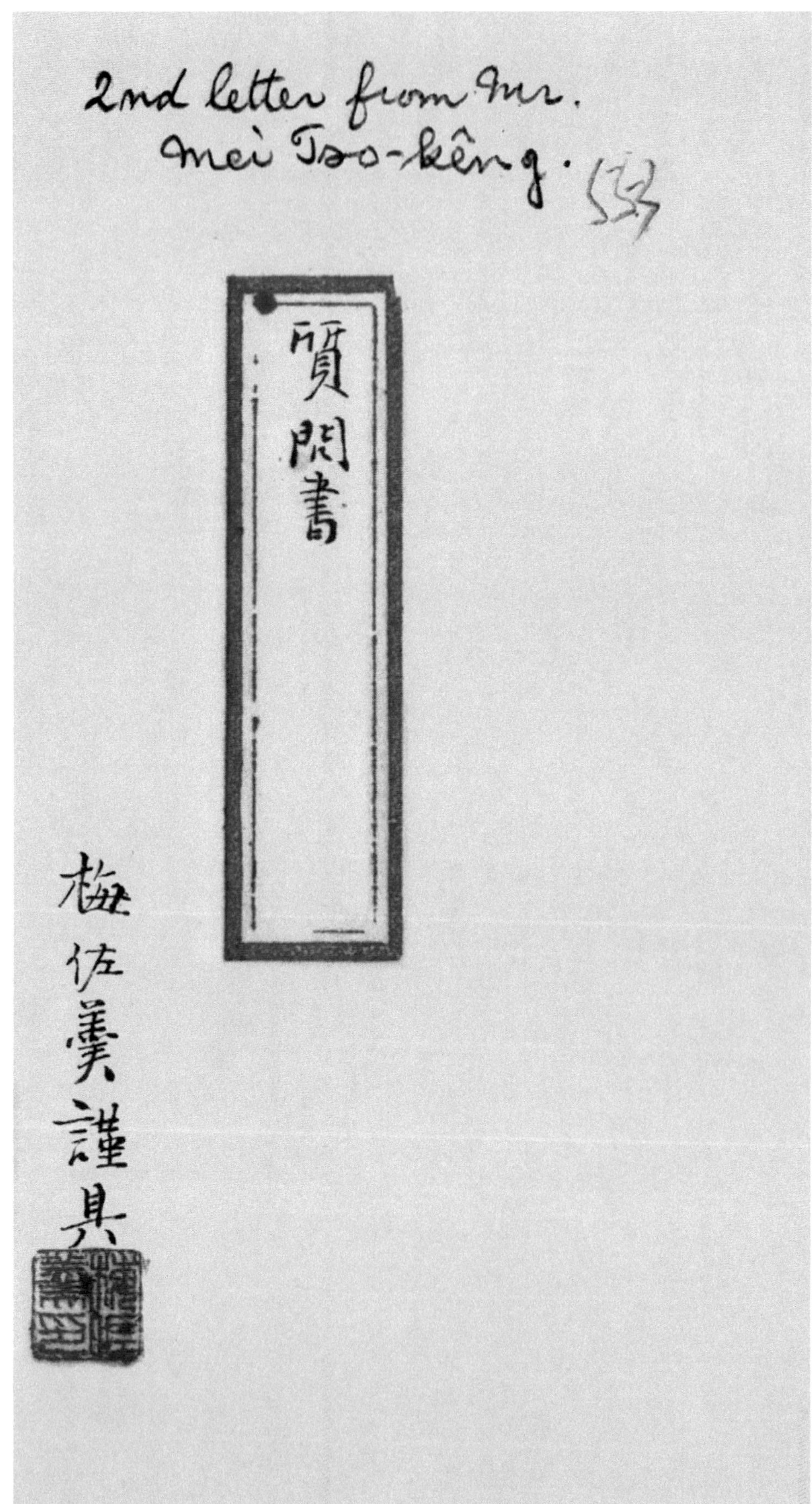
2nd letter from Mr. Mei Tso-kêng. 533

賀閱書

梅佐羹謹具

2nd letter from Mr. Mei Tso-kêng. 553

質問書

梅佐羹謹具

554

為再提質問事、竊佐羹前因海關處分新角、有違定章、於上月三十日、具函質問未承 示復、除已于本月五日正式向 監督署提起呈訴外、合再向貴稅務司提出質問如下、

(甲)、查獲新角、例應銷燬、何以上月下旬間、

裕源等並私運新角、為數極鉅、既經查獲、竟由呂文起、楊雨農說情、關中即准其繳款贖回、免予銷燬、是否銷燬章程、可以任意變更、抑係呂楊二人、別有方法、能使令中外關員、為此違法屬之事、此應行質問者一、

516

(乙)、中国任用外国人為稅務司、原持以整飭関章、事事依法而行、使国内関員不敢舞弊、何以此次查獲新角、監督擅自處分、免徵、發還、是否已徵得 貴稅務司同意、貴稅務司何竟不拒駁、聽其違章辦理、究係是何用意、此應行質問者二、

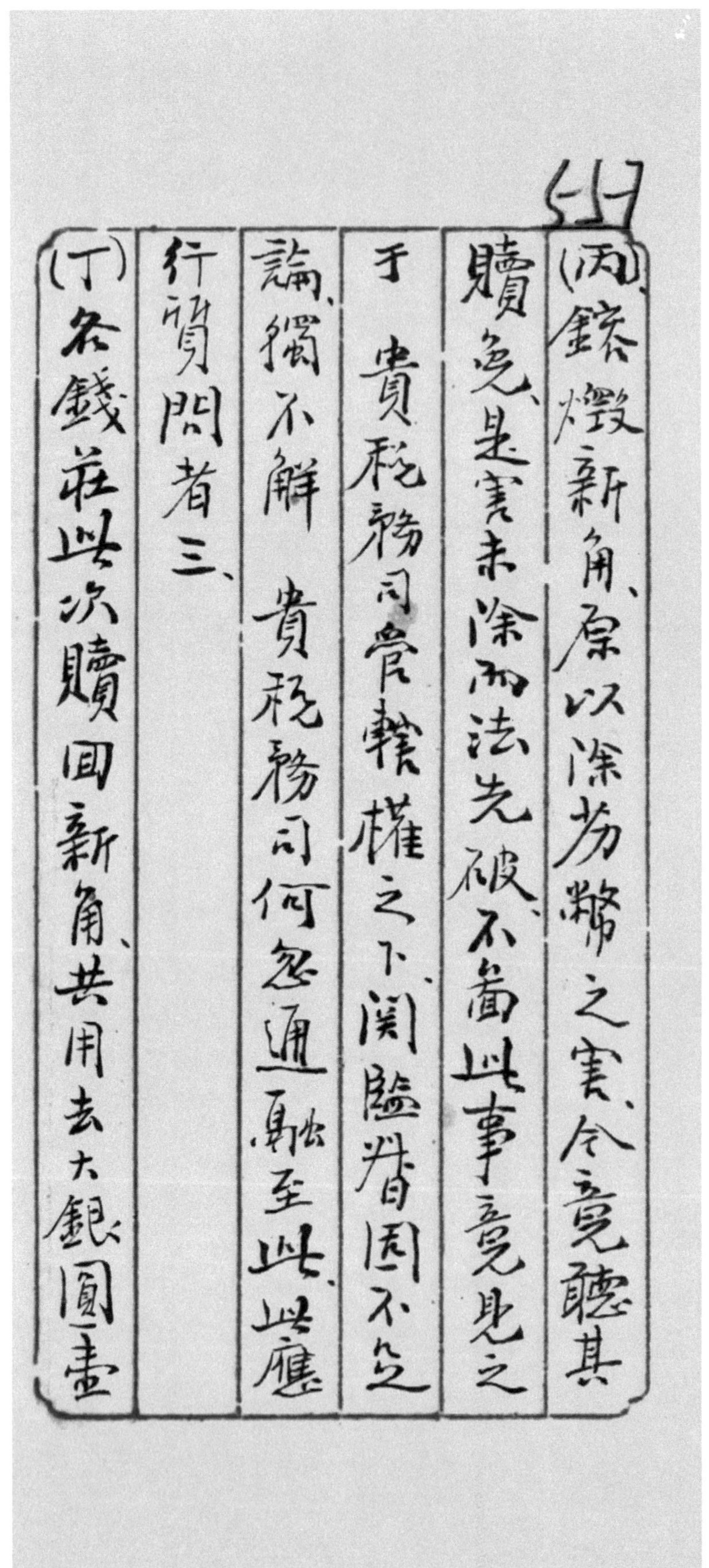

（丙）鎔燬新角、原以除劣幣之害、今竟聽其贖免、是害未除而法先破、不啻此事竟見之于 貴稅務司管轄權之下、関監督固不足論、獨不解 貴稅務司何忽通融至此、此應行質問者三、

（丁）各錢莊此次贖回新角、共用去大銀圓壹

558

萬元、関中僅收四千元、餘六千元、莫名用途、中间自有絕大之黑幕、究竟関中有無別項開費、柳、呂、楊二人借運動関署為名、從中詐取、事関海関聲譽、地方物議紛紜、想貴稅務司當有所聞、何以置耳不一究、與應行質问者四、

559

(戊)閩源莊所運新角、係為案查獲、迭經該莊稟求免繳、閩署已批不准行、何以此次一併發還、是直鬆繳新角之禁令、如同虛設、即 貴稅務司亦恬然收受、罸款不復爭議、誠屬咄咄怪事、此應行質問者五、

(己)奸商私運新角、事所常有、今既開此免繳

60

給還之惡例，設將來再有新角查獲，其將作何辦理，倘果照章銷燬，人自不免藉口莊棧照此次成案，流弊實復無窮。貴稅務司服官中国，于中国一切法令自有遵守之義務，銷燬新角，係 部處嚴重通令各埠海関，無不極力奉行，何獨于甌関破壞無餘，無怪各該莊額手相慶

56

均謂這一萬元花得值也、未知 貴稅務司聞之作何感想、此應行質問者六、

以上各項、敬乞逐一移知監督、切實解釋、並求

貴稅務司自行明白發表意見、

賜以答復、是所至盼、此上

甌海關稅務司

公鑒

民國十四年九月七日

[C.—32]

啟　事　簽

MEMORANDUM.

462

CUSTOM HOUSE,

關

年　月　日

, 19

To

查照

563

TRANSLATION OF 2ND LETTER FROM MR. MEI TSO-KÊNG.

Memorandum by Mr. Mei Tso-kêng.

In view of the illegal settlement by the Customs of the case of the silver coins, I wrote to you on the 31st ultimo, but no reply has yet been received, therefore, I, beside on the 5th instant taking up legal proceedings with the Superintendent of Customs, now again set forth the following queries to you.

(a) In accordance with regulations, when new silver coins are seized, they are to be melted down. Why was it that in the last 10 days of the ultimo, a large quantity of new silver coins, which, clandestinely shipped by local banks, Yü Yüan, etc., had been seized by the Customs, were then released through the mediation of Messrs Lü Wên-ch'i and Yang Yü-nung? The release was effected by ransom and thus the coins escaped melting. Was it because the ruling governing melting of inferior silver coins may be changed at will or was it due to the fact that both Chinese and foreign members of the Customs Staff were induced to commit the unlawful act of settling the above question by Messrs Lü and Yang? This is the

first

564

first matter which requires explanation.

(b) The reason why China employs foreigners as Commissioners of Customs is simply that the foreigners may carry out Customs regulations strictly and act everything in accordance with the requirements of the law, so that Customs Officials dare not to exercise malpractice. Why was it that the Superintendent of Customs this time arbitrarily released the silver coins without melting them? Was the case approved by the Commissioner of Customs? Why did the Commissioner of Customs not object to such an act and why did he allow such illegal treatment? What was the idea? This is the 2nd query which requires explanation.

(c) The idea of melting inferior silver coins is to get rid of inferior coins in the market. Now, if the practice of ransom is allowed to be carried on, not only the evil is not done away but the law has been violated. The case is within the scope of the Commissioner's authority. It is needless to speak of the Superintendent of Customs in the matter. Why did the Commissioner of Customs suddenly allow such an act to be carried out? This is the 3rd question which requires explanation.

(d) The banks spent $10,000 for the sake of redeeming

565

redeeming the seized silver coins. The Customs has actually received only $4,000, while the use of the remaining $6,000 is unknown. There is evidently a great piece of corruption in the matter. Whether the Customs had any other expenses in this connection or whether Messrs Lü and Yang extorted the above sum in the name of the Customs - a matter which concerns the reputation of the Customs, and of which there has been discussion among the public - this must have been known by the Commissioner of Customs. Why do you not look into the matter? This is the 4th point which requires explanation.

(e) The new silver coins smuggled by the bank Jun Yüan were seized separately. The Customs refused to release the coins to the said bank in spite of its repeated requests. Why were they then later released too at the same time as the others? This evidently shows that the instructions governing the melting of inferior silver coins are merely a scrap of paper. Even the Commissioner of Customs accepted the fines without any objection. It is ridiculous! This is the 5th head which requires explanation.

(f) It is quite a common occurrence that inferior silver coins are now and then clandestinely shipped

shipped by merchants of wicked character. Now the illegal practice of returning inferior silver coins without melting them is introduced, and in the future, if any seizure is made on such coins again, what will be the treatment? If they are melted down according to the regulations, there will no doubt be a protest evoked. If, on the other hand, this case is taken as a precedent, the evil will be endless. Since the Commissioner of Customs is an official of the Chinese Government, it is his obligation to observe all laws and orders of the country. The circular instructions re melting inferior silver coins are issued by the Tsai-chêng Pu and Shui-wu Ch'u and they are strictly observed by the Customs at the other ports. Why does the Wenchow Customs alone violate the ruling? It is not strange that the various banks have therefore congratulated themselves saying that it was worth while to spend $10,000 like that. What will the Commissioner of Customs think, when he learns that? This is the 6th question which requires explanation.

The above mentioned queries are kindly requested to be transmitted to the Superintendent of Customs for explanation and meanwhile the Commissioner

of

(567)

of Customs is requested to express his own definite opinion in reply. It is anxiously hoped for.

7th September 1925.

568

3rd letter from Mr. Mei Tso-keng

逕啓者前因海關查獲新角違章處分當於上月三十一日暨本月五日具函質問此係以地方士紳之資格因事質疑意欲得貴稅務司明白答復俾知該案是否為違章處分及其處分應歸何人負責以便向法庭告發治各該莊以應得之罪今貴稅務司竟儼以中國地方官憲自居視質問書如呈禀批令仰即來關候訊此等

569

措詞未免失態茲特鄭重聲明此案之

上陳

稅務處督辦
總稅務司 請為依法查辦關監督及

貴稅務司均列為被告人自無勞批候訊問

也此致

甌海關稅務司

梅佐羹啓 十四年玖月十日

570

TRANSLATION OF 3RD LETTER FROM MR. MEI TSO-KÊNG.

It was on account of the illegal settlement of the case of the inferior silver coins seized by the Customs, that I wrote to you on the 31st ultimo and 5th instant asking for explanations. This was done in my capacity as a member of the gentry of the locality, who is privileged to make queries whenever he has doubts. It was hoped that you would give me a satisfactory explanation with a view to letting me know whether the case was legally settled or not and who was responsible for such a decision, so that an action might be taken in the court against the various banks for the crimes they have committed. Now the Commissioner of Customs regards himself as a Chinese territorial official and treats my letters of inquiry as petitions with the reply, "Come to the Customs and wait for investigation". This kind of wording seems unsuitable. I hereby notify you that I have already petitioned the Minister of the Shui-wu Ch'u and the Inspector General of Customs requesting them to impose punishment on the Superintendent of Customs and the Commissioner of Customs according to law. Both the Superintendent of Customs and the Commissioner of Customs are now made

511

made the defendants. The latter will not be troubled any more to reply to my letter, "Wait for investigation".

(Signed) 梅佐羹 (Mei Tso-kêng).

10th September 1925.

INDEXED

CUSTOM HOUSE,

S/O No. 339.

Wenchow, 23rd Sept., 19 25.

Dear Mr. Stephenson,

Pilotage Service At Wenchow.

The instructions contained in your despatch No. 1345/104,541 of the 3rd September, 1925, are, "to make a local arrangement by which a pilot, on receiving his fee, shall turn it over at once to the common Pilotage Fund".

Up to the present, the money for bringing in or taking out vessels has been entered in our a/c D, which in this case forms a sort of Pilotage Fund. At the end of the quarter, 3/5ths of this collection is paid to the Customs employés who did pilotage work, according to the total number of feet of draft handled by each; the remaining 2/5ths is credited to Service accounts (I.G. Desp. No. 1036/85,458 of the 19th September, 1921). I shall be much obliged if you will let me know whether your instructions require the introduction of any changes into the present practice, or whether "common Pilotage Fund" means our a/c D.

Yours truly,

B. Bernadsky.

W. STEPHENSON, ESQUIRE,

Officiating Inspector General Of Customs, ad interim,

INSPECTORATE GENERAL OF CUSTOMS,

172

S/O

PEKING, 24th September 1925.

Dear Mr. Bernadsky,

I have duly received your S/O letter No.337 of the 7th September:

Standard Oil Company Case.

Please report this matter officially.

Yours truly,

J. W. Stephenson

Bernadsky, Esquire,

WENCHOW.

INSPECTORATE GENERAL OF CUSTOMS, 572

S/O

PEKING, 1st October 1925

Dear Mr. Bernadsky,

I have duly received your S/O letter No. 338 dated 14th September.

Staff and quarters: house vacant on Conquest Island.

Noted: remarks such as these are most helpful.

Yours truly,

J. W. Stephenson

E. Bernadsky, Esquire,

WENCHOW.

575

CUSTOM HOUSE,

INDEXED

/O No. 340.

Wenchow, 5th October 1925.

Dear Mr. Stephenson,

graph
oyès On
ke.

The operators of the Chinese Telegraph Administration went on strike on the 28th ultimo, asking for increase of pay. This strike, up to now still in force, is said to be led by workers in Shanghai, Tientsin, Hankow, and Peking. The local office will send messages within the province, but not those for other provinces.

ts In
ection
Shanghai
ble.

a. Some sugar owned by Chinese firms of the city, and suspected to be of British or Japanese origin, was confiscated by students and thrown into the river just in front of the Custom House on the 28th ultimo at 3 P. M. The value of this cargo was estimated at about $600.

b. The Wenchow Methodist College and the China Inland Mission Middle School for boys --

both

/. STEPHENSON, ESQUIRE,

Officiating Inspector General of Customs, <u>ad interim</u>,

P E K I N G.

2

516

both headed by principals of British nationality -- opened the middle of September. There are about 60 students in the former and 80 in the latter, as against 300 and 100 respectively last year. About half of this year's students are new, and half old.

Your S/O of 24th September, 1925.

lard Oil Case.

I have been informed by the Standard Oil Co. that the manager of their district head office at Ningpo will be here in a few days' time to discuss the case with me. Therefore, pending his arrival, I have postponed reporting the case to you officially.

.

Mr. J. W. Ryden, Tidesurveyor, B, left Wenchow on transfer to Harbin on the 29th ultimo, and Mr. C. Finch, Assistant Examiner, A, as senior outdoor officer here, is performing the duties of Tidesurveyor and Harbour Master. If the latter applies for Acting Allowance, I am not sure whether it is advisable to forward the application to you, or whether I should decline at once, as he has not been

3

been appointed by you to carry out the duties of the Executive Senior Officer during the absence of the latter from the port. I shall be much obliged if you will let me know by what principle I am to be guided in such cases.

Yours truly,

E. Bernadsky.

INSPECTORATE GENERAL OF CUSTOMS, 574

S/O

PEKING, 8th October 1925

Dear Mr.Bernadsky,

I have duly received your S/O letter No.339 dated 23rd September.

Pilotage Service: Accounts treatment of fees received.

No change in present Account practice required.

Yours truly,

J.W.Stephenson.

E.Bernadsky,Esquire,

WENCHOW.

CUSTOM HOUSE,

/O No. 341. 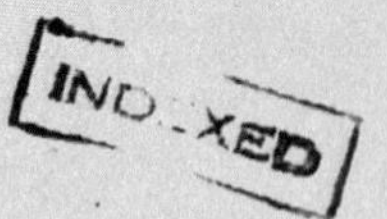 Wenchow, 17th Oct., 1925.

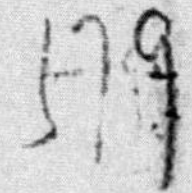

Dear Mr. Stephenson,

ration In
Of
er British
ılate
erty.

A few days there appeared in a local newspaper, the "Ta Kung Pao" (大公报), a note stating that the Magistrate and Gentry had held a meeting in the Magistrate's office for considering the lease of the site occupied by the former British Consulate property. It was decided that the lease should be renewed after a period of five years, but on account of certain gentry not being present, another conference is to be convened for re-considera-tion of the matter.

On the strength of this note, I approached the Superintendent privately and asked him to insist on the insertion of the words "renewable on the same terms on the expiry of a certain number of years." Privately he informed me that it would be very difficult to maneuver the question around to a situation favorable to the Customs, but he promised to do all he could.

Nil

W. STEPHENSON, ESQUIRE,
Officiating Inspector General Of Customs, ad interim,
P E K I N G.

2

560

In
ction
S/O
No. 49.

Nil report is not being sent by this office to the London office. Should this be done?

Yours truly,

E. Bernadsky.

INSPECTORATE GENERAL OF CUSTOMS,

S/O

PEKING, 22nd October 1925

578

Dear Mr. Bernadsky,

I have duly received your S/O letter No.340 of the 5th October:

Should an Acting Allowance be issued to Mr. Finch who is temporarily performing the duties of Tidesurveyor and Harbour Master ?

No. Mr. Cross, due from S. U. L. on 16th October replaces Mr. Ryden. It is not usual to give Acting Allowances for interim acting work. It was not anticipated that Ryden would leave so promptly.

Yours truly,

J. W. Stephenson.

Bernadsky, Esquire,

WENCHOW.

INSPECTORATE GENERAL OF CUSTOMS, 592

S/O

PEKING, 26th October, 1925.

Dear Mr.Bernadsky,

I am directed by the O.I.G.to say that an abnormal Staff situation compels him to ask members of the Foreign Indoor Staff whose leave is overdue to apply for it ; and to offer you your leave,if you desire it,from April 1926. In this case you are requested to forward your official application without delay.

I am to add that if you do not avail yourself of this opportunity your leave may have to be refused when you apply for it later and when conditions may be less favourable.

Please telegraph your decision.

Yours truly,

L. C. F. Holland

Monsieur Bernadsky,

W E N C H O W .

CUSTOM HOUSE,

S/O No. 342. INDEXED Wenchow, Oct. 30th 1925.

583

Dear Mr. Stephenson,

…ation In …Of …r British …late …rty.

On the 26th ultimo the Superintendent informed me by despatch that the Gentry of Wenchow city had decided that a note be put at the end of the lease as follows:

> "The lease is valid for 15 years, within which time the land cannot be rented to any other person";

therefore the Superintendent returned the proposed lease and asked me to make the required alteration. By S/O No. 341 I informed you that I had privately asked the Superintendent to bring the case to a more desirable arrangement; but, as I understand, he could do nothing, as the majority of the Gentry are youngsters, who at present are eager to make all possible objections to foreigners and to the Customs. I told the Superintendent that the proposed note, as stated in his despatch, was very unsatisfactory from

our

W. STEPHENSON, ESQUIRE,

Officiating Inspector General Of Customs, ad interim,

P E K I N G.

2

184

our point of view, but that if the Gentry insist on its insertion, we must discuss the question of our property; i. e., all constructions on the leased land; and I made a proposal as follows:

> "After the expiration of 15 years, the agreement is to be renewed on the basis of the original agreement, otherwise the cost of all constructions on the leased land must be repaid to the Customs."

The Superintendent's idea was that my proposal would be unacceptable, and he made a counter-proposal as follows:

> "After the expiration of the lease, if it is necessary to let the land to any other person, the concurrence of both parties must be obtained."

I pointed out to him that we must take steps to secure our property on the island against loss in the event that the owner of the land should, after expiration of the lease, be unwilling to make a suitable agreement with us. The Superintendent seems to disagree with me, mostly on account of the difficulty in passing my proposal through the Gentry; but

3

585

but still he promised to discuss the question with the Taoyin and Magistrate, and to find a way of settling it.

All this interview took place with the Superintendent's Chief Secretary, Mr. Chang, who is at present in charge of the office. The Superintendent himself is with General Sun, probably in Nanking.

ard Oil Case.

I have just received a letter from Mr. Daniels, sub-manager of the Standard Oil Co.'s office at Ningpo. He writes:

> "Sorry that it is taking a little longer than expected for us to reply -- but the matter has been put before our General Management and we will give you an answer shortly now, or Mr. Lilley (Ningpo manager) or I will come to Wenchow."

On receiving the Company's reply, or after interview with the manager of their office at Ningpo, I shall report to you.

Yours truly,

E. Bernadsky.

INDEXED

CUSTOM HOUSE,

No. 343.

Wenchow, Nov 4th. 1925.

486

Dear Mr Stephenson,

..ation In ... Of ...r British ...late ...rty.

On the 31st of October Mr Chang, who is in temporary charge of the Superintendent's office here called upon me and advised me to agree to insert on the lease without any alteration the note proposed by the Gentry, which reads as follows;

"The lease is valid for 15 years within which time the land cannot be rented to any other person."

The reasons why he takes such an attitude in this question, as he explained to me, were :-

1. There are no grounds for any fear of loss of the property. If after expiration of the lease of the land for which a rent was paid regularly, the Ground-Landlord wishes to use it for his own purposes or to rent it to another person, then according to the Chinese custom and law

.W. STEPHENSON, ESQUIRE,
Officiating Inspector General of Customs, ad interim,
PEKING.

2

187

he is obliged to refund the cost of all constructions to the owner of the buildings.

2. If we want to alter the proposed wording of the note, as was suggisted by me and mentioned in my S/O letter 342, then a Gentry meeting must be held. It will take again several months time with a very uncertain result.

I told Mr Chang that if he can give official assurance that we cannot lose anything after the expiration of the lease, then I shall be able to refer this question to you. He agreed to my proposal requesting me to send him a despatch enquiring whether the cost of construction shall be refunded, if the land is claimed back after expiration of the lease. He will forward this query to the magistrate instructing him to reply and he expects that the reply will be the same as that which has just been stated by him. And he expects that the wording of the lease supported and explained by the official correspondence will satisfy the Customs.

3.

I was asked by him to refrain from raising the question of renewing the lease on the same or desirable terms after expiration of the 15 years as :-

a. The magistrate will not dare to give any reply without referring the question to the Gentry and also because :-

b. This question is included in the original query

Though this system of working is not the usual European practice, it is possible that it is just as good when applied to the Chinese, therefore I have decided to send the required despatch to the Superintendent. After receiving a reply, I will forward the whole to you officially

Yours truly,

E. Bernadotz

390

INSPECTORATE GENERAL OF CUSTOMS,

S/O

PEKING, 5th November 1925

Dear Mr. Bernadsky,

I have duly received your S/O letter No. 341 of the 17th October.

S/O Circular No. 49:

Nil reports are not required.

Yours truly,

[signature]

E. Bernadsky, Esquire,

WENCHOW.

CUSTOM HOUSE,

S/O

Wenchow, 6th November 1925.

Dear Mr. Holland,

I am very grateful to the Officiating Inspector General for his willingness to grant me long leave from April 1926, but I am sorry to state that my present financial state does not permit of my applying for such leave. I must confess that since my arrival at Wenchow this situation is gradually improving but it requires time to be able to raise from the ruined financial state when practically every cash of the saving and the first Retiring Allowance was lost owing to the Russian revolution. I shall be obliged if you will bring to the O.I.G. attention that the present political situation of Russia - my native country where it would be easier for me to support my wife and 6 children - is not very attractive for going there.

Yours truly,

B. Bernadsky

C.F. Holland, Esquire,

PEKING.

(91)

INSPECTORATE GENERAL OF CUSTOMS,

S/O

PEKING, 14th November 1925

Dear Mr. Bernadsky,

I have duly received your S/O letter No.342 of the 30th October:

Alteration in lease of former British Consulate Property.

We are safeguarded for a period of 20 years by our agreement with H. B. M.'s Board of Works. As the present temper of the local gentry is clearly antagonistic it may be best not to press for an immediate settlement in the hope that the Superintendent will of his own volition let the matter rest until a time when the local temper has changed.

Yours truly,

J. W. Stephenson

Bernadsky, Esquire,

WENCHOW.

CUSTOM HOUSE,

S/O No. 344. INDEXED Wenchow 19th Nov. 1925.

596

Dear Mr. Stephenson,

Alteration in Lease of Former British Consulate Property.

Continuation of S/O No. 343 of the 4th Inst.

Mr. Chang, who is in temporary charge of the Superintendent's Office, has just privately informed me that the Magistrate cannot give the official assurance that the Customs will not lose anything after the expiration of the 15 years lease without referring this question to the gentry. His opinion at present is that if we do not want to sign the agreement with the remarks proposed by the gentry inserted on it then the best thing under the present circumstances is to leave the question open and to pay the annual rent $72.00 without signing any lease. Later on when the gentry will consist of members more favourably

disposed

J. W. STEPHENSON, ESQUIRE,

Officiating Inspector General of Customs, ad interim,

PEKING.

2.

591

disposed to the Customs then the question of having a lease will be raised again.

Staff. (a) Mr. C. Finch, Assistant Examiner A, is on the sick list suffering from dysentry since the 16th instant. Mr. G. E. Cross, Acting Tidesurveyor, is attending to the Examiner's Office in addition to his ordinary duties.

(b) Messrs. Ng Shiu Hung (3rd (Chi.) Assistant, B) and Wang Cok Man (1st Clerk C) who are transferred here have not arrived yet. The Kongmoon Commissioner notified me by a telegram that he will detain there Mr. Ng Shiu Hung for a few weeks more. In my reply I told Mr. Talbot that the transferred Assistant is urgently required here and at the same time I informed the Shanghai Commissioner by a letter, copy of which is appended, that Mr. Chü Kam Po will accordingly be detained here for sometime.

Yours truly,

E. Bernadotz

3.

598

APPEND.

S/O

Wenchow, 14th Nov. 1925.

Dear Mr. Maze,

I have just received a telegram from the Kongmoon Commissioner stating that the Chinese Assistant transferred from that port to Wenchow cannot be spared for a few weeks more. This Assistant is for the Native Customs here and his delay in arriving causes me to retain there Mr. Chü Kam Po, the Chinese Assistant in charge of the Wenchow Native Customs, who is transferred to your port. I am sorry that on account of the pressure of work and shortness of the staff I cannot detach anybody from the Maritime Customs Staff to take over the temporary charge of the Native Customs and I shall be obliged if you will let me keep Mr. Chü here up to the time that the Assistant from Kongmoon arrives. I am in hopes that the latter will not be kept for a long time as I have notified the Kongmoon Commissioner that the transferred Assistant is urgently required here.

Yours truly,

(Signed) E. Bernadsky.

[A.—42]

589

/o

INSPECTORATE GENERAL OF CUSTOMS,

PEKING, 24th November 1925.

Dear Sir,

I am directed by the Inspector General to inform you that your S/O letter No. 343, dated 4th November, has been duly received.

Yours truly,

for Personal Secretary.

~~Private Secretary.~~

Bernadsky, Esquire,

WENCHOW.

590

INSPECTORATE GENERAL OF CUSTOMS,

PEKING, 5th November 1925

dsky,

duly received your S/O letter

17th October.

No.49:

eports are not required.

Yours truly,

E.Bernadsky, Esquire,

WENCHOW.

CUSTOM HOUSE,

S/O No. 345. Wenchow, 1st December 1925

INDEXED

600

Dear Mr. Stephenson,

Position of junk "Chin Shun Hsing" being measured N.C. Staff for junk dues.

On the 21st of November the Native Customs Examiner at Chuangyuanchiao station Mr. Tu Chi-chiang (杜志强) arrived here and reported as follows.

On the 20th of November at about 5 p.m. he was asked by a fisherman of a fishing junk Chin Shun Hsing (金顺兴) to clear the junk. He together with a Native Customs Watcher Wang Yün (汪云) proceeded by a sampan to that junk for taking measurement for the assessment of Liangt'ou Dues and examination. When our officers asked to open the hold of the junk the fishermen refused to do so on the pretext that the junk was in ballast and that therefore there was no necessity for her examination. As it

J W. STEPHENSON, ESQUIRE,

Officiating Inspector General of Customs, ad interim,

PEKING.

2.

601

it was difficult to understand the fishermen - who were all Fukien people - our officers decided to take the measurement for Liangt'ou Dues expecting that the question of the examination would be settled when the owner of the junk came. But to their great surprise the crew opposed the measuring of the junk for Junk Dues. They probably thought that the vessel might be exempted from such dues as no export cargo was taken. At this time the fishermen called their people from ashore. While the Examiner tried to explain to the crew that Liangt'ou Dues have to be collected indiscriminately whether the vessel takes cargo or not, some fishermen together with the laodah and the owner of the junk boarded the junk and without asking any questions from our officers began to push and beat them. The latter shouted for help. This call was heard by our officers' two servants, who took a sampan and reached the junk. The fishermen at once seized and brought them on board of the junk and pulled them together with the Watcher into the hatch leading to the sleeping room of the junk. But they

could

3.

602

could not pull into that room the Examiner who strongly resisted this violence and who again began to call for help. An employe of the Likin Station who heard this call went to the Maritime Police Boat, which was at a distance at about 30-40 yards from the place of the incident, and asked them to protect the Customs people seized by the fishermen. The Police Boat raised anchor and approached the junk to about 10 yards distance. The fishermen seeing the move of the Police Boat shouted: "let us kill the seized people and fight the police". At this moment a sampan carrying two men from ashore approached the fishing junk and these two unknown persons began to persuade the fishermen to stop the fighting and to release the Customs people. Noticing that the situation at that time looked suitable for escape the Examiner jumped into the sampan carrying these two persons and proceeded to the Police Boat where the case was explained by him to the officer in charge of the boat. At this time the brother of the owner of the fishing junk boarded the Police Boat, appologized and asked the officer in

4.

603

in charge of the boat to forgive the fishermen and the owner of the fishing junk for the accident. The Police officer told him that an appology in such cases can be accepted only from the owner of the junk. A few minutes later the owner of the junk and his brother appeared on board of the Police Boat. Then the first one was detained and the second one was instructed to bring the Customs employees and their servants to the Police Boat. Soon after this the brother of the owner of the junk brought there the Watcher Wang Yün and stated that the servants would be released at once after the release of the owner of the junk. The officer in charge of the Police Boat explained to our officers that in view of the absence of instructions from his Superior about this case and also in consequence of the late hour of the day - it was about 11 p.m. - he did not dare to do anything before the next day but would keep a special watch on the fishing junk to prevent her leaving the place. Under these circumstances our officers left the Police Boat. The Examiner instructed the Watcher to

carry

5.

604

carry out his duties and himself left Chuang-yuanchiao for Wenchow by a sampan and arrived here on the 21st of November in the early morning.

The Superintendent was notified of the case and asked to instruct the Police to help us in releasing the servants of our employees and in bringing the junk and guilty persons to Wenchow for investigation and it was done by him on the same day.

On the 23rd of November at about 3 p.m. I was inform by Mr. Chü Kam Po, Assistant-in-charge of the Native Customs at Wenchow, that the servants of the Customs employees were released on the 21st of November at about noon and that the junk, fishermen and the brother of the owner of junk were brought to the Native Customs here. The owner of junk was released by the Police under the guarantee. I notified the Superintendent of their arrival and forwarded them to him. On the next day the Superintendent called upon me and asked to have a pity to these poor people who had made such a disturbance owing to their ignorance. He told me that the present time is the beginning of the fishing season and if if a fisherman is detained now he loses all of his earnings. If all these people should be handed to the Chinese court then without speaking about the punishment which would be meted out to them in accordance with the law, the investigation of the case only would take such a long time that they would lose their annual earnings, and several fishermen's families would be left without means of livelihood. Therefore he asked me to take this case in my hands and to punish them financially. Though such cases should be investigated and settled by the Chinese authorities, in view however of the special circumstances as explained by the Superintendent I agreed to his proposal. Such was my reply.

On the 25th of November I investigated the case and found that (1) the owner of the junk did not insult our officers. (2) fishermen pushed and insulted our officers by order of the laodah, therefore they were all released without punishment but under guarantee. (3) the laodah - the only responsible person for the things which happened on board the junk - was convicted and punished by being made to pay Hk.Tls. 75.00 and

released

7.

606

released also under the guarantee.

The particulars of distribution of the above amount are:

			Hk.Tls.
(1)	Fine		20.00
(2)	Food-money to Maritime Police for the time when they were watching the fishing junk and bringing her to Wenchow	$40.00	
(3)	Bill produced by the Chuang-yuanchiao Customs employees in connection with the case: sampan hire, replacing lost things and medical expenses	$44.26	
	Total:	$84.26 @ 1.532 =	55.00
	Grand total Hk.Tls.		75.00

The reasons for such a light punishment were :

(a) The ignorance of the man in question.

(b) The evening when the incident occurred, was the fishermen's festival before departure, and they were all under the influence of alcohol.

(c) Fishermen's superstition calling for the non-admittance of officials in uniform during the festival, if they want to have good luck in their fishing during the

3.

607

the season, whereas our Watcher was in uniform.

(d) Our officers were asked to clear the junk at about 5 p.m. - before festival - but it seems they went on board the junk at about 7 p.m.

(e) The fishermen stated that our officers threatened to take the rope off the sail, if the fishermen refused to comply with the Customs formalities and that made them excited.

Yours truly,

E. Bernadsky

[A.—42]

511

INSPECTORATE GENERAL OF CUSTOMS,

/o

PEKING, 3rd December 1925.

Dear Sir,

I am directed by the Inspector General to inform you that your S/O letter No. 344, dated 19th November, has been duly received.

Yours truly,

Personal Secretary.

~~Private Secretary.~~

Bernadsky, Esquire,

WENCHOW.

CUSTOM HOUSE,

Wenchow, 1st December 1925

600

on,

of November the Native Customs gyuanchiao station Mr. Tu Chi- arrived here and reported as

of November at about 5 p.m. a fisherman of a fishing junk (金順興) to clear the junk. a Native Customs Watcher Wang eeded by a sampan to that junk ement for the assessment of d examination. When our open the hold of the junk the fishermen refused to do so on the pretext that the junk was in ballast and that therefore there was no necessity for her examination. As it

W. STEPHENSON, ESQUIRE,

Officiating Inspector General of Customs, ad interim,

PEKING.

CUSTOM HOUSE,

S/O No. 346. INDEXED Wenchow 12th Dec. 1925

Dear Sir Francis,

pplication to rent
he Customs property,
..

A few days ago one of the Customs broker here applied to me to allow him to rent for godown purposes the land on the North-west side of the Custom House compound, between the public jetty and China Merchants Steam Navigation Co.'s property. This piece of land was originally intended to be used for examination of cargo, as was reported to you by despatches Nos. 3672 and 3710, but the practice of the last three years has shown that this ground has been left unused for any purpose. The present situation does not promise much development for the port in the near future and probably we shall not use the land in question for 5-10 years at least.

Sir Francis Aglen, K. B. E.,
Inspector General of Customs ,
P E K I N G .

2.

610

least. The building, which he proposes to make on it must be of such construction that our bunding will not be spoiled in any way. The applicant agreed to this and also to restore the land after 5 years, if we want to use it for our own purposes, but the time for the expiration of the lease will be after 10 years. If he would agree to my proposal to pay $700 per year, the question would be referred to you officially for consideration and approval. But the applicant found that the requested amount was too high and offerred $245 only per year. Probably I can come to an agreement with him for $300-400 per year, but as I have no means of arriving at a good commercial agreement except by throwing open the question to the public, I propose to issue a notification to the effect that this piece of land can be rented for godown purposes and that the highest bidder will obtain it. If you approve of my suggestions, then I shall try to make a suitable agreement, a copy of which will be forwarded to you together with a report of the case for consideration and approval.

On

3.

611

ikin on postal
arcels.

On the 7th instant Mr. Chang, who is in temporary charge of the Superintendent's Office, called upon me and asked if there was any objection on my part in allowing the Likin Authorities instead of the Maritime Customs collecting Likin on postal parcels at Wenchow Post Office. The question has been brought before him by the local Likin Authorities, as they expect to make certain improvements in this direction. I replied that this question must be referred to Peking. If the Superintendent thinks that this demand is reasonable and if he is ready to support it, then I should be glad to have a despatch from him in which should be stated the reasons for such an innovation and proposed improvement. I could not obtain from Mr. Chang any good reason for this proposal but it can be guessed that the local Likin Authorities are dissatisfied with the sum collected by us, which approximately amounts to $25.00 per month. If Likin was collected on every postal parcel, as they would probably want to do, then the amount would be considerably increased.

Wenchow

4.

612

esssels in peril
t sea.

Wenchow Summary of Non-urgent Chinese Correspondence, October, 1925, Subject No. 5. Chinese Secretary's Memorandum of the 24th of November 1925.

The question will be referred to you officially after the collection of due information about the subject.

pening of District
ssembly.

The Wenchow District Assembly (永嘉縣議會), Special Session, has been convened on the 10th instant.

I and my family send you Christmas greetings and all good wishes for the New Year.

Yours truly,

E. Bernadsky

INDEXED

CUSTOM HOUSE,

S/O No. 347. Wenchow, 24th Dec. 1925.

619

Dear Sir Francis,

ccusations against mployės of Native ustoms.

During the last few weeks I have spent much of my time in an investigation of cases brought by Chinese against Native Customs Examiners and Watchers, in which they accuse the latter of bribery and of handing over to the Customs only a part of their collections. On the 22nd instant I instructed Mr. Ng Shiu Hung, the 3rd Assistant B now in charge of the Native Customs and Mr. K'o Yu-p'ing, 2nd Clerk B, in the Maritime Customs to proceed to Ningtsun, Chuangyuanchiao and Puchow and to bring me, if possible, figures taken from brokers' account books of payments made by them to the Native Customs. I am glad to state that as far as I could discover in the course of my investigation there were no proofs that the accusations were well grounded. There is a rumour that all the

SIR FRANCIS AGLEN, K. B. E.,
Inspector General of Customs,
PEKING.

2.

615

the different tax-stations except the Native Customs will be closed soon and it is probable that the employés of the offices expected to be closed are trying to guarantee themselves for a position in the Native Customs by bringing accusations and thereby creating vacancies in that office.

taff. 14 days' leave (from 22nd December 1925 to 4th January 1926) was granted by me to Mr. B.S. Abramoff, 3rd Class Tidewaiter, to proceed to Shanghai for dentist treatment. A medical certificate was produced.

Yours truly,

E. Bernadsky

A.—42]

608

INSPECTORATE GENERAL OF CUSTOMS,

PEKING, 31st December 1925.

Dear Sir,

I am directed by the Inspector General inform you that your S/O letter No. 345, ted 1st December, has been duly ceived.

Yours truly,

Personal Secretary.

Bernadsky, Esquire,

WENCHOW.

CUSTOM HOUSE,

Wenchow, 12th Dec. 1925

606

ago one of the Customs broker me to allow him to rent for the land on the North-west side House compound, between the public Merchants Steam Navigation Co.'s piece of land was originally used for examination of cargo, to you by despatches Nos. 3672 the practice of the last three that this ground has been left purpose. The present situation does not promise much development for the port in the near future and probably we shall not use the land in question for 5-10 years at least.

Sir Francis Aglen, K. B. E.,

Inspector General of Customs,

PEKING.

1926 年

CUSTOM HOUSE,

S/O No. 348. Wenchow, 8th January 1926.

INDEXED

Dear Sir Francis,

Standard Oil Co. case.

Your despatch No. 1363/105,796 of 9th December 1925 §§ 3 and 4.

Ever since the Chekiang Kerosene Additional Tax Bureau at Wenchow started negotiations with the oil companies to try and make them understand that the acceptance of the regulations of this bureau would be to their advantage, the oil companies have not been so interested in Transit Passes issued by the Maritime Customs as before. Therefore the arguments advanced by the Company to the effect that the tank is an unbonded one, and as such is not under the Customs control, could be more easily disqualified if the position of the

SIR FRANCIS AGLEN, K. B. E.,
Inspector General of Customs,
PEKING.

the tank had been discussed from the Native Customs point of view.

I am sorry to state that during the discussion of the case with the S.O.Co's representatives, it became evident that the company understands its obligations only when the latter were advantageous to it.

Piracy.

On the 5th instant the Steam Launch "Li-tai" was pirated just off Wenchow Point. The 12 pirates boarded the steam launch as passengers and seized the launch and took over $6,000.00 in cash and clothing, etc. to the value of over $1,000.00. Four persons were wounded, two by shot wounds and two by stabbing. The case was reported to the Superintendent at once when it was known to us.

The activity of the Reds.

There is a rumour here that the local students have deputed about 50 of their number to go for 3-18 months training to the Canton Military Acadamy opened by the Reds. They all expect to be back soon with the rank of captain

3.

captain to form and train a Red army here. One of the Bolshevicks' leaders at Canton, General Chiang Chieh Shih (蔣介石) is a Chekiang man and will its appears take a great part in the process of bringing this province under the influence of the Reds through these new recruits. To draw the students - boys and girls - into the sphere of their influence, to form a Red army at the various centres, and lastly to attract the mob by tempting promises are the three usual steps taken by the Bolshevicks to gain control. The Chekiang province is therefore now reaching the second stage.

Yours truly,

E. Bernadsky

[A.—42]

S/O

INSPECTORATE GENERAL OF CUSTOMS,

PEKING, 21st January 1926.

4

Dear Sir,

I am directed by the Inspector General to inform you that your S/O letter No. 348, dated 8th January, has been duly received.

Yours truly,

Personal Secretary.

~~Private Secretary.~~

Bernadsky, Esquire,

WENCHOW.

CUSTOM HOUSE,

Wenchow, 23rd January 1926.

5

[...]ED

cis,

21st instant two leaflets issued t Country-saving Association were the streets of Wenchow by the he local schools.

original copies of these their translation are enclosed

ng Hsi-wên (程希文), Superin- stoms, Wenchow, returned from e 28th December 1925, having spent nths time (left Wenchow on 3rd September 1925) in Marshal Sun Ch'uan-fang's Office.

Yours truly,

E. Bernadsky

SIR FRANCIS AGLEN, K. B. E.,

Inspector General of Customs,

P E K I N G .

[A.—42]

616

S/O

INSPECTORATE GENERAL OF CUSTOMS,

PEKING, 21st January 1926.

Dear Sir,

I am directed by the Inspector General to inform you that your S/O letter No. 347, dated 24th December, has been duly received.

Yours truly,

Personal Secretary.
~~Private Secretary.~~

Bernadsky, Esquire,

WENCHOW.

CUSTOM HOUSE,

S/O No. 349. Wenchow, 23rd January 1926.

INDEXED

Dear Sir Francis,

Events in connection with
(a) Shanghai trouble and
(b) Manchuria affairs.

On the 21st instant two leaflets issued by the Student Country-saving Association were distributed in the streets of Wenchow by the students of the local schools.

The two original copies of these leaflets and their translation are enclosed herewith.

Return of Superintendent of Customs, Wenchow.

Mr. Chêng Hsi-wên (程希文), Superintendent of Customs, Wenchow, returned from Nanking on the 28th December 1925, having spent over three months time (left Wenchow on 3rd September 1925) in Marshal Sun Ch'uan-fang's Office.

Yours truly,

E. Bernadsky.

SIR FRANCIS AGLEN, K. B. E.,
Inspector General of Customs,
PEKING.

LEAFLET DISTRIBUTED BY THE LOCAL STUDENT COUNTRY-SAVING ASSOCIATION RE SHANGHAI AFFAIR OF MAY 30TH.

親愛的同胞們！五卅慘殺是帝國主義者真面目出現的始期我國近幾十年來受帝國主義者的侵略壓迫剝削種種苦痛已達到極點而帝國主義者對於五卅所施之嚴酷手段謀壓燬中華民族之獨立運動置我民族生命於不顧實為我中華民族極大之恥辱所以滬上工商學聯會提出最低限度之十三條件令其承認以為解決滬案標準稍雪五卅之大恥辱而最近北京使團竟敢以我國人始終所否認反對之滬案重查為根據作片面之處置未經我政府與民眾之同意即以七萬五千元區區之數欲了結五卅懸大之案此種非法解決之敷衍舉動寧為我國民眾所甘受五卅死難先烈所甘心為今之計對於使團發表解決滬案之妄舉只有誓不承認須得滬上工商學聯合會所提出之十三條件完滿解決慰藉死難先烈之英靈挽中華民族之危機尚希各界同胞一致奮鬥始終否認與列強作強有力之反抗奮鬥奮鬥願各勉之

LEAFLET DISTRIBUTED BY THE LOCAL STUDENT COUNTRY-SAVING ASSOCIATION RE JAPAN DESPATCHED HER TROOPS TO MANCHURIA.

親愛的同胞們！此次日本帝國主義者公然出兵南满名為保護僑民實則為助其走狗張作霖侵害主權破壞公理莫此為甚我中華人民年來受喪心病狂之軍閥所施苦痛已無可再忍望和平如同飢渴方以郭氏倒戈張賊危急成敗之決指日可待孰料日本乘机進兵助長内亂陷人民於水深火熱之中拯張賊於一髮千鈞之危循環不息之紛爭使我國民氣奄然一息此而不爭國運益危尚希各界同胞一致竭力反抗非達到退兵目的誓不退轉特此宣言

中華民國浙江温州學生救國联合會啓

8

LEAFLET DISTRIBUTED BY THE LOCAL STUDENT COUNTRY-SAVING ASSOCIATION RE SHANGHAI AFFAIR OF MAY 30TH: TRANSLATION OF.

Dear brothers! The dreadful disaster of May 30th is a revelation of the real characters of the imperialists. During recent years, our country has suffered to the utmost by usurpation, repression, despoilment, and such like insults inflicted by the imperialists. In the case of the inhuman action of May 30th, the imperialists plotted to suppress the independent movements of the nation of the Republic of China regardless of the lives of people of our race. It was really the greatest disgrace to the Republic of China: therefore the association of labourers, merchants and educational bodies put forward 13 simple articles and asked them (the imperialists) to consent to these as a basis for the settlement of affairs in Shanghai and for the redressing of the great disgrace of May 30th. But, recently, the Ministers of the foreign powers at Peking, making the 2nd inquiry of Shanghai affairs which has not been recognised by our countrymen from the very beginning to the end, their basis, put forward a

one-sided

2.

9

one-sided decision without the consent of our government and people in offering a small sum of $75,000.00 for conclusion of the big case of May 30th. How can this unlawful decision cheating us of our rights be accepted by all of our countrymen and give satisfaction for the deaths of May 30th? The best plan for us under these circumstances is not to recognise the unlawful decision on the Shanghai affair expressed by the deplomatic bodies but to arrive at a satisfactory decision on the 13 articles delivered by the association of labourrers, merchants and educational bodies so as to appease the spirits of the dead and to rescue China from her critical condition. Our brothers of various circles are requested to fight strongly and unanimously, and not to recognise this offer up to the last. Use great efforts to resist the Powers. Fight strongly! Fight strongly! Hoping that every one will make the greatest effort he can.

3.

10

LEAFLET DISTRIBUTED BY THE LOCAL STUDENT COUNTRY-SAVING ASSOCIATION RE JAPAN DESPATCHED HER TROOPS TO MANCHURIA: TRANSLATION OF.

Dear brothers! The Japanese imperialists have this time openly despatched their troops to Manchuria on the excuse of protecting her nationals living there but really to assist their stalking horse Chang Tso-lin. This action is most seriously detrimental to China's rights and international principles. In recent years our people of the Republic of China have suffered at the hand of cruel and mad militarists so much damage that we cannot endure any more and long for peace. The revolution of General Kuo made the condition of the Traitor Chang very dangerous. The success of Kuo and the destruction of Chang could have been decided in a moment. Japan unexpectedly seizing this opportunity despatched her troops to extend the boundaries of this rebel, causing considerable destruction and loss and rescuing the Traitor Chang from instant annihilation. This endless fighting has brought our people to their last gasp. If we do not fight on account of this, it will bring greater dangers on our country. Hoping that our brothers

4.

brothers of each class will unanimously put forth their greatest efforts to resist until these Japanese troops are withdrawn. This is the proclamation.

The Student Country-saving Association,
Wenchow, Republic of China.

[A.—42]

12

INSPECTORATE GENERAL OF CUSTOMS.

S/O

PEKING, 17th February 1926.

Dear Sir,

I am directed by the Inspector General
o inform you that your S/O letter No. 349,
ated 23rd January, has been duly
eceived.

Yours truly,

Personal Secretary.
~~Private Secretary.~~

rnadsky, Esquire,

WENCHOW.

INSPECTORATE GENERAL OF CUSTOMS,

S/O

PEKING, 29th January 1926

613

Dear Mr. Bernadsky,

I have duly received your S/O letter No.346 of the 12th December:

Proposal to lease Customs property.

If the land in question is not required for Customs purposes it should of course be leased out as advantageously as possible. Please report officially in the matter. But don't issue any notification.

Christmas and New Year Greetings.

Many thanks.

Yours truly.

F. A. Aglen

rnadsky, Esquire,

WENCHOW.

CUSTOM HOUSE,

19

S/O No. 350.

Wenchow, 1st February 1926.

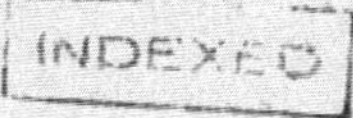

Dear Sir Francis,

uthority for issuing round-rent.

In accordance with the Superintendent's request I have forwarded to him on the 30th January 1926 $72.00 - the annual ground-rent for the period from 6th September 1924 to 5th September 1925 for the land on which the Tidesurveyor's and Senior Examiner's Houses are located (Former British Consulate Property) without signing any lease (your S/O of the 14th November 1925). I used your Despatch to Wenchow No. 1267/100,079 of 23rd August 1924 as the authority for this payment but I am not sure if it is sufficient.

wards for Chuang-anchiao Case.

My S/O Letter No. 345 of the 1st December 1925.

I

SIR FRANCIS AGLEN, K. B. E.,

Inspector General of Customs,

P E K I N G .

2.

I have just received a petition from the employe of the Likin Station who informed the Maritime Police that the Native Customs Officers were detained on board of junk "Chin Shun Hsing" at Chuangyuanchiao Station. This man asks me now to issue to him 3/10 of fine imposed on the junk, as a reward for the service given to us by him. It is probably right that he helped us a great deal by going to the Maritime Police Boat and insisting that the officer in charge of the boat should give us protection, and it is probably quite just from the Chinese point of view to get a reward for such a service, but I cannot issue it to him without knowing your point of view on this matter.

Yours truly,

E. Bernadsky

CUSTOM HOUSE,

22

S/O No. 351.

Wenchow, 11th February 26.

INDEXED

Dear Sir Francis,

Alteration in lease of former British Consular Property.

Mr. Chêng Hsi-wên (程希文) the Superintendent of Customs told me few days ago that he had held a private meeting of leaders of the Gentry and that they had agreed to insert on the ground lease the following note

"After the expiration of 15 years, if the owner of the land wants to take it back, then the estimated value at that time of all constructions on the leased land is to be repaid to the Customs".

Though the insertion note is not as good as that

SIR FRANCIS AGLEN, K. B. E.,

Inspector General of Customs,

PEKING.

2.

23

that required by us

"Renewable on the same terms on the expiry of a certain number of years"

but still it looks as acceptable. After receipt of this letter from the Superintendent the question will be referred to you officially.

Superintendent's Allowance issued before Chinese New Year's Holiday.

The Superintendent's Allowance for February, according to his verbal request, has been issued on the 11th instant before the Chinese New Year.

Leaflet in connection with Manchuria Affairs.

Please find enclosed herewith a leaflet dealing with warnings to Chinese on the despatch of soldiers to Manchuria by the Japanese Government and distributed by the Wenchow Kuomingtang Executive Committee through the local Bolshevick Newspaper 大公報. The original copy of leaflet and its translations are enclosed.

Yours truly,

B. Bernadsky

5

TRANSLATION OF

LEAFLET DISTRIBUTED BY THE WENCHOW KUOMINGTANG EXECUTIVE COMMITTEE REGARDING WARNINGS TO CHINESE ON THE DESPATCH OF SOLDIERS TO MANCHURIA BY THE JAPANESE GOVERNMENT.

Dear Fellow Countrymen! We must wake up to the fact that the Japanese have within these few days availed themselves of the opportunity presented by the fighting between Chang Tso-lin and Kuo Sung-lin by sending an army corps to Manchuria under the pretext of protecting their citizens living there. They have also despatched more than ten gunboats to Tientsin, Chinwantao and neighbouring ports.

The Chinese militarists who are throwing China into such confusion have been aided by the Japanese to further their agressive policy. Now without any warning the Japanese have demonstrated their agressive imperialism by swooping down like a robber band in an attempt to annex China.

We must realise that this sudden despatch of Japanese troops into Manchuria is an invasion of our territory and a violation of our sovereignty. It is to help that cowardly traitor Chang Tso-lin. It is an offence against international morality, and by disturbing the peace of Asia is enough to bring a world

2.

26

world war, which will end in the loss of Manchuria and perhaps the subjugation of China.

Fellow Countrymen; we are Chinese and as we do not violate the rights of others, so should our own be respected. We must resist every country, whichever it may be that tries to invade us. We must remember that we are all citizens of China, we must put aside our quarels and unite to resist invaders, who are now the Japanese.

(1) The Japanese imperialism must be overthrown.

(2) " " military Government must be dissolved.

(3) The traitor Chang Tso-lin must be expelled.

(4) The Japanese people must hasten to revolt against their own government.

(5) Chinese and Russian citizens must unite on the same footing of equality against Japan.

(6) All the peoples of Asia must adopt the same attitude in resisting the Japanese militarists.

(7) Korea must declare its independence and Formosa its autonomy.

(8) The peace of Asia must be maintained.

(9) The independence of our Country must be preserved.

(10)

3.

27

(10) Every one must unite to the utmost in order to sever forever economic relations with Japan - not to purchase Japanese goods, not to use Japanese banknots, not to deposit in, and to remit through, Japanese banks and not to sell Chinese goods to Japanese.

[A.—42]

28

INSPECTORATE GENERAL OF CUSTOMS.

/o

PEKING, 9th March 1926.

Dear Sir,

I am directed by the Inspector General ɔ inform you that your S/O letter No. 351, lated 11th February, has been duly eceived.

Yours truly,

Personal Secretary.
~~Private Secretary.~~

Bernadsky, Esquire,

WENCHOW.

INSPECTORATE GENERAL OF CUSTOMS,

21

S/O

PEKING, 22nd February 1926

Dear Mr. Bernadsky,

I have duly received your S/O Letter No. 350 of 1st February.

Authority for issuing ground-rent:

I.G. Despatch No. 1267/100,079 is not sufficient authority for this payment, for which sanction should now be applied officially.

Rewards for Chuangyuanchiao Case:

Follow the instructions of I.G. Circular No. 2268!

Yours truly,

For Inspector General.

E. Bernadsky, Esquire,

WENCHOW.

CUSTOM HOUSE,

S/O No. 352. Wenchow 26th February 1926. 31

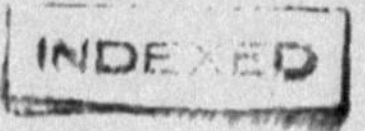

Dear Sir Francis,

S.S. Haean searched by Police.

On the 25th the Chief Secretary of the Superintendent called upon me and stated that there is a strong rumour here about the proposed piracy of the S.S. Haean this trip to Shanghai. According to his statement the ship will have on her board a treasure about $400,000 and the Wenchow Chamber of Commerce asked the local authorities to give due protection to the ship. The local authorities decided to search the suspicious passengers and their luggage before departure of the ship and they asked the Superintendent to communicate with me of the subject. As the matter was urgent the Superintendent instructed

SIR FRANCIS AGLEN, K. B. E.,
Inspector General of Customs,
P E K I N G .

32

instructed his Secretary to come and see me and to explain the situation. He promised also to send me the necessary letters later on. I replied that it did not lie with me to permit or object to such a search, but that the Superintendent must understand that he takes all responsibility for it. Then I instructed the Tidesurveyor to witness the search by Police. The Tidesurveyor in his report book for 26th February stated as follows: "4 a.m. Acting on instructions from the Commissioner I visited S.S. "Haean" to witness the search by Police for pirates or bad characters. These Police, who were not armed, had a walk around the vessel but did not search or even speak to any passenger. Then they proceeded to the entrance gate to pontoon where they made themselves comfortable in the Police rooms there. No passengers were searched, the whole thing was a farce". That was the kind of protection given by local Police authorities.

Continuation

3.

33

Customs Property to rent.

Continuation of S/O No. 346.

The Manager of the China Merchants Company here wishes also to rent this piece of our land for godown accommodation, but he cannot settle the question without referring it to the Company's authorities at Shanghai, therefore he asked me to give him a time to go to Shanghai and to discuss the matter there. He left the port this morning and only after his return it will be possible for me to report to you officially.

Yours truly,

E. Bernadsky.

[A.—42]

34

S/O

INSPECTORATE GENERAL OF CUSTOMS,

PEKING, 16th March 1926.

Dear Sir,

I am directed by the Inspector General to inform you that your S/O letter No. 352, dated 26th February, has been duly received.

Yours truly,

[signature]

Personal Secretary.

~~Private Secretary~~.

Bernadsky, Esquire,

WENCHOW.

CUSTOM HOUSE,

S/O No. 353.

Wenchow 9th March 1926.

36

INDEXED

Dear Sir Francis,

Delay in reply to I.G. Despatch No. 1373.

Your Despatch No. 1373/106,406, N. C. No. 241, re intention of the Superintendent to collect duty on goods passing Kuant'ou - Checking Barrier - under his control within 50-li radius.

I shall be able to reply to this despatch only after receiving definite answer from the Superintendent. I proposed to him a system of control to be introduced on goods destined within 50-li radius, and he agreed to it but he asked me to give him time to consult with Weiyuan of P'uch'i Native Customs Station,

SIR FRANCIS AGLEN, K. B. E.,

Inspector General of Customs,

PEKING.

2.

37

Station, under whose control this Barrier at present is.

Temporary detention of Mr. K'o Yu-p'ing.

Your telegram of the 8th instant re transfer of Mr. K'o Yu-p'ing to Harbin. According to instructions he must proceed immediately. At present here there is in the General and the Secretary's Office so much work in hand that it is practically impossible to relieve him from duty before the arrival of his successor. The work in preparing the comparative tables for the annual returns for 1924 and 1925 in accordance with instructions contained in the Printed Note No. 509 occupies now a clerk who helps him in Secretary and Accountant's Office. If Mr. K'o is to be relieved from duty immediately I am afraid that the current work cannot be finished in time, but I shall try to do so at the end of this month in hope that his successor will arrive at Wenchow about that time.

Yours truly,

E. Beinadtky

[I.—42] 38

S/O

INSPECTORATE GENERAL OF CUSTOMS.

PEKING, 23rd March 1926.

Dear Sir,

I am directed by the Inspector General to inform you that your S/O letter No. 353, dated 9th March, has been duly received.

Yours truly,

[signature]

Personal Secretary.

~~Private Secretary.~~

E. Bernadsky, Esquire,

WENCHOW.

CUSTOM HOUSE, 391

S/O No. 354.

Wenchow, 23rd March 1926.

Dear Sir Francis,

Pilotage Service at Wenchow.

Since the beginning of this year the new scheme for the pilotage fees as authorised by your Despatch No. 1345/104,541 of the 3rd September 1925 has been introduced here and at the end of the Quarter 3/5th of this fee will be issued to the Customs Boatmen who performed pilots' duties (I.G. Despatch No. 1036/85,458 of the 19th September 1921 and your S/O Letter of the 8th October 1925). The amount due to them for the March Quarter will be about $850.00 to the No. 1 Boatman and $250.00 to the No. 2 Boatman.

Mr.

SIR FRANCIS AGLEN, K. B. E.,
Inspector General of Customs,
P E K I N G .

2.

40

Mr. G. E. Cross - the Harbour Master - in conversation about the pilotage at Wenchow stated to me that there is no foreigner or Chinese Customs employe anywhere else in China enjoying such favourable conditions as the pilots at Wenchow, i.e. no risk, no expenses, monthly boatman's salary, uniforms, quarters, Customs benefits, 3/5th of the pilotage and sampan hire, and that therefore it is obvious that the pilotage will never be a separate institution when conditions are so favourable to the pilots. If the full amount of 3/5th of the increased pilotage fee is issued to them, then only two or three individuals will profit whereas a part of this sum might be more profitably employed in raising the general conditions under which pilotage in this port is performed to a better status.

In view of the fact that during this year as compared with the previous years there has been no change to make the duties of a pilot more difficult it seems that there is no reason why the issue of the increased amount of the pilotage fee should be issued

to

3.

41

to our boatmen and it would probably be more reasonable to reserve this extra amount received from the increased fee in the pilotage fund to the end of the year when the question of the separation of the pilotage will be settled. In case the pilotage will be separated from the Customs then this detained amount will be handed over to the pilots concerned and in the contrary case this amount can be used for the benefit of the pilotage accommodation as well as that of the Customs for the supervising of this branch of navigation. This money can be used for purchasing a motor-boat or constructing a hut at the Wenchow Point, etc. If a motor boat could be obtained it would be used also for Harbour work: rough survey work, visiting triangulation marks etc. and by the Native Customs for visiting outstations, patroling work etc. which would without doubt greatly facilitate the Customs work.

The pilotage fee to boatman-pilots for the March Quarter will be issued after receipt of your reply to this letter.

On

4.

42

Strike.

On the 14th instant the rice shops raised the price of rice from 20 to 23 copper cent per sheng (升). To stop this speculation the local coolies on the same day rushed into a rice-mill, smashed everything there and then made a street demonstration, trying to urge the shops to close their doors as a sign of their sympathy with them. The police arrested some leaders of the demonstrators and advised the shopkeepers to open their shops. When some of these refused they were also arrested and as a result all the other shops closed their doors. After the gentry, the Chamber of Commerce and the officials had held a meeting and had found a way how to lower the price of rice to its former level, the arrested people were released. The City returned to normal life on the 19th instant.

Yours truly,

E. Bernadsky.

CUSTOM HOUSE,

S/O No. 355.　　　　Wenchow, 5th April 1926.

64

INDEXED

Dear Sir Francis,

S.S. Haean landing passengers *en route*.

Mr. Chang, who is temporarily in charge of the Superintendent's Office, called upon me on the 26th of March last and stated that the China Merchants Steam Navigation Company's "Haean" - a regular steamer between Shanghai and Wenchow - anchored on the 25th March at the mouth of the Ou river (entrance to Wenchow) and discharge cargo into sampans alongside the ship. When an examiner of the P'an-shih Native Customs Station - which office is under the Superintendent's supervision - noticed this he took a sampan and proceeded to the ship and asked the crew of the ship to stop this illegal discharge, but his request

SIR FRANCIS AGLEN, K. B. E.,
Inspector General of Customs,
P E K I N G .

request was ignored and he was badly beaten by some members of the crew of the ship for interference with their business. This examiner arrived at Wenchow to report the case to the Superintendent and to obtain medical treatment. For this last purpose he went to the Blyth Hospital which is in the charge of Dr. Stedeford - the Customs Medical Officer - and asked there to be given a statement of the injuries he had received, but the doctor refused to do so, therefore now Mr. Chang came and asked me to help him in obtaining such a letter from the doctor. I promised to write to the doctor, but I asked Mr. Chang to send me this examiner of P'an-shih Office to take this letter in hope that I should be able to obtain from him some particulars of the discharging of cargo. Two hours later Mr. Chang informed me by telephone that the examiner of P'an-shih had reported the case to the court and he will be examined there

3

46

there by the authorities concerned and that therefore it is unnecessary now for him to go to the foreign doctor. When I met Dr. Stedeford I raised the question of the injuries inflicted on that Native Customs examiner, but the doctor told me that he did not know anything of the case. The Captain of S. S. "Haean" in his statement of the case said that the ship anchored at the mouth of the river on accdount of a low tide. He stated also that no discharging of cargo took place there but some passengers landed at that place and to avoid such illegal landing he promised to anchor the ship in future at White Rock - a place about sixteen miles farther out to sea - to wait for flood tide. The compradore of the ship in his statement says that the fighting between the people in the sampan and a Chinese in no distinct uniform or badge took place on account of a demand by the latter of $5.00 from each

passenger

4

47

passenger before they could leave. The compradore of S. S. "Haean" promised also to take all necessary precautions to prevent any passenger from landing at unauthorized places. Therefore no punishment was inflicted by me on the ship in this case, but the Captain, Compradore and China Merchants Steam Navigation Company were warned. On the 29th of March I received a despatch from the Superintendent in which he in accordance with the statements of P'an-shih examiner and P'u-chi Native Customs station - the head office of P'an-shih station - repeated what he had told me on the 26th March and asked me to take the necessary steps. In my reply of the 31st March I stated that the Captain and the Compradore of the ship denied the fact of any discharge of cargo but they admitted that some passengers were landed there, and that they promised to take in future all steps to prevent such landing of passengers at unauthorized

5

48

unauthorized places. They and the China Merchants Steam Navigation Company were warned by me. The question of the insulting of the examiner by some members of the crew of S. S. "Haean", as stated in the Superintendent's despatch, is to be investigated and dealt with by the Chinese Authorities concerned.

Yours truly,

E. Bernadsky

[A.—42]

49

INSPECTORATE GENERAL OF CUSTOMS.

10

PEKING, 28th April 1926.

Dear Sir,

I am directed by the Inspector General inform you that your S/O letter No. 355, ated 5th April, has been duly ceived.

Yours truly,

F. W. Lyons

Personal Secretary.

~~Private Secretary.~~

ernadsky, Esquire,

WENCHOW.

CUSTOM HOUSE,

S/O No. 356.

Wenchow, 14th April 1926

55

Dear Sir Francis,

Application for Sunday, Holidays work junk cargo without paying Special Permit Fees.

Last March 67 firms dealing in timber and paper sent me a petition asking me to allow them to work junk cargo on Sundays and Holidays without paying Special Permit Fees, which are equal here to Hk. Tls. 3.00 per day. I invited the leaders of this petition to come to my office and on the April 6th two of them - who are leading petitioners and Native Customs brokers at the same time - came and discussed the points put forward in the petition: i. e.

a. There are only two suitable tides in a month when big junks may leave port and therefore if these tides coincide with Sundays or Holidays then they lose 15-16 days in case they do not wish to pay Special

SIR FRANCIS AGLEN, K. B. E.,
Inspector General of Customs,
PEKING.

56

Special Permit Fee.

b. If only two or three junks asked for examination on ordinary days the Native Customs would not examine them until the next day when more junks put in request for examination.

c. They suffer great loss on account of their not being allowed to work cargo on Sundays and Holidays.

d. It may happen that junks owing to the existence of non-working days may lose their chance of joining the police boat escorting junks through the area infested by pirates.

During the discussion they confessed that the first two items do not represent true statements, as there are two tides every day during which the biggest junks can leave port without any difficulty and no examination of cargo has been postponed up to the next day if application was presented to the Native Customs General Office before 4 p. m.

As

3.

57

As to the amount of "great loss" that they suffer, the applicants could not give any figure, while our account books stated that the total annual amount of Special Permit Fees collected on junks working cargo on Sundays and Holidays was Hk. Tls. 120 for the whole of the last year.

The question of losing the chance of joining the escorting boat is worthy of attention, but the applicatants could not give me any concrete facts, therefore even in this item there is probably no more truth than in the previous ones.

Taking into consideration that the closing of the Native Customs on Sundays and Holidays is not detrimental to trade or revenue here and the fact that the petitioners are really the Customs brokers who, according to the local practice always pay these fees for the merchants and want now to reap these trifling sums into their own pockets. I refused their request.

Rewards

4.

58

Rewards to fire-brigades for their services.

On the 10th instant the Likin Office next door to the Native Customs Head Office was burnt down completely but our Native Customs building was untouched by fire, though part of the wall nearest the Likin Office was broken down. The approximate cost of repairing it will be about $ 15. According to the local practice the fire brigades are to be rewarded by us whose building was saved by their services and the Assistant in charge of Native Customs recommended to me to issue to them $ 5-6. It is advisable to do this but I doubt if I can issue such a reward; but if you are of opinion that this amount may be paid from Petty Cash Account or if our account instructions page 20, 7 miscellaneous, section 93, can be used in such cases as the authority for such a gratuity then the amount recommended will be issued.

Demonstration in connection with the deaths of students in Peking.

A few days before the demonstration different associations instigated by the Stud-

ent:

5.

59

ent Association inserted in the local newspapers a general invitation to the city to join the memorial service for the Peking students shot by the government's guards.

In the morning of April 12th at the parade ground of No. 10 Middle School Mr. Ching Jung (金 嵘) head master of the school opened the ceremony by giving a speech describing the case; he was followed by several others, who gave their views.

After the funeral orations had been given; the students and their followers over 1,000 in number paraded through the main streets of the city, and passed round the Custom House. They carried flags and banners, the inscriptions on which, appended herewith, they shouted out. Leaflets were distributed; of these five were obtained and are attached.

Yours truly,

C. Bernadsky.

60

A P P E N D.

The inscriptions on banners carried by students, etc. on demonstration of 12th of April 1926 were:

1. (討伐殘殺愛國同胞的段祺瑞) To fight against T'uan Chi-jui (段祺瑞) who slaughtered our patriotic brethren.
2. (取消辛丑條約) To cancel treaty of 1901.
3. (打倒延長內亂之吳佩孚) To fight down Wu Pei-fu (吳佩孚) who prolongs the internal disturbances.
4. (召集國民會議) To call a national assembly
5. (打倒媚外軍閥) To fight down the militarists who fawn on foreign powers.
6. (打倒帝國主義) To fight down monarchism.
7. (愛國烈士不死) The souls of patriotic heroes never die.
8. (國民革命萬歲) May the revolution of the people reap 10,000 years' happiness.
9. (誓雪國恥) To swear to revenge the national shames.
10. (中華民國萬歲) May the Republic of China stand 10,000 years longer.

S/O No. 356 of 1926.

ENCLOSURE.

(一)基於反對宗教的理由，當然要反對基督教。

(二)基督教教義如上帝造物造人，如靈魂不滅，我們可據星雲說，進化論、心理學，生理學來反對。　如有罪而又可贖罪，則不但是造謊，而且是獎勵作惡。　如博愛犧牲，固非基督教所專有，而基督教的說法為尤不可通。(如打臉脫衣等說。)

(三)基督教是帝國主義者侵略我中國的先鋒隊。　為了傳教，發生多次賠款割地的事實，而且他們利用傳教，根本破壞中國民族的獨立性。

我們尤其要反對基督教會，理由是：

(一)做事假借名流，聯絡官場，奉迎財主。

(二)收教徒利用物質的引誘與虛榮的心理。

(三)牧師們教徒們多是『吃』教者，而且言論矛盾，行為詐偽。

(四)牧師們恃帝國主義的後盾，恐嚇官吏，武斷鄉曲，袒庇罪犯，包攬詞訟；有時且為土匪私運槍械，助長中國內亂。(襄陽有此事。)

(五)利用金錢，收買役使男女教徒，有時甚至干涉婚姻，逼成慘禍。(成都一教會學校女生因此自殺。)

(六)在中國傳教四百餘年的影響，祗把一部分鄉人的『菩薩』換了個『上帝』，而且養成他們崇拜洋人，此外別無好處。

反對宗教！

反對基督教！

反對基督教會！

危險。人命朝露。

銷我國民賣身契之

起圖之。謹此宣言。

反對基督教運動

我們要反對宗教，理由是：

(一)我們要謀學術進步，而宗教則重保守，重因襲，對於教義絕對不許疑難，且對於違反教義者處以極刑。

(二)我們要謀人類和諧，而宗教則重派別，重門户之見，增長人間的隔膜與仇視。（如十字軍的異教的戰爭，新舊教的三十年戰爭。）

(三)我們要謀科學昌明，而宗教則神道設教，徒然養成迷信。（上海三育大學師範班還要力辯人是上帝造的，不是由進化來的。）

(四)我們要謀自我實現，而宗教則禱告、懺悔，無往而非依賴。

(五)我們要謀人性發展，而宗教則賤視肉體，叫勞動者甘心受苦，無往而非毀滅人生。

我們特別要反對基督教，理由是：

S/O No. 356 of 1926.
ENCLOSURE.

●中國國民黨浙江永嘉縣黨部對北京段祺瑞殘殺愛國民衆宣言

日本帝國主義。豢養其走狗張作霖。自五卅慘案發生。對愛國運動種種壓迫。至反奉戰爭郭將軍松齡。爲民衆起而討賊。勦匪作霖。行將授首。日本帝國主義因在我國之勢力搖動。不顧國際公理。公然出兵南滿。干涉內爭。使郭氏討賊之舉。功敗垂成。直系軍閥吳佩孚。以討奉始。而英日兩帝國主義從中鼓惑。使奉直兩相妥協。反奉戰線。遂歸破壞。實深著明。近大沽口事件。國民軍爲防奉軍上陸。佈置防禦。事理平常。彼日本帝國主義。使日艦砲擊大沽砲台勾引奉軍上陸。以破國防而延內爭。此顯係日本帝國主義爲貫澈武力侵略政策。而加我國家民族之奇恥大辱。乃猶以單獨侵略爲未足。更進而聯合英美帝國主義。藉口辛丑條約。向我國提出哀的美敦式之通牒。限十八小時答覆。威脅詐嚇。無所不至。北京愛國民衆。痛外侮頻仍。內亂長延。因舉行抗爭駁覆列強通牒。於三月十八日爲廢約禦侮之運動。奮起外外交後援。赴政府請願。實爲國家爭生死民族圖自存之舉。乃段祺瑞不獨不接見代表。接受民衆意見。更指揮衛隊。立卽開槍向羣衆射擊。四十分鐘之久。死者五十餘人。傷者更不計其數。血花飛舞。除尸纍纍。此種殘暴行爲。桀紂幽厲不敢爲。中外古今所未聞。較之五卅慘案。尤爲重大。不過五卅是帝國主義之直接慘殺我民衆。此則帝國主義假手於殘酷不仁之段祺瑞。以屠戮我民衆。實在同是英日帝國主義在中作祟也。

北京政府。如此屠戮民衆。罪大惡極。尚不知悔。更祕密集議。嫁禍於少數羣衆領袖。以轉移國民視線。誣此正大光明之愛國運動。爲「赤化」「共産」而芟戮之。嗚呼。父母兄弟。妻子朋友。人皆有之。此不抗爭。國亡無日。全國同胞。將無噍類矣。

際此帝國主義相聯合。殘暴軍閥相攜手。互行勾結。內外交攻。國家危險。人命朝露。欲圖生存非喚醒民衆聯合戰線。內則非驅逐殘民之段祺瑞吳佩孚張作霖。外則非取銷我國民賣身契之辛丑條約不可。本黨爲人民利益而奮鬥。生死存亡。在所不問。願與愛國同胞。共起圖之。謹此宣言。

S/O No. 356 of 1926.
ENCLOSURE.

去年五卅運動。滬案竟有重聲結果。段賊帖耳不爭。金佛郎案。損失國庫三萬萬元之鉅。段賊也承認了。外崇國信尊重條約。把中國人的賣身契延長下去。召集軍閥分贓式的善後會議。把真正國民會議要打消了。張吳馮造成三角式的局勢。把中國的內亂發展了。種種事實。那裏有些將意為人民謀利益。民衆的愛國運動。反不許他。是應該用鎗屠殺麼。這般的政府。中外古今所未有。亡國的禍。真迫在目睫了。全中國的民衆實死無葬身之地。本會誓為死者後援。寧為玉碎不肯瓦全。盡國民驅國賊祛外敵的責任。共申義憤。願賦同仇。特此宣言。

職工研究會對北京慘案宣言

段祺瑞為北京政府的執政。三月十八。竟對民衆為大沽口事件很正當之請願。用鎗掃射。死傷纍纍。真不愧為帝國主義者。駐華的經理人。是帝國主義者對中國人民的劊子手

S/O No. 356 of 1926.
ENCLOSURE.

▲溫州京案後援會成立宣言

我國連年內亂多次。每經一次的戰爭。帝國主義的侵略。也緊迫一次。亡國的禍。就迫在目睫了。

其實我國的內亂。皆帝國主義濟款給械與彼所豢養的走狗軍閥。甲勝則甲對所豢養的帝國主義者忠於賣國的行爲。乙勝則乙對所豢養的帝國主義者盡其走狗的能事。皆沒有能代人民謀一分的利益。

此年來很顯着的事實。盡人不能否認的。所以人民愛國的運動。彼帝國主義者和其豢養的走狗！軍閥。嫉視如眼中釘。加以摧殘慘戮屠殺了。

此次大沽口事件。曲在日本帝國主義。爲不可掩的事實。乃日本帝國主義。竟唆使辛丑條約的與約國各帝國主義者。反以哀的美敦式之最後通牒。限十八小時答覆。用其威嚇脅迫的手段。對我們要求。北京愛國民衆、痛正義不伸國亡無日。羣起作愛國運動。爲抗爭駁覆的請願。這是爲民族存亡國家榮辱關係的動擧動。世界各文明國中所常有的事。我國人民更且是必要的表示。

三月十八那一天。羣衆向北方政府推舉代表入內請願。北方政府。拒絕不見。媚外賣國的段祺瑞和安福派爪牙。竟下令開鎗。向徒手的羣衆射擊。歷十分鐘之久。當場立斃五十多人。受傷者不計其數。反欲因此大興黨獄。要以共產赤化等名詞。掩盡天下耳目。使愛國志士的鮮血。熱騰騰；亮晶晶；白流一淌。將其餘愛國志士一網打盡。這是何等殘暴毒辣的一回事。很顯出他帝國主義劊子手的威風。帝國主義經理人的面目。世界那裏有這樣的政府？人民更何用這樣殺人的政府？同胞們！我們若不趁此覺悟；實力團結；爲最後決死的抗爭。何以對已死愛國的烈士。更何以解決我們現在生存的危險。比那高麗安南還不及。

親愛的同胞們！烈士的鮮血。染遍了大地。快起來吧！趁他的血流前進！

S/O No. 356 of ,1926.
ENCLOSURE.

中國國民黨永嘉縣黨部爲北京慘案告國民書

國民軍在大沽敷設水雷，日英各國，爲賣國軍閥張作霖張目，藉口辛丑條約，對我作最後通牒，干涉內爭，蔑視國權，全國人民，均應一致抵抗，嚴詞駁覆，乃段祺瑞諂媚列强，甘心賣國，對八國之通牒，不予駁覆，對不平等條約，履行惟恐不力，仇視國民愛國運動，以博帝國主義之歡心，嗾使衛隊，開放排鎗，殺傷請願羣衆達二百十一人之多，國務院前，血流成渠，屍骸枕藉，稍有人心，詎能容忍，奈段祺瑞殘殺不足，繼以構誣，通電全國，毫無顧忌，尙冀全國人民，弗與所惑，整我隊伍，遵循我

總理孫中山先生之遺教，作打倒帝國主義、打倒軍閥廢除不平等條約等工作，驅逐殘民以逞賣國求榮之段祺瑞，懲辦北京慘殺案之首要凶犯，以伸烈士之冤，全國國民，宜一致援助，聲罪致討，使賣國殃民之軍閥，帝國主義之走狗張作霖段祺瑞輩．不得逞其毒燄，愛國同胞、盍共圖之，

中國國民黨永嘉縣黨部中華民國十五年四月十二日

CUSTOM HOUSE, 62

S/O No. 357. Wenchow, 28th April 1926.

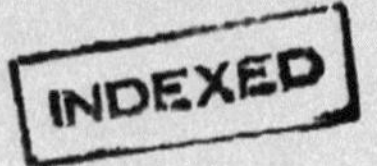

Dear Sir Francis.

Petition to establish C. M. Customs at Juian and Pingyang.

A few days ago I received a petition from the tea-merchants of Pingyang (平陽) in which they stated that they had petitioned the Shui-wu Ch'u to send suitable instructions to Juian (瑞安) and Pingyang tax-offices to exempt from duty "tea for abroad" or to open there a Chinese Maritime Customs Office which will pass such tea duty free, and they asked me to help them. I doubt that I can do anything in this direction, but the opening of sub-stations of Chinese Maritime Customs at Juian and Pingyang or handing over the Native Customs at these places would be very timely. At present these two ports deprive us of about 15%

SIR FRANCIS AGLEN, K. B. E.,
Inspector General of Customs,
P E K I N G.

2.

63

15% of the Wenchow revenue and in future the percentage will probably be higher, therefore, if the question of establishing a Chinese Maritime Customs Office or handing over to us the Native Customs at these two ports will be raised before you I would recommend you to do everything possible to push it forward. The question of desirability to obtain control over the Native Customs at Juian was referred to you by despatch No. 3883, N. C. 365 of 6th December 1924. I am sorry I cannot give you any statistics to make the situation plain, but the Shanghai Native Customs can supply you with full particulars.

Standard Oil Co. case.

In your despatch No. 1386/107,157 of the 14th April 1926 you have instructed me to call upon the Company to pay the fine of five times the duty evaded in respect of the oil removed from bond without payment of Native Customs duty or

Transit

3.

64

Transit Dues and without Customs Release Permit. If the fine is to be imposed for the cargo exported from 4th September 1922 to 30th September 1925 then the punishment will be heavier after the production the books by the Company than when they refused to do so, therefore I think the fine according to your instructions is to be imposed from 1st January to 30th September 1925 only. But to be sure that my interpretation of the period of time is correct I prefer to ask you of it. I am not sure also if the duty on the other goods is to be assessed for the same period. Herewith are particulars of the duty evaded for each year :

Year	Duty on Kerosene Oil Hk.Tls.	Duty on other goods Hk.Tls.
From 4. Sept. to end of year 1922	7.748	11.359
1923	240.732	57.757
1924	321.088	27.072
From 1. Jan. to 30. Sept. 1925	396.055	145.040

Anti

4.

65

nti British propaganda.

A critical article printed in North China Daily News of 20th February under heading "Absurd Allegation of Britain's Supposed Intention to Invade China" (page 11) appeared here in Chinese and English under the heading "British Plans for Intervention in China" and has been spread amongst students and labouring classes during the last few days. A copy of this leaflet in a form suitable for Anti-British propaganda (i.e. without criticism) is enclosed herewith.

Yours truly.

E. Bernadsky.

S/O No. 357 of 1926.

Enclosure.

"BRITISH PLANS FOR INTERVENTION IN CHINA".

"The plans for a war of Intervention to smash the Chinese National Movement have already been thought out in some detail.

"The struggle in diplomatic circles is between those who believe in 'negotiation', e.g. conferences, promises, delays, etc., and those, on the other hand, who believe that 'Force' alone can restore British domination in China.

"Experts have already considered this position and have recommended that only 100,000 men are necessary. Many of those could be speedily brought from India, where there are 80,000 European troops. Also the Hongkong garrison has already been strengthened.

"The plan is to divide China into two commands - North and South. The major portion of the troops would be divided between Tientsin and Shanghai. The first portion would be landed at Tientsin and would endeavour to come to an early and decisive engagement with Feng Yu-hsiang. The tacit support of Chang Tso-lin has already been obtained

67

obtained.

"At Hankow only British gunboats would be necessary to reduce the Chinese town.

"At Canton it is considered that it would be necessary to land only about one battalion of European troops. This can easily be done on the Island of Shameen which is still held by British and French volunteers. From the island of Shameen the attack on the Chinese town would be launched - equately supported by gunboats and cruisers, which have been collecting on the China Station from other parts of the globe for some months.

"Financial experts have estimated that the cost to the British taxpayer can be reduced by seizing the Chinese railways (of course after the war is successfully terminated). Allowing that the war would last for two years, which was the period of intervention in Russia, and would cost £150,000 per day, this sum can be recovered by a mortgage on the whole Chinese railway system if an additional £50,000,000 is invested in Chinese railways to extend the present trackage from 7,000 to 12,000 miles. It is understood that with a thoroughly defeated

and

3.

and subdued China and with increased 'settlements' and 'concessions' certain banks backed by the bank of England would be prepared to invest this sum. It should be remembered that the Chairman of the Hongkong & Shanghai Bank is also a Director of the Bank England.

"It is believed that as all the news services can be controlled and cables censored, the major operations can be effectively launched before British Labour or any other radical, organisations likely to protest, will know of it.

"Already the Bank of England has transferred £600,000 sterling to the Hongkong & Shanghai Bank in Shanghai for use in beginning a vast propaganda campaign in the East to 'overcome Chinese antagonism' (? nationalism) 'and Soviet propaganda."

69

英國進攻中國之計畫

譯二月二十日上海字林西報倫敦通信

干涉中國撲滅中國民族運動的戰爭計畫已經過詳細的考慮其範圍尚未爲外間所完全了解外交界有兩種意見的爭執一派相信「協商」即會議許諾延宕可以恢復英國在華的宰治而另一派則唯信賴武力依專家的計算征服中國只須用十萬大軍隊半可由印度（該處有八萬英兵）調遣香港的警備亦已增强此戰爭的計畫進攻中國分南北二部多數軍隊將配置於上海天津之間第一部分軍隊將在天津上岸將力求早與馮玉祥決戰且已獲得張作霖之默許在漢口祇需數兵艦即可征服此外英兵一團從沙面上岸護以數月來從各地調集之軍艦巡洋艦即可向廣州進攻依財政專家之計算戰爭目的達到戰爭停止以後英國可以攫取中國的鐵路英國人民的納稅可以減輕假定此戰爭需時二年（亦即從前干涉俄國所需的時期）以克服中國軍費每日十五萬磅此數可由將來全國鐵路抵押給英國時補償但必須再投資五千萬磅加造鐵路自今之七千英里增加至一萬

Enclosure.

"BRITISH PLANS FOR INTERVENTION IN CHINA".

二千英里屆時中國既已完全戰敗屈服租界割讓均有增加則各銀行得英國國家銀行之幫助必樂投資況今滙豐銀行行長亦為英國國家銀行董事之一因為郵電可施檢查可以控制大部分戰爭行動可以在英國工人及別的激烈團體知道消息以前迅速有效的實行目下英國國家銀行已寄款六十萬磅交滙豐銀行以為在東方開始廣大宣傳戰勝中國的民族主義與蘇維埃宣傳的費用

INSPECTORATE GENERAL OF CUSTOMS,

S/O PEKING, 5th May 1926.

Dear Mr. Bernadsky,

I have duly received your S/O letter No.354 of the 23rd March:

Pilotage Service at Wenchow.

You should adhere to the 3/5-ths proportion hitherto issued. You should, however, submit the matter officially, putting forward your proposals for a change in the existing practice.

Yours truly,

[signature]

Bernadsky, Esquire,

WENCHOW.

CUSTOM HOUSE, 72

S/O No. 358. Wenchow, 8th May 1926.

INDEXED

Dear Sir Francis,

E. Bernadsky's application for long leave.

In reply to your telegram query of April 14th asking if I was going to apply for leave in October I informed you that I was not going to do so. The main reason for this is the financial difficulty. If I go to Europe with my family consisting of wife, 6 children and nursery-governess I shall have to spend from my own resources, £400 for passage there and back in addition to the official allowance granted by the Service. This sum is more than I can spare at present and I am doubtful if I shall be able to find it for some little time. Also I do not expect that we shall be allowed to go to

SIR FRANCIS AGLEN, K. B. E.,

Inspector General of Customs,

P E K I N G.

2

73

to Russia, where though life would not be very attractive at present, it would be easier I think for me to support my family than in any other foreign country.

This telegram of April 14th in connection with your previous queries made to me on the same subject and your last Circulars Nos. 3677 and 3678 brought me to the understanding that from the Service point of view it is very desirable that employee whose leave is due should take it and that such private reasons as financial difficulties, etc. are not good ground for postponing long leave. Therefore if I am not mistaken in my opinion I am prepared to apply for leave from any moment convenient to the Service, i.e. from 16th October 1926 or 16th April 1927 or any other time. But in view of my present financial difficulties I cannot afford to take all the

members

3.

74

members of my family to Europe and during the period of my leave they will stay probably in Tsingtao or Harbin and I shall apply for your permission to stay in China with my family for a part of my leave. If the suggestion will meet your approval kindly inform me from what date I can get my leave and the official application will be forwarded to you at once.

Yours truly,

E. Bernadsky.

CUSTOM HOUSE,

S/O No. 359. Wenchow 12th May 1926. 76

Dear Sir Francis,

Return of Superintendent of Customs. Wenchow.

Mr. Chang Hsi-Wen (程希文), Superintendent of Customs, Wenchow, returned on May 6th, having stayed about two months time (left Wenchow on March 12th) in Marshal Sun Ch'uan-fang's (孫傳芳) and Governor Hsia Ch'ao's (夏超) Offices at Nanking and Hangchow.

Arrival and departure of Mr. Soothil.

Professor Soothil, the member of the British Boxer Indemity Commission, and his wife and daughter, Lady Hosie visited Wenchow. 19 years ago Mr. Soothil was a head of the United Methodist Mission here. On April 26th Mars. Soothil and Lady Hosie arrived at Wenchow. On April 29th Lady Hosie left Wenchow for Shanghai as

SIR FRANCIS AGLEN, K. B. E.,

Inspector General of Customs,

PEKING.

2

71

as Lady Hosie had intended to go to Manila and as at Shanghai she was taken ill with German measles could not go there. On May 6th Professor Soothil arrived here and on May 9th he and Mrs. Soothil left for Shanghai. They expect to stay in China up to September at least.

Meeting in connection with the 21 demands and the deaths of students in Peking.

The 9th May in Wenchow is the day when demonstrations or any other action used to be taken in connection with the 21 Japanese demands. This year on this day in the afternoon a meeting took place at the parade ground of the No. 10 Middle School with the usual speeches in connection with the case. This meeting was called by the Association Extending Assistance toward Peking Slaughtering Case (京案後援會). The following inscriptions were made at the entrance to the

3.

78

the ground. At the top of the door were written 五九雪耻大会 (The great meeting for wiping away disgrace of 9th of May) and at the sides 人而無耻不如早死 (It would be better for certain people to die if they have no sense of shame). Paper tablets with the characters 誓雪五九國耻等字樣 (Swearing to wipe away the national disgrace of 9th of May, etc.) were raised high in the ground.

On that day some students gave their speeches in different parts of the city and in some temples.

Leaflets were distributed; of these nine were obtained and are attached.

Yours truly,

P. Bernadsky

S/O No. 359 of 1926.

Enclosure.

79

Notice of "The Association for Saving Country" exhorting not to use British and Japanese goods, neither to smoke cigarettes of British and Japanese make but only Chinese.

警告同胞

嗚呼吾中國　英日時侵迫
可憐諸烈士　流盡多少血
五四又五九　五卅更慘烈
可恨惡政府　相與惡軍閥
嗚呼吾中國　奄奄在一息
嗚呼國存亡　匹夫皆有責
警告各同胞　快把利害識
英日貨莫用　英日煙莫吃
提倡中國貨　以為對待法
我今告國人　短歌代痛泣

今日是何日　諸君須記得
屢次捨性命　無非為救國
交涉到如今　依然無解決
公然反民意　媚外良心黑
若非賴民氣　亡國在眉睫
國亡做奴隸　苦頭吃不出
不必動干戈　但使經濟絕
但須三五載　彼必財力竭
救國須愛國　効力同一轍
牢記此心頭　莫把天良沒

全甌救國團泣告

Declaration of "Wenchow Association Extending Assistance toward Peking Slaughtering Case" (温州京案後援会) stating that Japanese Government has endeavoured to put the 21 demands in force by supplying the militarists with money and arms. For saving ourselves and country we must stop the financial intercourse with Japan and strike down the Japanese monarchism as well as the militarist Chang Tso-lin (張作霖).

S/C No. 359 of

Enclosure.

為「五九」國恥第十週紀念哀告同胞

十五年五月九日

同胞們！、蠻橫的日本在民國四年的今日、用威逼利誘賣國賊袁世凱簽字他提出二十一條的條件、這二十一條損害我國主權、非基于平等的原則、已應當然無效的、且當時簽約、不過是他一兩個走狗的同意、我人民即熱烈抗爭、發起救國儲金、對日經濟絕交、始終沒有絲毫承認的、凡契約成立、根於雙方的同意、民國主權在民、載在約章、公布世界、此條件既非我人民所同意、又為國會所不通過、乃袁世凱和日本私相授受的契約、應與我國家和人民影響無及的、五卅慘案發生、日本無產階級、也深表同情于我們的廢約運動、此不僅我們國民所絕對否認、且彼國人民亦未嘗有同意的、以双方不同意的條約、損害主權破壞和平的條約、決沒有發生効力、自不待言、而日本帝國主義屢次扶助我國軍閥、欲相攫取、以圖實行、如袁世凱段祺瑞及安福派、以及現在奉系軍閥張作霖、那一個不是日本帝國主義借餉給械助他謀叛的、致我全國人民、士失於學、商困於市、工喪其業、農廢其時、流離失所、輾轉溝壑、這皆是吃日本帝國主義的虧、真真不少了、日本既為我全民衆的敵人、我們為民族爭生死、為國家圖存亡、決不自貶人格、與他往來、經濟絕交、堅持到底、打倒日本帝國主義、同時打倒其走狗奉系軍閥張作霖、這是我、國民現在唯一的任務、自救的方法、同胞們！、急迫時機到了、快起來作一致的行動吧！、

温州京案後援會謹告

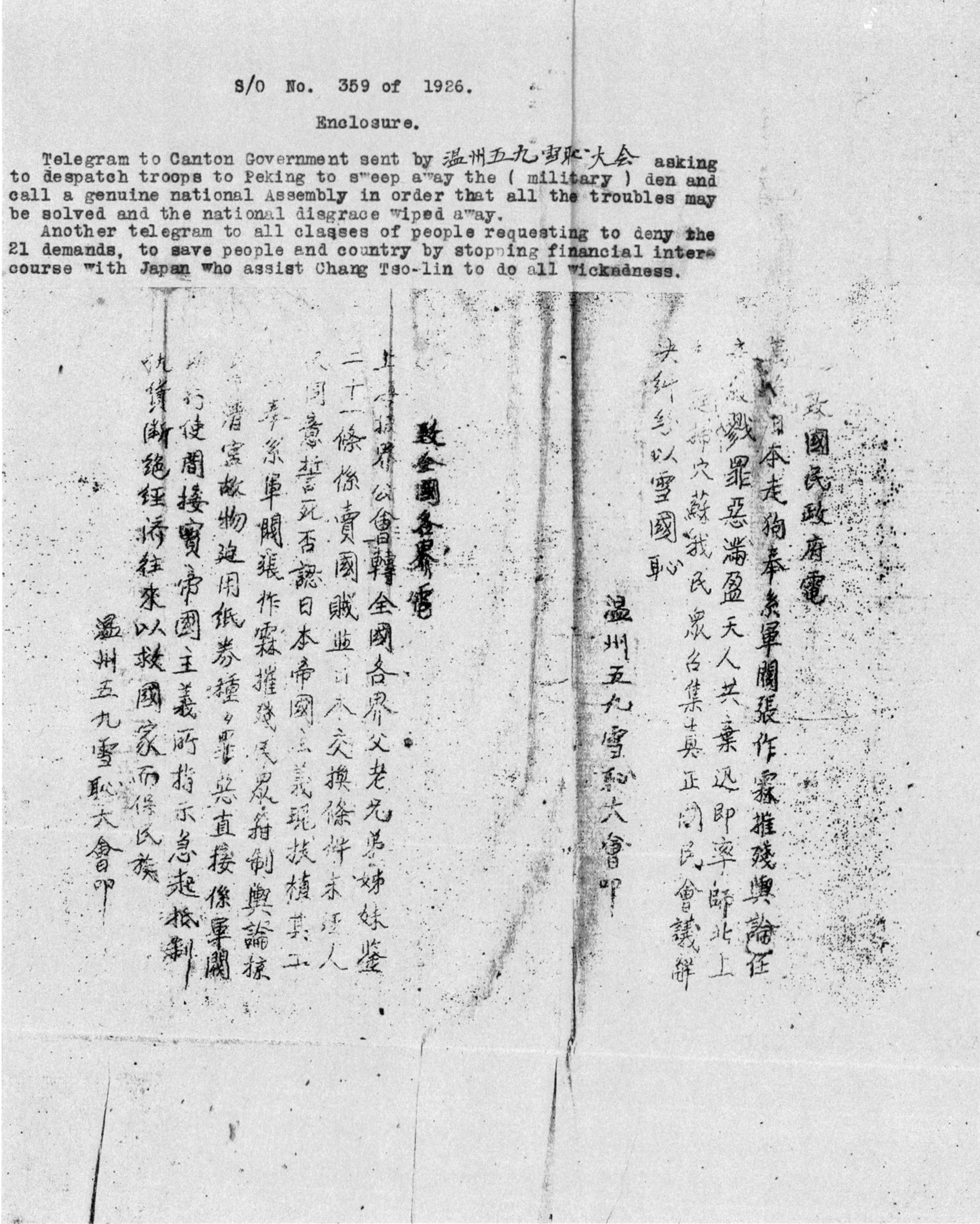

S/O No. 359 of 1926.

Enclosure.

Telegram to Canton Government sent by 温州五九雪耻大会 asking to despatch troops to Peking to sweep away the (military) den and call a genuine national Assembly in order that all the troubles may be solved and the national disgrace wiped away.

Another telegram to all classes of people requesting to deny the 21 demands, to save people and country by stopping financial intercourse with Japan who assist Chang Tso-lin to do all wickedness.

致國民政府電

日本走狗奉系軍閥張作霖摧殘輿論任意殺戮罪惡滿盈天人共棄迅即率師北上直搗巢穴蘇我民衆召集真正國民會議解决糾紛以雪國恥

溫州五九雪恥大會叩

致全國各界電

上海各報界公會轉全國各界父老兄弟姊妹鑒

二十一條係賣國賊與日本交換條件未經人民同意誓死否認日本帝國主義現扶植其工奉系軍閥張作霖摧殘民衆箝制輿論掠潛害斂物濫用紙券種種罪惡直接係軍閥行使間接實帝國主義所指示急起抵制仇貨斷絕經濟往來以救國家而保民族

溫州五九雪恥大會叩

S/O No. 359 of 1926.

Enclosure.

Announcement of the Wenchow Commercial School urging to strike down the monarchism, traitors of flattering foreign powers and unruly military oligarchs.

五九國恥的宣言

今日何日豈非五九之日耶撫今追昔能不黯然神傷是故愛國同胞熱血滿腔於是日有開會紀者有露天演講者有終日啼噓不齊餐者此可見國民雪恥之心仍未絕也然徒知紀念雖效君山之淚倩長沙之痛哭有何益哉雪恥之道除發憤自強與實行革命外無他術也願我國胞抱百折不撓之精神打倒帝國主義媚外國賊擁護軍閥凡一切為國家前途之障礙皆與視之為公敵遠之若蛇蠍類蝗蟲去而快此萬世不易之理也則此莫大之國恥雖無西江之水無不難境滌得矣矣否則國之不存民將焉附事者此國勢風雨飄搖之時願我同胞急宜奮起中

舊溫屬聯合縣立商業學校啟

S/O No. 359 of 1926.

Enclosure.

Suggestions submitted to the great meeting of wiping away disgrace, for approval, conjointly made by the "Wenchow Association Extending Assistance to Peking Slaughtering Case." (温州京案後援会) and the "Society of Urging the opening of National Assembly" (國民会議促成会): 1. to stop financial intercourse with Japan and 2. to unify all the union.

提案大綱

(一)二十一條係日本帝國主義與袁世凱私行換契約，人民抗爭至今，絕對[illegible]府否認。日本帝國主義現決植[illegible]國利用其工具奉系軍閥張作霖[illegible]進行實施侵略，係與我民族存亡有絕大關係。

(一)日本帝國主義鐵路不被壓迫之無廢除[illegible]，對中國二十一條亦所不認，我們應以經濟絕交的手段督促其政府悟醒，並對政府之隊伍為實施解[illegible]。

[illegible]之步驟

根據以上理由，我們所應實行者是：

(甲)經濟絕交

(1)自今日起抵制日本貨物，拒絕輸入

(2)為日本人雇員以至夫役立即退出日本機關及家庭住宅，不再服務。

(3)不賣給日人貨品食物，不許日人與用中国房屋

(4)禁止原料出品售與日本。

(乙)統一團體

(1)向內地各處宣傳

(2)統一內地各體一致行動

(3)與國內各團体共同合作

此請

[illegible]雪恥大會公決

提出者：京案後援会

国民会議促成會

十五年五月九日

S/O No. 3

S/O

Statement of "encho" Publi
communities not to forget the n
away the disgrace which can be
the people.

卒建興漢之功。吾同胞苟以句踐之志為志，何患無昆陽之一戰時，以韓信之心為心，何患無興漢之日。同胞勉乎哉！同胞勉乎哉！

同胞呀！

現在正是卧薪嘗膽的時候，同胞應該曉得日本人的野心，乘歐戰各國無暇東顧，趁時打劫，提出條件，以威嚇的手段迫袁世凱總統承認，這真是吾國的奇恥大辱哪！同胞呀！牢記五月九日國恥紀念！！

[illegible]宣言

No. 359 of 1926.

Enclosure.

lic School (甌公學) students to remind the
national disgrace of May 9th and to wipe
e done only by education extended to all

告同胞文

痛莫甚於亡國，辱莫大於忘恥。世界雖無血
物乃刺之而亦知痛。亦惟心死者乃冥然而不知辱。安
有共和國民受彼邦人之侮辱而不知恥者耶。
吾國自開海禁以還，所遭國恥凡三，曰甲午，曰
庚子，曰五月九日。噫，甲午之國恥，吾同胞未忘也，
而庚子之國恥胡為乎來哉。庚子之國恥，吾同胞
未忘也，而五月九日之國恥胡為乎而來哉。一言
以蔽之曰：民智未開也。民智未開，縱有雪恥之
心而無雪恥之術。然開民智之道，首在教育。
鄙子慕俟教育家也。然五月九日之恥，今將
一讀再讀，而應所以處此也。且思潮來，密鄰陳深
濬民智，冀同民智漸開，恥安有不雪者哉。昔
句踐當國恥會稽之恥，而卧薪嘗膽，卒
沼吳之志。韓信受胯下之恥，而卒為名將
[illegible]

Notification of Kuo
inviting all people to be

育訓練的大黨，每個黨員能夠一致進行去宣傳主義，運動羣衆，同時聯合國外革命勢力，以至於聯合帝國主義國家中的革命勢力，我們可以使一切被壓迫的中國人民乃至各國人民，都變成我們的同志；帝國主義軍閥掌握中的海陸軍隊捕探警察，都有一天會覺悟到他們與我們的利害一致，而站到我們一方面，像辛亥年滿清的軍隊站到我們一方面一樣。要希望有這一個日子，必須大家加入國民黨幫着宣傳主義，運動羣衆，不好站在國民黨外面。我們是要與帝國主義軍閥作戰的軍隊，你若贊成我們作戰的主旨，不但要幫同作戰，而且要受我們軍隊的編制，以求步伍的整齊。步伍不整齊的作戰，是不易取勝的，我們希望要有一個更大更整齊的軍隊，讓我們可以更有把握以取得勝利。

被壓迫的民衆是站在同一地位，革命的民衆是要歸入一個旗幟底下的！

革命的民衆們，大家加入中國國民黨！

拿着青天白日旗向前去！

打倒帝國主義！

打倒軍閥！

中國國民革命萬歲！

中國國民黨浙江省執行委員會 十五年五月

杭州頭髮巷十五號

附入黨須知

(一)凡中華民國之國民，志願接受本黨黨綱，實行本黨主義者，不分男女，皆可請求入黨。

(二)在徵求期內(五月一日至卅一日)入黨者，手續如下：

1. 填寫黨員應徵表一張，送至本地的本黨黨部，或直寄寄交本省黨部。(應徵表可向本黨黨員或各黨部索取)

2. 應徵表經本黨黨部審查，認爲合格後，即發給黨表二張

3. 接到入黨表後，即須逐條填寫清楚，送交本黨區分部，請求通過。

(倘本地無區分部，可直交上級機關或直接寄交本省黨部)

4. 區分部報告通過入黨後，再填志願書一張，繳本人二寸相片一張，便正式入黨爲本黨黨員，由本省執行委員會發給黨証。

(三)本省黨部通信處爲杭州頭髮巷十五號

(四)本地黨部通信處爲

S/O No. 359 of 1926.

Enclosure.

...Min Tang (國民党) of Chekiang Province
...members of the party.

大家加入中國國民黨

同胞們！

你感覺得你的生活安寧麼？你感覺得你所經營的事業，商務，實業，教育等都能發達麼？你見到各地有許多流離顛沛，痛苦無告麼？你也感覺得今日的中國，完全是帝國主義者之殖民地麼？全國人民們所受的痛苦都是帝國主義者所賜予啊！我們每年全國稅收四萬一千萬元，支付賠款內外債便需二萬一千萬元，供應軍閥又需一萬八千萬元，可供政費與教育實業費用的款項，不過二三千萬元。 全國農民完錢粮，商人納厘金，此外如房捐，舖捐，關稅，鹽稅，烟酒稅，印花稅等，莫不直接間接增加人民的負担；然而這些金錢十之八九只是供所謂中央政府拿去供獻給帝國主義者與軍閥，全國人民不但得不着一點好處，而且爲自已造出許多壓迫與禍亂。 現在，官吏教員技師兵士拖欠薪餉動輒數月；教育實業不能振興，使許多人找不着事做；國家無力管理水利墾荒等事業，農民常受水旱蟲災及缺乏田地的痛苦；然而同時因爲捐稅繁重，生活程度却增高起來。 帝國主義者不但每年向我們要幾萬萬元的賠款外債，而且把持着我們海關，限定我們不許加增洋貨入口稅，使洋貨完稅比本國貨所完厘金不及十之一二，於是洋貨流行全中國，奪了許多本國貨的生意，每年洋貨入口價值一二三萬萬兩，洋米入口價值一萬萬兩，使中國工人農民失了職業，本國工廠又因爲受了他們的[illegible]，以收容他們，於是他們只得化爲兵匪游民，爲帝國主義軍閥供奔走。 全國有一百二十萬兵士，爲各省軍閥保障而且爭奪地盤，帝國主義者藉個專制軍閥的保護，經營私運軍械，鬧得全中國鷄犬不寧，人民生活更趨于悲慘而不安定。各種事業既都衰敗，於是大中小學畢業學生乃至歐美留學生都要互相傾軋排擠，纔可以有一個飯碗位置；一切缺了職業的人，非花費一大部分金錢精力，以從事奔走應酬，便會很容易受人家的傾軋排擠，中國的貧農與工人，在衰敗的農場工廠中工作，所受地主資本家的壓迫，比各國格外利害。

帝國主義者宰治了中國，就產生許多軍閥，官僚，買辦階級，土豪，直接以剝削壓迫我人民，間接以滅亡我國家。中國的北洋軍閥，與其分化以後之皖系軍閥，直系軍閥奉系軍閥以及趙恒惕，陳烱明等都是帝國主義者所卵育着的，歷次的軍閥戰爭，袁世凱之稱帝，段祺瑞之武力政策，民九之直皖戰爭，民十一十三之兩次奉直戰爭，陳烱明之叛變，楊劉之內寇，以及最近吳佩孚張作霖之反國民軍，誰不是受了帝國主義之主使，大借款之給予，槍械之接濟。可是他們——帝國主義者——還借此以干涉中國之內政強訂剝削中國之條約，現在帝國主義者除利用軍閥外，覺親自動手了，英國帝國主義者之五卅屠殺，沙基慘殺，日本帝國主義者進兵奉天，砲擊大沽，熱血的中國人民，何能一日忘之。帝國主義者之手段更狠，其走狗之气燄也更凶了，段祺瑞屠殺北京的愛國民衆，張作霖李景林張宗昌之封閉學生會，工會，殺死工人學生；吳佩孚之屠殺京漢路工人，拘捕武漢學生，陳廉伯等買辦之反動，章太炎章士釗等亡國夭孽，破壞愛國運動，楊實甫，潘冬林等工賊之破壞工人團體，誰不是帝國主義者主使操縱之。全中國的人民，無論其爲欲創辦實業，經營商務之資本家，實力爲活的勞動者以及智識階級，自由職業者，誰不是陷在痛苦的黑暗地位中。

這有甚麼辦法呢？這只有依照國民黨的主張，打倒帝國主義與軍閥，建設國民革命的政府，實行國民黨的對內對外政綱。

你爲甚麼不加入國民黨呢？你受的痛苦己經多了，只有國民黨的革命能夠救拔你。你要知道國民黨爲我們反抗一切壓迫，所以凡以壓迫我們爲利的人總不願我們相信國民黨，總不願我們加入國民黨。帝國主義與軍閥，和他們的走狗，常常要爲國民黨造出許多謠言，尤其是在本黨統一兩廣，削除一切反叛分子，帮助香港的罷工委員會，使香港帝國主義無能再在廣東站足的時候。去年五卅以後，本黨努力宣傳，中國國民革命之潮流高漲，打倒帝國主義，打倒軍閥之口號，遍於全國，於是帝國主義者，和他的一切走狗，國內的反動分子更千方百計的誣衊國民黨，破壞國民黨。他們要使一般人認不清國民黨的眞正性質，以妨害國民革命的發展。你不要受他們的欺騙呢！只有國民黨第一次第二次在廣州發表的全國代表大會宣言是國民黨的眞正面目，一切不合於所宣言中精神的，都係假冒國民黨招牌，故意破壞國民黨對於國民的信用。我們要加入眞的國民黨，要使眞的國民黨得着全國國民的信用，打倒一切誣衊破壞國民黨的卑劣行爲。

有些人還有兩種不願入黨的理由，第一是以爲國民黨的主張是很好的，但是打倒帝國主義軍閥，終究是不可能的事；第二是以爲他可以照着國民黨的主張做事，不一定要加入國民黨。打倒帝國主義與軍閥，果眞是不可能的事麼？從前人家說我們打倒滿清是不可能的，然而滿清已被我們打倒了！…我們今天若是有了一個有數

Handbill of Wenc
ment stating that the
and equality of China
cancellation of unequ
Pei-fu and the monarc

日接日寇，便教使張作霖與吳佩孚攜手，進攻素接近民意的國民軍，發生大沽事件，殘民三一八慘案，本都最近進攻北京，好像掠不用，勒逼上海市民用一文不值的軍用票二千萬元，使商店倒閉，兵匪光天化日搶燒殆盡一空，鎗斃京報主筆邵飄萍，監視大陸晚報記者張鵬，並大肆黨獄。

吳賊佩孚幾年來做武力統一的惡夢，使我們中國北部中等的同胞，無日不在槍林彈雨之中！於去年十二月七日，在萬縣殺害鐵路罷工工人有餘人，傷者無數，還借英人勢力的協助背解國條約盡，民生凋殘。前年殺戮了！！便將英國帝主義者長江流域的勢力，逍遙法外，斷送祖中國。五卅時死殺愛國市民，及解散愛國團體，今年為日本張作霖奔了不共戴天的國仇，也投了軍，開始從湖南部下的葉開鑫，向本自治的國民軍總司令部，並要推翻廣東國民政府，先攻湖南，幸得唐生智部的一面，當做唐八十萬兄，充作殺人放火，兩湖人民真是不堪其苦！

我們之同胞受帝國主義及軍閥雙重的壓迫，要救我同胞離開這雙重壓迫之下，只有大中華國民黨領導前去北上接防直隸的速開國民會議及廢除不平等條約，是真的為國民謀利益！及中國自由平等的唯一出路！讓今日大家高呼道：

取消二十一條及一切不平均條約！打倒吳佩孚及其他軍閥的孽！

打倒走狗軍閥的張作霖和吳佩孚！打倒帝國主義！

速開國民會議！

永嘉……部第一區三分部印

S/O No. 359 of 1926.

Enclosure.

l of Wenchow Kuo Min Tang No. 1 Division, 3rd Branch Depart-
that the only way to obtain people benefit and freedom
of China is by an early opening of national assembly,
of unequal treaties, and striking down Chang Tso-lin, Wu
he monarchism.

廿一條先用小夢之的大軍閥袁世凱，竟膽敢承認了；
以為借款等備做皇帝的抵押品：當時全國民同

一致反抗，未得勝利；八年五四運動發生，收回青島
問題，尚為懸案；十一年華府會議，青島虽收回，
而二十一條不得取消，東三省及福建南部的同胞，俱
被日本帝國主義鎖鍊的鎖住。
二十一条何以尚未得取消呢？因因中国民族運動未達
高潮的緣故，要知道日本帝國主義勾結國內的軍閥
，实為致命傷！看！大惡棍袁世凱死了，還四年
至八年的賣國賊段祺瑞繼着；段祺瑞下台了！
關外的強盜張作霖又繼起了！
張作霖陰謀滿州完全送給日本，又構成了幾次的奉
直戰爭，擾亂人民尤甚；去年反日帝国主義大浪
最高時，還施其高壓手段，禁止愛国運動，解散
愛国運動的機關，學生会工会等等……十一月
郭松林為民意而反戈，日本便親自出馬，戰敗郭松林
破壞民族革命戰的第一陣；三月間，英日兩帝国
主義因中国反帝国主義的運動，……反英反日，
日接日厲，便教使張作霖與吳佩孚攜手，進攻
北方較接近民意的國民軍，發生大沽事件

(1) 五九國恥紀念日告同胞們!!!

我們真苦啦!!受了八十年來外國帝國主義不平等條約——海關鹽關領事裁判權租界權賠款割地鐵路建築的束縛,和帝國主義所豢養的軍閥政客剝削宰割同胞們!我們的苦楚,想已無可再忍了!!快起來反抗!!反抗!反抗!

今天是大家會操的日子,檢點我們勇猛的戰鬥力,反抗日本帝國主義貪嚇我辰寸凌我的哀的美敦書——二十一條,雪洗十一週年尚未伸雪莫大恥辱的紀念日!民國四年五月七日,日本帝國主義乘歐戰方酣列強未暇東顧的時候,進兵便佔據德國在華的管轄地,提出廿一條,於是,帝制夢夢的大軍閥袁世凱,竟膽敢承認了!!以為借款籌備做皇帝的抵押品;當時全國學生們一致反抗,才得勝利;八年五四運動發生,收回青島問題,尚為懸而未決;十一年華府會議,青島雖收回,而二十一條不得取消,東三省及福建南部的同胞,但[illegible]

S/O No.

E

Notice of Kuo Min Tang (國
Japanese goods, to stop financ
to strike down the militarist

着一着的進行很明顯地看出来、單就温州一隅而言、沿海的漁民、
炭啦、米啦、我們養命的物品、他又用累進購買的方法、勾串奸紳、私自漏去、鬧得滿地飢荒了。
同胞們！ 我們是不是有理性的人類呢、是中華民國的人民呢、日本對我們已亡被保護國的朝鮮和被割的臺灣、那是怎樣呢、 日本於民國成立以來煽惑我國的內亂又是怎樣呢、彼豢養奉系的軍閥張作霖在北京摧殘輿論姦淫搶奪逼用奉天庫券又是怎樣呢、 我們要中華民族的獨立自由脫離半殖民地地位、最大的障礙、於各帝國主義中尤其是日本帝國主義、 我們要打倒殘民賣國的張作霖、尤須先打倒日本帝國主義。
同胞們！ 日本帝國主義對我們種種的侵畧、這二十一條的關係、不僅是國家存亡的問題、實是文化上經濟上歸到民族生死的問題、日本一國貨物的銷售地、以我們作唯一的尾閭、用的吃的、都以脆薄不耐久的貨品、換我們的食物供給、我們果不落「五分鐘熱度」的恥辱、拿出細微的良心、果能堅持三個月的斷絕經濟往來、他全國的工廠就要倒閉、能堅持六個月他政府就能摇動、果能堅持到一年兩載、不怕他不屈服了、因為他們被壓迫的民衆、也認識他政府的罪惡、我們果由此督促整齊他向政府的隊伍、這不僅我們唯一自救的方法、并且是東亞和平絕大的關係、親愛的同胞們！ 亡國滅種的禍、臨到頭上了、我們的双肩應負着責任、、

抵制日貨！

實行經濟絕交！

誓雪國恥！

否認廿一條！

打倒走狗張作霖！

打倒帝國主義！

國民革命成功萬歲！

中華民國獨立自由萬歲！

十五年五月九日

S/O No. 359 of 1926.

Enclosure.

Notice of Kuo Min Tang (國民党) of Wenchow advising to boycott Japanese goods, to stop financial intercourse with Japan, to strike down the militarist Chang Tso-lin (張作霖).

厚的、實足制張作霖的死命、張作霖也要逃走、日本怕在東三省勢力的……

兵南滿、襲擊郭軍後方、使走狗張作霖勢力又經興起來。

今年三月國奉兩軍相持在京奉路線、日本的海軍、竟率奉系軍艦來襲大沽口、國民軍實施檢查、彼竟反行射擊、並運動各帝國主義國相據什麼辛丑條約向段祺瑞下哀的美敦式的通牒、限十八日時答覆、北方民衆、知國亡無日、羣起抗爭、日本又以利餌安福餘孽、暗結屠殺民衆的條件、所以有「三一八」的慘劇、並加愛國民衆以赤化的徽號、並使我們結實的由其予取予求、任他宰割。日本為經濟侵略的便利、在中國設立工廠、苛待我們做工的同胞、真慘無人道、去年五月在上海打死中國工人顧正紅、激起全國公忿、又聯合英法帝國主義者演成五卅的大慘殺。

同胞們！ 我們受着日本的恥辱、已罄竹難書、日本要消滅我們的民族和國家的野心、事實上一着一着的進行很明顯地看出来、單就溫州一隅而言、沿海的漁民、漁業權被他的侵害已有發見、炭啦、米啦、我們養命的物品、他又用累進購買的方法、勾串奸紳、私自運去、鬧得滿地飢荒了。

同胞們！ 我們是不是有理性的人類？、是中華民國的人民？、日本對我們已亡被保護國的朝鮮和被割的臺灣、那是怎樣？、日本於民國成立以來煽惑我國的內亂又是怎樣？、彼豢養奉系的軍閥張作霖在北京摧殘輿論姦淫搶奪逼用奉天庫券又是怎樣呢？、我們要中華民族的獨立自由脫離半殖民地地位、最大的障礙、於各帝國主義中尤其是日本帝國主義、我們要打倒殘民賣國的張作霖、尤須先打倒日本帝國主義。

同胞們！ 日本帝國主義對我們種種的侵畧、這二十一條的關係、不僅是國家存亡的問題、實是文化上經濟上歸到民族生死的問題、日本一國貨物的銷售地、以我們作唯一的尾閭、用的吃的、都以脆薄不耐久的貨品、換我們的食物供給、我們果不落「五分鐘熱度」的恥辱、拿出細微的良心、

sing to boycott
Japan, to swear
).

中國國民黨永嘉縣黨部為「五九」國恥紀念警告全民眾書

親愛的同胞們！最痛的五九國恥、到第十週紀念了、我告訴你、我們國家的危險和現在應來克爭的方法呢？

民國四年五月七日、日本帝國主義趁歐戰英法德等國不暇東顧的時候、對列強均勢下半殖民地的中國、趁袁世凱要做皇帝、攫取獨霸的權利、提出最無公理損害中國主權二十一條苛約、並發最後通牒、限四十八小時答覆、到五月九日就是袁世凱私行簽字、留下這軍閥賣國的「五九」國恥絕大紀念。

同胞們！這二十一條的內容、沒一條不是亡國的條件、到了巴黎和會、我國申訴又是失敗、差幸「五四」學生運動、拒絕簽字、做一度消極的抵抗、其實關於山東的、關於南滿洲東部內蒙古的、漢冶萍公司的、全國沿岸港灣及島嶼與山東省內並其沿海一帶土地及各島嶼均已斷送了。

日本帝國主義要完全達他目的—滅亡中國—起見、勾引賣國的軍閥、利用袁世凱以後、便利用段祺瑞和安福派、最近幫助奉系軍閥張作霖、去年郭松齡將軍為民眾利益而倒戈、他是奉軍實力最厚的、實足制張作霖的死命、張作霖也要逃走、日本怕在東三省勢力的危險、便揭去中立面具派兵南滿、襲郭軍後方、使走狗張作霖勢力又經盛起來。

今年三月國奉兩軍相持在京奉路線、日本的海軍、竟率奉系軍艦來襲大沽口　國民軍實施檢查、

[A.—42]

88

INSPECTORATE GENERAL OF CUSTOMS.

S/O

PEKING, 27th May 1926.

Dear Sir,

I am directed by the Inspector General

, inform you that your S/O letter No. 359,

ated 12th May, has been duly

ceived.

Yours truly,

F. W. Lyons

Personal Secretary.
~~Private Secretary.~~

ernadsky, Esquire,

WENCHOW.

INSPECTORATE GENERAL OF CUSTOMS,

S/O PEKING, 21st May 1926.

Dear Mr. Bernadsky,

I have duly received your S/O letter No.357 of the 28th April:

Standard Oil Company Case.

Please officialise in order to complete the despatch correspondence on this case.

Yours truly,

F. A. Aglen

Bernadsky, Esquire,

WENCHOW.

CUSTOM HOUSE,

S/O No. 360. Wenchow 21st May 1926. 79

Dear Sir Francis,

Phosphorus matches case.

On the 14th of January last 200 gross boxes of matches uncovered by any Customs documents were found by a searching party on board S.S. "Hua Feng" upon her arrival from Shanghai. Our examiner stated that the cargo was "phosphorus matches" and therefore it was confiscated as contraband. The Superintendent was approached on the 18th of January with a request for treatment of such cargo. In reply he stated that the question was referred to Shui-wu Ch'u. On the 28th of January a merchant came to me and brought samples of matches, which were similar to those confiscated, and asked if this kind of matches as they did not

SIR FRANCIS AGLEN, K. B. E.,

Inspector General of Customs,

PEKING.

2.

90

not contain phosphorus, could be imported into Wenchow. To settle the question whether the matches contained phosphorus, samples were forwarded to the Shanghai Appraising Department. The reply was that the matches were free of white or yellow phosphorus. Therefore the merchant was informed that the matches as per samples brought by him to us could be imported. On the 27th April came the decision of the Shui-wu Ch'u that the phosphorus matches seized from "Hua Feng" were to be destroyed. In view of the information obtained from the Appraising Department that the matches do not contain phosphorus I informed the Superintendent that the nature of the seizure had ipso facto transferred from contraband to ordinary smuggling and asked him to request the Shui-wu Ch'u to cancel its decision though in future the Ch'u's instructions re destruction of phosphorus matches will be carried out.

Seizure

3.

91

Seizure of copper cents at South Gate Station.

According to the Memorandum on the working of the Wenchow Native Customs (page 73) forwarded to you under Despatch No. 3833, merchandise imported by Juian from other coast ports, if conveyed to Wenchow by Juian canal, pays duty at the South Gate Station. The practice of the last few years has shown that no duty has been collected by that station on such cargo, though there is a rumour that the Shanghai cargo used to take this route to Wenchow. I instructed Mr. G. E. Cross, Acting Tidesurveyor, to proceed to the South Gate Station, to choose there the most suitable place for checking purposes and to verify if any goods liable to duty are being imported into Wenchow <u>via</u> Juian canal. On the 29th of April he took one tidewaiter, one watcher and two boatmen and proceeded to the South Gate Station and even about 10 li farther to the place where the network of local canals and creeks begins and kept watch there until the

92

the 2nd May without any result.

But on the 30th of April they boarded a boat towed by a motor-launch the "Hui-chang" at about 1½ miles away from the South Gate and found there 12 packages of copper cents, valued to $590.00. They detained and brought these copper cents to the Custom House. Two-three days later four owners applied to me to release the cargo on the ground that the motor-launch traffic was never interferred with before by the Customs and therefore the merchants did not know that the movement on Juian canal of this kind of cargo was prohibited. As the excuse was a good one I told them that there would be no objection on my part to release the cargo if they could produce me a Huchao from the Superintendent. On the next day Mr. Chang, who was temporarily in charge of the Superintendent's Office, came to me to discuss the question. I told him that the instructions of the

Currency

93

Currency Bureau sent here under your Circular No. 3211, § 2 should be taken as a basis for a decision in this case. But he was of opinion that the Wenchow-Juian traffic was a local movement and that therefore the copper cents should not be detained by the Customs though he was ready to issue the required Huchao if I insisted on it. On the 8th of May I received a letter from the Superintendent requesting me to release this cargo without Huchao as no restriction has been placed on the movement of such cargo in the interior canals. In my reply letter I stated that I was still of the opinion that these copper cents should be covered by the Superintendent's Huchao, but as he insists on their release without a Huchao I prefer to send this cargo to him to dispose of. In reply the Superintendent asked me by a letter of the 13th of May to release the copper cents without sending them to him and he expressed at

the

6.

94

the same time an opinion that I was mislead in my interpretation of the instructions issued by the Peking authorities. The cargo was released by me on the 14th instant but I told Mr. Chang, who called upon me on the same day, that it was desirable to bring the case to the notice of Peking authorities so that they could settle the question of movements of prohibited articles in interior canals. This seizure can be put under series of Native Customs Seizure Reports (as we have Native Customs Station at the South Gate) and also under the series of Maritime Customs Seizure Reports (Juian canal traffic is under the Harbour Master's control). If this Seizure Report will bear the Native Customs number then it will not be mentioned in Fine and Confiscation Report. But if you are of opinion that it is advisable to bring the Shui-wu Ch'u's attention to this case then please

7.

95

please let me know and a Chinese Maritime Customs number will be given to this Seizure Report.

Yours truly,

E. Bernadsky

75

INSPECTORATE GENERAL OF CUSTOMS,

S/O

PEKING, 27th May 1926.

Dear Mr. Bernadsky,

I have duly received your S/O letter No.358 of the 8th May:

Commissioner's Long Leave: May part of it be spent in the East?

Circular No.3678 only applies to leave for Outdoor Staff employees, and I regret that I cannot extend it to cover Indoor employees in your situation as a general rule. Before deciding the matter, however, I should like to know what amount of leave and how much of it you would like to spend in the East. But I can promise nothing, and in any case leave in October 1926 is out of the question now.

Yours truly,

F. Aglen

ernadsky, Esquire,

WENCHOW.

CUSTOM HOUSE,

S/O No. 361.

w Wenchow, 2nd June 1926.

97

INDEXED

Dear Sir Francis,

Attempt to establish efficient control over lorchas movement.

In the first part of May last Mr. G. E. Cross, the Harbour Master here, asked my permission to go down river in a houseboat and try to establish a more efficent control over the movement of lorchas, when the port work allowed him to do so. He stated that several lorchas had been fined last year for discharging imports and loading exports at points down river and that there were rumours that this year import cargo had been transhipped from lorchas and other vessels into craft for conveyance to Wenchow, and as a proof of this he pointed out that import manifests of

some

SIR FRANCIS AGLEN, K. B. E.,

Inspector General of Customs,

PEKING.

2.

98

some lorchas were showing very little cargo. I allowed him to do so on condition that the expenses of this trip should not exceed the petty cash expenditure. On the 16th of May he reported that according to official records some of lorchas were about due to arrive, therefore he took a watcher and four boatmen and on the 17th ultimo at 2 a. m. proceeded to "Rocky Point", anchored there out of sight and organized and kept a watch night and day up to 23rd of May. Though during this time several lorchas passed nothing suspicious was noticed in their movement and the party returned to the port without result.

Events in connection with Shanghai trouble.

There appeared an insertion in the newspaper "Hsin Ou Chao" (新瓯潮) of the 24th ultimo of instructions issued conjointly by the Commander-in-Chief of five provinces and the Civil Governor of Chekiang to all Police Stations of Chekiang province

3.

provinces to prohibit students from making demonstrations, making speeches and distributing leaflets on the occasion of the 30th of May.

In spite of these instructions the meeting was held, demonstrations were made, etc. but on a small scheme, probably owing to the precautionary measures taken by the local authorities, who combined prohibition and permission by attaching a strong police guard to each of the demonstration party.

The article in the Wenchow Pao (温州報) of the 31st of May describing the 30th of May in Wenchow stated:

Some soldiers and police with arms having been stationed at the front door of Chekiang 10th Middle School on the 30th of May, the number of attendants meeting at the parade ground of the school in memorial of the people slaughtered in Shanghai on this day of last year was

not

101

not as great as that in the other previous meetings. The ceremony was opened at about 1 o'clock p. m. After the bell had been rung the community honoured the national flag then sung the national song. Mr. Lin Sheng-chung (林省中) stated the object of the meeting; made offerings to the seats of the slaughtered heroes; funeral music was played; the national song of swearing to wipe away the disgrace was sung; there was silence for 3 minutes; then several school teachers and students made speeches which were applauded by all the hearers. After the orations Mr. Chen Chun-lei (陳仲雷) lead the shouting by the community of watchwords, i.e. "to overthrow imperialism", "to cancel all the unequal treaties", etc. Then the meeting was closed. They went out of the ground and were divided into four parties for demonstration purposes. One party formed of the primary school students went in

one

5.

101

one direction taking a short circuit; another of middle school students went in another direction and took a longer route (passing the Custom House). Along the streets they sang the song of swearing to wipe away national disgrace and shouted watchwords at intervals. Another party went out specially to distribute leaflets (4 of which were obtained and are attached herewith). Another party of orators each went to their appointed places and made speeches there. They all returned to their schools at about 5 p.m

Yours truly,

E. Bernadsky

S/O No. 361 of 1926.
Enclosure.

An announcement was made by the Self-governing Society of the Chekiang 10th Middle School regarding the "Slaughter" of May 30th in which they urge the people to rise against the aggressive imperialism of England and Japan by boycotting the goods of those countries, by refusing their religious systems and by forbidding children to enter their schools.

102

◉浙江十中學生自治會爲五卅大慘殺週年紀念泣告民衆

同胞們！你還記得今天是什麽日子？去年今日，在上海的南京路上，不是有一大隊學生，同老百姓，在那裡叫破了喉嚨，哭損了眼睛的麽？不是有一隊紅頭巾的巡捕，聽着那碧眼睛高鼻頭的命令，舉槍向着遊行隊亂放的麽？不是那無辜的學生，老百姓，受了他們雨一般的槍彈，流出鮮紅的血，斷了臂，穿了胸膛，橫死在那裡的嗎？不是他們眼裏含了熱淚，心裏埋着了痛哭，直挺挺地竟斷送了他們可愛的生命嗎？啊！這是怎麽一回事？你們可也曾記得？

他們也有親愛的父母的；他們也有和諧的妻室；他們也有兒子，也有兄弟！尤其是那整天勞苦的工人，他們的父母妻子，都依他們過活；他們死了，他們父母妻子，是要餓死凍死的！啊！他們爲了國家，爲了同胞－他們是無罪的－但是，犯了洋大人的虎威，他們竟不得不拋掉了慈愛的父母，和諧的妻子，兄弟，讓他們餓死凍死！啊！這是怎麽一回事？你們也是有父母兄弟妻子；那件事臨到了你自己頭上，又將怎樣？

同胞啊！請廓大了你的眼睛！我們中國死了一個人，便是你們自已的兄弟死了一個！今天是你慘死的兄弟底週年的日子了！你們至少也要流一點熱淚，感覺了一些苦痛，再想謀報仇的方法。這是生者對於死者，對於國家，對於同胞，應該的責任呵!!

同胞啊！你親愛的死者，是那洋鬼子英人所殺的！他們是我們第一個仇人－我們半文不値的政府，除向他們鞠躬俯伏外，沒有他法！還有誰力去替我們報仇麽？死了一年，政府那裏有說半個不字！什麽國會法會都是仇人所弄的鬼呵！還有不平的，今年三月，竟連政府也殺起學生來！原來政府同洋鬼子，一鼻孔出氣；他們都是來殺我們老百姓，亡我們祖國的！你們也要自已不被殺，國家不被亡嗎？

要知帝國主義（便是英日等總稱）用了強大的海軍，及許多資本，來侵略我們；只爲我們的祖國，有廣大的土地，豐富的物產。他們爲滿足自已的發財慾；故不得不使我們－中國的主人翁－做了他們的奴隸！於是任其宰割，任其屠殺，半毫也不許我們做主人的反抗！可憐前清末季；到了現在，那一天不是他們在滅亡我的日子！我們故國已割得破碎不堪！我們老百姓也弄得叫苦連天了！他們用剩餘的貨物，借自巳手下的關稅權，盡量地運過來；於是百姓的錢財，被他刮個光！於是居然開起銀行，操縱中國經濟之命脈－又把鎗子炸彈，運給我們萬殺不可赦的軍閥，假他們的手，來剝百姓的皮，吃百姓的肉！民國以來，我們苦也吃盡了！是不是我們要掙一掙身，醒一醒呢？去年今日，正是我們百姓夢中猛醒的時候！雖是流了這許多的血，餓了這許多的工人，沒有得到了一點自由；然我們不可灰心！我們不買他們的劣貨？我們不信他們的宗教！我們不入他們的學校！使他們的工業商業的中心，都成了荒址！－香港便是一個樣子。使我們覺到自巳是一個中國人，應該有打倒侵略者的必要！我們努力掙脫身上的繩索！我們努力來殺這張牙舞爪的虎狼!!

其次便是禍國災民的軍閥了！在去年五卅慘殺以後，封了總工會的，不是奉系的邢士廉嗎？在漢口殺人的，不是直系的蕭耀南嗎？他們（軍閥）勾結了洋鬼，各爭地盤，刮百姓的血，是我們中國人中的盜賊！我們應該互相團結起來，以實力抵抗！

同胞啊！南京路上的血滴還沒有乾哩！帝國主義同軍閥的罪惡，更日甚一日了！我們爲了慘死的同胞，祖宗的國土，同自己的生命起見，快高呼那

全中國人團結起來，
用民衆實力，
打倒一切帝國主義!!
打倒一切賣國軍閥!!
建設了健全的中華民國！

S/O No. 361 of 1926
Enclosure.

A notice was sent round to the women of Wenchow by the Women's department of Wenchow People's Association urging them to support the men in resistance to imperialism, to take an equal responsibility, to show a strong spirit, to assert their personality, and fight for the independence of China

五卅慘案週年紀念告婦女書

親愛的女同胞：

去年今日—五卅—上海學生市民，爲替被日本人搶殺的顧正紅呼寃，爲反對工部局越界築路，在公共租界講演，這是爲中華民族爭人格，爭主權，是一種極有意義的民族運動。誰料那帝國主義者，嗾使他的巡捕開放排槍轟擊我們手無寸鐵的學生市民？登時死者十餘人，傷者無數，血肉橫飛，言之心傷，而帝國主義者，毫無悔禍之心，又於六月一二兩日接連的打死我們的民衆十餘人。這種喪權辱國的案子，假使發生於任何稍能獨立國家，至少也預備一番血戰。而在我們失了獨立性的半殖民地的中國，雖也激動全國人民的公憤，一致起來反抗，然而媚外的軍閥橫行，人民處處受壓迫，那有實力積極的同他們—帝國主義者—對抗呢？所以只得隱忍吞聲用消極的罷市罷課罷工對付。犧牲了三十餘條生命不算，還要犧牲光陰和金錢。而所要求的十三條，到現在非特沒有實行，並且帝國主義者，逼緊的向我們進攻；請看去年六月廿三日廣州沙基死難的烈士，以及今年三月十八日北京國務院前的大屠殺，無一不是帝國主義者的借刀殺人。回想昔日我國山東爲教案的屠死兩個德國教士，賠了他們一千萬兩銀子；並割讓了靑島數百方里的土地的往事，及近年英日帝國主義者殺死我們愛國同胞數百人之多，輕輕的十三條要求，還不能履行。如此强權抹殺公理，怎不令人怒髮衝冠，憤氣塡胸呀！

親愛的姊妹們！我們中國的人民，眞是羞恥極了！國外的帝國主義者，不許我們作愛國的運動，國內的敗類的軍閥，還要向我們壓迫摧殘，慢說自由平等享不到，簡直連一日半日的一條生命誰都不敢爲我們保險、回想那死難諸烈士、當去年遊行講演的時候，，誰會夢到一去不返、罹這不測之禍呢？然而烈士之死，是爭人格爭主權而死，是死得其所死得其榮的，可是中國失了這許多精粹份子，實堪痛惜！不過在這重重鐵蹄踐踏之下的中國民衆，從此也得了不少底經驗和教訓，就是覺得；雖處處失却自由和有生命底危險，同時處處也可以恢復自由利求生，這條是什麼路呢！就是「國民革命」

在國民革命歷程中，是不分階級，不分男女；一致聯合起來向帝國主義者進攻底。我國底民衆，經了五卅慘案後，底確站在戰線上去了。然而一般底婦女，在這革命高潮之中，還相安無事底在那裏做夢似底，雖然也有少數婦女站在聯合戰綫上，很勇敢底爲工作，但是數量太少，實力自然不見增加。那末革命就難能成功了。

親愛的姊妹們！我們知道中國的民衆，把不平等的條約束縛住動踏不得自由了、而我們女子受這種公有的束縛以外還要受舊禮教束縛，其苦痛當較男子們爲更深。其欲解除痛苦也較切，但是要達到解除痛苦的目的非認淸自己的地位，檢閱自己的力量，急起直追、參加國民革命不可。姊妹們！勿妄自菲薄，大家要負起責任來，表現自己强固的神精，健全的人格，謀民族的獨立，及自身的利益呀！努力罷！

S/O No. 361 of 1926.
Enclosure.

An announcement was made by the Wenchow Kuo-min Tang on May 30th, the anniversary day, stating that the case of the Shanghai "slaughtering" had not yet been settled, but that the issue had been shelved by the opening of the Tariff Conference and Extraterritoriality investigation, both likewise insincere; and that to do away with the suppression of anti-foreign demonstration the people should keep alive the spirit of May 30th, should overthrow imperialism and militarism, revolt strenuously against their policy and get rid of foreign influence

親愛的同胞們！「五卅」的恥辱紀念，不幸到了週年了！

大家都曉得「五卅」是日商在華紗廠虐殺我們親愛的工友顧正紅等而滬上工、商、學友們的悲奮，漢口、九江、重慶、沙基的影響，共同罷工、罷市、罷課，反抗示威，因此激動強暴的帝國主義妒忌我們中華民眾在無產階級領導下的民族運動伸張、列強壓迫的解脫，遂演成了這場破天荒的大屠殺，各地同胞死難者凡數百人，此種空前的國恥，凡[illegible]我們四萬萬同胞[illegible]都不會泯滅的。

同胞呀！帝國主義侵畧的手段愈見猛了，[illegible]學閥媚外的面具越顯了，「五卅」慘案發生今已一週年，尚無正式的解決，什麼六國調查團，司法調查，等等的美名來緩和中國民氣，關稅會議，庚款退還，等等的假意來籠絡高等華人，又強以「赤化」誣我來恫嚇愛國同胞，且假借軍閥工具來壓迫反抗運動，日帝國主義又出兵滿洲，攻擊大沽，助長中國內亂，撮合張吳，最後又嗾使[illegible]外的老狗段祺瑞，來屠殺首都的民眾，演成了第二次「三一八」的大流血，睥睨世界的形勢，東方的形勢，將由「五卅」事件展開了，我們要切實地負起責任，努力向前，繼續「五卅」「三一八」的工作，如果再不醒，不覺悟，那末，我們弱小民族是沒有復生的路地了！現在，大家快一致團結起來，我們國內的各界，和國外的以平等待我的民族，聯成一條堅固的大戰線，為我們民族爭平等國家的要求，擯除一切不平等條約，脫離了帝國主義的羈絆，跳出強暴者的圈套，達到我們最後的勝利而後止。

親愛的同胞們！快醒吧！起來

繼續「五卅」革命精神！

打倒帝國主義及媚外軍閥！

努力革命工作！！

[illegible]

S/O No. 361 of 1926.
Enclosure.

An announcement was made by the Students Self-governing Society of Wenchow Public School regarding the tragedy of May 30th, in which they advised the people to overthrow militarism before imperialism, and stated that the offer of $75,000 in compensation is far from pacifying the dead and clearing away the shame, and urged them never to forget the anniversary of this most painful day of shame.

五卅宣言

同胞呵，殘暴的英國賊在去年的今天幫助日本，兩個帝國主義，表裏作奸，在上海英租界內，槍擊死了我們愛國無數同胞，橫屍山積，流血遍地。當那個時候，正是天悲地慘，日月無光的時候，全國異常悲憤，罷工、罷市、罷課，游行講演，群起反抗，為國民自己爭真正的自由，過了數天，漢口、沙面[illegible]又遭他們屠殺，這樣情景真是空前的慘劇，古今無度的奇恥。同胞們呀！同是世上人類，英國賊以這種兇狠手段，壓迫我們中[illegible]民族，視我國家，就是殖民地一樣，視我國民如雞犬還不如，着實是喪天良，滅公理的胡兒。我國內一般無賴軍閥，都抱袖旁觀的態度，非但不肯為國民伸冤雪恥，反做英日帝國主義的走狗，禁止學生愛國運動，殺戮無辜工人，種種是媚外的證據，好像為老虎作倀鬼一樣。這些軍閥一天不撲滅，中國的乱就一天多一天，帝國主義在中國勢力，天天擴張一天，同胞應当知道，若要打倒帝國主義，須先應該打倒媚外軍閥。唉！唉！光陰很快，烈士死難的時候，轉眼已经一年了，交涉直到今天，也沒有完善的结果，只有七萬五千元以作賠償撫恤各費，試問以這區区的款，怎能安慰可悲可敬的英靈，然我國民莫大的恥辱麼？同胞應當曉得今天要算我國有史以來，極可痛憤的一大國恥紀念日，願我們同胞永遠勿忘！

甌公學生自治會印發

[A.—42]

106

S/O

INSPECTORATE GENERAL OF CUSTOMS,

PEKING, 19th June 1926.

Dear Sir,

I am directed by the Inspector General o inform you that your S/O letter No. 361, lated 2nd June, has been duly received.

Yours truly,

F. W. Lyons

Personal Secretary.

~~Private Secretary.~~

ernadsky, Esquire,

WENCHOW.

INSPECTORATE GENERAL OF CUSTOMS,

S/O

PEKING, 9th June 1926

96

Dear Mr. Bernadsky,

I have duly received your S/O letter No.360 of the 21st May:

Seizure of Phosphorus Matches reported to Shui-wu Ch'u which orders their destruction: Appraising Department, however, states matches do not contain white or yellow phosphorus: Superintendent is accordingly asked to request Ch'u to cancel its instructions.

What was the final decision ?

Seizure of Copper cents at South Gate Station: Released at request of Superintendent: Is this to be treated as an M.C. or N.C. seizure?

The Superintendent evidently does not want the question raised here and as the goods have been released you had better treat it as an N.C. seizure.

Yours truly,

F. W. Aglen

nadsky, Esquire,

WENCHOW.

CUSTOM HOUSE, 107

S/O No. 362. Wenchow, 11th June 1926.

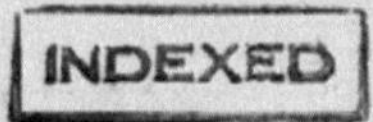

Dear Sir Francis,

Complaints regarding Examination and loading of cargo. I.G. Despatch No. 1388.

I consulted the Superintendent twice and he was of the opinion that this question could not be settled quickly.

Duplicate Applications system. I.G. Circular No. 3686.

With the agreement of the Superintendent it will be introduced here from 15th instant.

Commissioner's long leave. I.G. S/O letter of 27th June.

I am going to apply for one year of leave of absence and probably shall stay with my family 2 months time in the East to help them to make arrangements for housing accommodation, etc.

Change in Seizure Reward system.

At the beginning of this quarter Mr. G. E. Cross, Acting Tidesurveyor prepared a

SIR FRANCIS AGLEN, K. B. E.,
Inspector General of Customs,
PEKING.

2.

108

a memorandum, a copy of which is appended herewith, recommending a new system in distribution of seizure rewards, which I found quite reasonable and approved.

Yours truly,

E. Bernadsky

APPEND.

MEMORANDUM FROM TIDESURVEYOR TO COMMISSIONER

Wenchow, 6th April 1926

(Re Seizure Rewards)

The present system of seizure rewards does not seem to be quite as fair as it might be and I suggest alterations.

The present system is:-

Foreign Officers receive 4 shares each.

Chinese Officers and Watchers receive 3 " "

Weighers

109

Weighers receive 2 shares each.

Boatmen " 2 " "

By the boatmen receiving two shares each it means that the shares of the officers who actually do the hardest work decrease in proportion to the number of boatmen employed. These boatmen do very little actual work but are mostly used to look after the seized goods. They don't even carry the seized goods to the godown, coolies being employed for this purpose. My proposal is the following:- (including examination seizures)

Maritime Customs.

Foreign and Chinese Officers to receive 1 share each.

Weighers and Watchers to receive ½ " "

Boatmen " " one tenth of seizure reward, irrespective of number.

This means that one tenth of seizure reward will be deducted for boatmen and the remainder to be divided by the number of shares represented by the individuals engaged in the seizure.

****

Native

4.

11/2

Native Customs.

Present Practice:-

Foreign Officers	receive	4 shares	each
Chinese Examiners	"	3 "	"
" Weighers	"	3 "	"
" Watchers	"	3 "	"
Boatmen	"	1 share	"

Proposed Scales:-

Foreign and Chinese Tidewaiter to receive	2 shares	each
Chinese Examiners " "	1 share	"
" Weighers " "	1 "	"
" Watchers " "	½ "	"
" Boatmen " "	1/10th of seizure reward.	

(Sgd.) G. E. Cross,
Acting Tidesurveyor.

TRUE COPY :

E. Bernadtz.

Acting Commissioner.

112

CUSTOM HOUSE,

S/O No. 363.

Wenchow 15th June 1926.

Dear Sir Francis,

Reply to S/O Circular No. 51.

A memorandum to S/O Circular No. 51 is enclosed herewith.

Yours truly,

E. Bernadsky

SIR FRANCIS AGLEN, K. B. E.,

Inspector General of Customs,

PEKING.

S/O No. 363 of 1926.

Enclosure.

MEMORANDUM RE S/O CIRCULAR NO. 51.

1.- Substitution of Duplicate Applications for Cargo Certificate.

(a). Will save the clerk most of the time employed by him actually in writing the Cargo Certificate, unless as is likely numerous corrections will be required on the applications.

(b). But as each Shipping Order will require a separate application, the extra number of applications will double the work of assessment of duty and duty sheet. Therefore the system as far as the clerk is concerned will not save much time.

II.- Abolition of Coast Trade Duty.

(a). As there are on the average 20 Duty-paid Certificates per ship arriving here the Import clerk will save a little time in assessing duty but too little to matter.

(b).

2.

114

(b). The abolition of Duty-paid Certificates will save at least half the time of Lushih II but the increase in the number of Duty Memo's will double the work of Duty Memo Lushih I. Therefore as the two cancel there will not be much difference in the time spent.

(c). If by the enforcement of the Washington surtaxes the export duty will be increased to a bigger amount than the present Export and Coast Trade Duty and if no increase is made in Native Customs Tariff it is almost certain that a considerable amount of the native goods now coming to or leaving Wenchow will be sent instead to Juian or Pingyang.

III.- Transit Passes.

(a). The main items going inland are foreign or Special Exemption Certificate goods, and the new system will have no effect on them as the interior is economical

economical and buys only what it needs regardless of cost.

(b). If it could be made possible for merchants to bring goods under Transit Pass from the Interior to Wenchow, it is quite possible that their preference for fixed dues will bring about increased export.

IV.- No direct Re-export cargo goes abroad from the Port.

V.- Staff.

(a). Head Lushih: keeps Chinese accounts and prepares all Duty Memo's; as under new system every Shipping Order will require a Duty Memo, his work will be at least doubled.

(b). Lushih II prepares Special Exemption Certificates and Chinese Coast Trade documents; the time saved by the latter cancels with the extra time of Lushih (a).

(c). Lushih III helps the writer and Lushih

I

4.

118

I and II when required in addition to Transit Passes.

It seems that unless there is a large increase in Transit Passes, no alteration in staff will be required.

E. Bernadsky

Acting Commissioner.

[A.—42]

117

INSPECTORATE GENERAL OF CUSTOMS.

/O

PEKING, 24th June 1926.

Dear Sir,

I am directed by the Inspector General

inform you that your S/O letter No. 363,

ted 15th June, has been duly

ceived.

Yours truly,

F. W. Lyons.

Personal Secretary.

ernadsky, Esquire,

WENCHOW.

CUSTOM HOUSE,

S/O No. 364. Wenchow 21st June 1926. 118

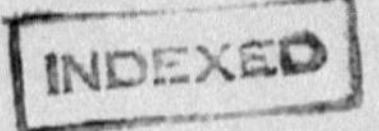

INDEXED

Dear Sir Francis,

Rewards to fire brigades for their services.

I shall be glad to know if I may issue the rewards to the fire brigades in such cases as that stated in my S/O No. 356 of 14th April 1926.

Customs property to rent.

The terms proposed in your Despatch No. 1393/108,065 were communicated to the Agent of the China Merchants Steam Navigation Company here. The latter will send me an official reply after communication with the Head Office at Shanghai. But according to his opinion the proposed terms are unacceptable, though the Company has already spent $ 800 in different preparations for building a godown. Certainly they

SIR FRANCIS AGLEN, K. B. E.,

Inspector General of Customs,

PEKING.

2.

119

they recognize that they must blame themselves for these preparations which were made before your sanction was obtained.

Phosphorus matches Case. I.G. S/O of 9th June 1926.

After receiving reply from the Shui-wu Ch'u cancelling its previous decision the owner of the unmanifested imported native cargo will be fined five times duty in accordance with the port practice that was reported to you in Despatch No. 3907 of the 13th of April 1925 :- enclosure - handing over charge memorandum, "Seizures" column.

Yours truly,

E. Bernadsky

INSPECTORATE GENERAL OF CUSTOMS,

S/O

PEKING, 25th June 1926

Dear Mr. Bernadsky,

I have duly received your S/O letter No.362 of the 11th June:

Change in Seizure Reward System.

There appears to be no objection to the change made.

Yours truly,

[signature]

...rnadsky, Esquire,

WENCHOW.

INSPECTORATE GENERAL OF CUSTOMS, 170

S/O

PEKING, 2nd July 1926.

Dear Mr. Bernadsky,

I have duly received your S/O letter No.364 of the 21st June:

Rewards to Fire-brigades for their Services.

Requests for instructions regarding accounts should always be submitted officially.

Yours truly,

[signature]

ernadsky, Esquire,

WENCHOW.

61

INSPECTORATE GENERAL OF CUSTOMS,

S/O

PEKING, 2nd July 1926

Dear Mr. Bernadsky,

I have duly received your S/O letter No. 356 of the 14th April:

Suggested issue of Rewards to Fire-brigades for their Services: Commissioner enquires whether certain Accounts Instructions apply to this case.

Submit this case officially. The instructions quoted do not apply.

Yours truly,

[signature]

Bernadsky, Esquire,

WENCHOW.

CUSTOM HOUSE,

122

) No. 365

Wenchow, 3rd July 1926.

Dear Sir Francis,

Bernadsky's
ave of absence.

Since my arrival at Wenchow I ~~have~~ have tried to solve locally the difficulty of educating my children, but I am sorry to state that all my attempts in this direction have not been very successful, and now I have decided to send my three girls of 8, 10 and 13 years old to a school outside Wenchow. As the Shanghai School for girls does not provide board I cannot send them there and therefore I am going to put them into the Tsingtao convent School. To take them there I have forwarded to you to-day my application for a month's leave of absence from 20th-25th August. In view of the uncertainty of

R FRANCIS AGLEN, K. B. E.,
Inspector General of Customs,
P E K I N G .

2.

123

of steamer traffic between Wenchow and Shanghai I cannot state the exact date from which I shall be able to take this leave. I apply for a month's leave as the maximum time but if I can arrange to put my girls into the School and provide them with what is required by the School regulations then I shall be back in a shorter time. I shall be much obliged if you will grant me this leave of absence.

ents in connection
th Shanghai trouble,
c.

Please find, herewith enclosed, two pamphlets (and their summary in English) which have recently appeared here and called the "May-30th Special" and the "June-8th Special" (June 8th being the date the students left the Methodist College last year) and representing a collection of the local anti-foreign, anti British and anti-Christian propaganda.

Yours truly,

E. Bernadsky.

114

Wenchow S/O No. 365 of 1926.

Enclosure.

Published by the Students' Self-governing Society of the Wenchow College (甌海公學學生自治會編輯科出版.

The May - 30th Issue. (Special)

1. The foreigners have attempted to subjugate China first by means of force, then by money and thirdly by civilisation - religion and education which the Chinese ought to resist.

2. The causes of the Shanghai May-30th Affairs: attack on sovereignty; and results which are only $75,000.00 as compensasion.

3. The Chinese have awoken from a dream of horror. It is necessary to keep on struggling against the foreign devils with the hope eventually of eating the flesh and drinking the blood of the imperialists.

4. Chinese youths should know that their country will cease to exist if they do not reject the religion and education of the foreigners.

5. Referring to the history of the world, one may judge that whenever powers want to extend their colonies,

125

colonies, they always send missionaries as their advance guards. In looking at Chinese history itself, the same story is to be found.

6. The May-30th Shanghai Affairs have aroused the spirit of the working class not only in China but also all over the world.

7. Most of the unconscious Chinese have learned lessons from the Shanghai tragedy and have come to realise that their lives are endangered, if they do not wake up.

8. Although the May-30th activities were not successful, yet they were sufficient to let the foreigners know the existence of a public opinion in China.

9. If Chinese were well united, China's enemy might be defeated.

10. The disgrace of Shanghai, Hankow, etc. must not be forgotten and must be revenged.

11. The month of May should be observed as the Anniversary Days of the Shanghai, Hankow and Canton tragedies.

12. In reality, it is not the students' business to talk about a declaration of war against China's enemy.

3.

enemy. But owing to the dangerous state of their country, they are willing to sacrifice their lives like those who were killed.

The June - 8th Issue. (Special)

1. The Wenchow College students warn those who are still in the Wenchow Methodist Union College that they must sever relations with the latter college in order to maintain their personality and to show true citizenship.

2. It shuuld be remembered that the 8th of June is the day when the students left the Wenchow Methodist Union College for good that they might not be betrayed by the hypocritical missionaries.

3. Foreign educationists, after the May - 30th Affairs, in order to keep their schools open have induced students to return by reducing tuition fees, establishing fine buildings, etc.

4. Foreign educationists are not here to cultivate young Chinese but to act as spies for their own countries.

5. The main aims of missionary schools in

China

127

China are to utilise Christianity as a weapon for peaceful penetration.

6. The doctrine of Christianity is nonsensical and all the Christian institutions in China are in reality hypocritical.

7. Foreigners have utilised education to deprive China of its civilisation which is more formidable than soldiers and warships.

8. The means of invading a country are three kinds (a) Force (b) Money and (c) Civlisation. The English have used force to invade China and then money; the French have used religion first and then civilisation.

9. The students of the Wenchow College announce why they left the Wenchow Methodist Union College and joined the Wenchow College.

10. The English missionaries in Wenchow have behaved unlawfully in robbing Chinese of their properties; Chinese missionaries should wake up and not remain in the English church.

11. The Wenchow branch of the Kuomintang encouraged those who left the Methodist College, by congratulating on the anniversary of their secession and saying that they had acted admirably.

12.

5.

120

12. Notice of regret at not being able to include in the June - 8th Issue all the articles contributed owing to lack of space.

129

邱祥

禎甫浙江鄞縣

是無賴出身的，無已遊民既被洋教閥豢養多年了，奴隸成性，心肝早已被挖去，自然是他槽中的豕，雖受宰割，亦毫無反對的，洋教閥恐他們的良心還活的，致受自立的影響，所以硬强以金錢及權勢極力撲滅其天理，使永遠屈服於帝國主義的魔力之下。

可哀那一班一班的花子班老鴇班哺啜班走狗班竭其光陰精力，爲洋教閥効忠，視愛國同胞如目中之釘，他們如咆哮之獅，欲把愛國同胞吞噬淨盡。

咳，此洋教在中華的成績—果子—賞賜我。總之爲惡魔的教，决不是耶穌的教。

●六八紀念萬歲

風雲變態　世事滄桑　五卅慘案　舉國張惶
類同狐死　禍怵鴟張　視英猶日　裂肝與腸
維彼藝文　異說披猖　宗教之蠹　帝國之倀
逝將去汝　遷地爲良　相率脫離　挈篋提箱
收回教育　士氣奮揚　巍峨公學　甌海稱强
莘莘學子　共萃一堂　春誦夏弦　日就月將
一週旋届　瞬息流光　舉行紀念　典麗裔皇
年年此日　個個健康　垂爲令典　永矢勿忘

中國國民黨永嘉縣黨部敬祀

●編輯科啓事

本刊限於篇幅，來稿不克備載，良深歉仄，尚乞投稿諸君原諒。

131

君民都是道德君子，如同天使，英國的社會，如同天堂；中國若屬英國，就是天國來到中國了！一般無知如蠢豕的教徒，都應聲說：心願如此！

用金錢當釣餌．

你們來聽道理吧！到每月初頭牧師必賞給你們洋錢，角子，到洋冬節之時，還有錢啦，米票啦，柑子啦，賞給你們的．於是鄭元和的子孫，及廣濟院裏的隊伍，都一齊調進去．你們來到藝文學堂讀書吧！堂宇講究，英文講究，學費免收，膳費減半，畢業後就有生意；到了耶穌生日，還有鳥鎗相送．於是一班哺啜流輩，孫山名族，都擁進去了．

你們這些虔誠老媽，我每月給你們三元，須每日到人家裡去招他們到我城西禮拜堂裡來，還要儆戒他們切勿進自立會，恐怕會落地獄，若你們能將自立會的教友，拉到我的教堂來，到冬天就有東西賞你，且下世到天堂更體面．於是徐慕心金馥祝氏吳陳唐[illegible]等許多女棍，每日分班做那老式生活．你們這班反自立的忠臣們！試看檯子上一共一共的是什麼？有一個說：是牧師賞給我們的銀洋，牧師說：誰要自立的，就沒有分，大家說：牧師啊：我們都不自立，而願永遠倚賴你，並且我們盡我的力撲滅自立會及其分子，牧師說：好呀！忠心的僕人！你們若更加努力，撲滅自立，直至完全肅清，我必提拔你們的位置，加增你們的薪水！他們說：牧師！我們已盡我力，到處反對，毀壞褻瀆，摧殘自立，不遺餘力了，請牧師就要賞賜些，牧師說：好我將華教友自籌的自立款奪來，加增你們的薪金，大家一齊叩首說感謝上帝感謝牧師．

咳！金錢的魔力，本來是大得很，再看我華人大都是見利忘義的，而且那些做牧師的百分之九九們平日口頭說幾句上帝救主．就以爲是功德無量遮掩萬惡了．實則他們的上帝．不是眞上帝．乃是洋人．是勢利．所以就洋化了．確象洋人兒．他們以爲洋大人作其師父．就驕傲凌人．肆無忌憚．

他們貼一張教會月份牌．就以爲姜太公在此百無禁忌．任何捐稅．都可免納．

他們以自爲天國百姓．羞與外教人爲伍．以爲自己必登天堂．別人不入洋教的．必下地獄．

他們把洋人當上帝．把中國人當做魔鬼．

他們說若中國瓜分．我們願分給英國．可見他們的心．已被收買．早種下奴隸種子．養成奴隸性質．

勸洋教徒醒醒吧．快些出來．你若託其勢力．他不久必被打倒．

你若貪其銅錢．這錢是釣餌．是鴆毒．是麻藥．

你若眞信教．中國自有教．也有自立會．

你若不回頭．將來洋人失敗．你就無地可容．

你們好像被洋神船擄了去．我們的非洋教運動正是要救們回國．

你們地盤被洋人佔去．若大家勿入洋教會裏禮拜．土地必有爭回的希望．

你們不要以賊爲友．不要把同胞當敵人．

看哪！我們是你們的救兵．

◉洋人果眞挖人的心肝了！

用宗教成語當麻葯

你們不要求地上的國，只要靈魂到天堂就得了；中國亡與不亡，有上帝做主，不是你們所做得到的；若中國滅亡，也是上帝的旨意，因爲中國百姓不敬上帝，不信耶穌，所以上帝把他們交給外國人責罰他．倘若上帝把中國交在英國手裡，就是上帝的福來到中國了！我們英國多少的富强，

133

△果眞藉傳教以行侵略

外人籍辛丑條約內傳教自由條爲護符・肆意橫行・包攬詞訟・引一般烏合之衆爲教徒・用無賴之類・充教師之職・於是托勢之徒蠭起・而民教之案疊出・致地方生出空前之惡感・

彼等每設一教堂・即侵爲己有之產業・如教堂基地費及建築費・雖十之八九捐自華信徒・總必攫其契據・送領事署蓋印・報交涉署註冊・契字載明英國某某會或法國天主教字樣・迨至華信徒欲謀自立・則英牧師出而拒絕・動曰教堂及英人產業・誰敢自立・昔年平陽宜山內地會建造教堂・基地及築費・百分之八十五出自平陽人・而堂契則爲英牧師持去・及至民國元年・信徒欲謀自立・全體同意擬在原有教堂開會・教料英人竟請警備軍來驅逐教徒・誣爲私佔英人產業・中國官廳素有媚外習慣・祇得聽其使喚而已・去年秋間・聞青田基督教徒欲謀自立・英人海和德及西溪人湯裕三盧元生省議員張煥紳等蜂擁而至・重演宜山故事・霸佔青田教堂・聞該堂地基是當地人所有・建築費亦半出於華人・再于同年冬間海和德湯復三盧元生陳金生等又到玉環坎門霸佔教堂、將自立會之國族會牌等什物搗毀斷碎・並用勢逼利誘之手段・運動各處已自立之會・復歸其節制・如有不聽其運動者・復派强悍惡徒强佔堂屋・近接青田新聞・謂海張湯盧等於强佔教堂之後・復强佔青田人自備的自立歟・引起青田全體教友及各法團公團之反對・現已激起交涉・而官廳反駁覆・不肯受理・於此可見戴假面具之牧師・是侵略主義的先鋒・願我同胞共起反抗、

信教徒爲勢利之外・亦有想討教會女學生而來入教會・此乃美人計引誘青年・

信教之人・以爲有上帝赦罪・就無惡不作・他

之術

尤樹勳

尤君與余素不相識．聞說原是基督教徒．然不與彼盲目喪心一味崇拜洋鬼子者比．且忿外人以傳教爲名．陰行其侵略之政策，毅然脫離外人教會之羈束．籌辦中華自立會．收回宗教權．與我校收回教育權之計畫．其取逕雖異．而熱忱救國則一也．今者承惠佳作．數英牧師之罪．語多翔實．不涉空洞．我同胞觀此．能不怒髮衝冠滅此朝食乎．

——編記識

溫州城西嘼道會會長英人海和德牧師．其平日講演中常帶帝國主義之色彩．一日語諸教友曰．五十年前上海及香港等處．皆是荒坵荒島．經吾英政府經營之後．卽成爲倫敦第二．且印度埃及等國．亦猶中國之野蠻．自歸英屬後．現已成爲第二之英吉利矣．中國斷無自治能力．非藉外力不可．

△英商與教會學校

某西人云．美國何以在中際營業之發達有如此者．吾知之矣．學堂之故．美人捐金所辦之學堂．暗中推廣其營業．故其畢業出來．非洋行買辦．卽公司經理．專門推廣洋貨．英商深悟箇中之理．故極力提倡．推廣教會學校．聞上海英商會慨助各處教會學堂之建築費．溫州藝文之建築費．亦出自英商會．此種學堂．不啻英商之廣告．亦洋奴之製造廠也．

△英牧師藉兵艦傳教

昔年因外人在華橫行無理．致生庚子之亂事．因此我國人遭八國聯軍之人恥辱．前年閩兵過甌．市民驚恐 英法教士藉保護教堂及教民之名．調兵艦來甌．水兵上岸．橫行霸道．辱我國體．莫此爲甚．去年五卅事起．溫州市民遊行示威．英人海和德語其教徒陳池等云．溫州若有遊行運動．我必請兵艦來示威．今年五卅週年紀念日．英人果調艦來示威矣．此確見外人藉武力傳教也．

追步其後・悔何及哉・今幸社會熱忱之士・以收回外人教育權・爲惟一目的・民國十四年・五卅慘案發生・大背人道道主義・故上海約翰大學・吾甌藝文中學諸生・忿外人之蔑視公理・皆相率脫離・作空前未有之舉・上爲祖國爭光榮・下爲地方爭幸福・誠可欽佩也・社會人士・倘皆奮爲一臂之助・將見十年教訓・十年生聚・臥薪嘗胆・誓雪國恥・庶幾他日獲安甯之可能・否則・堂堂神州・吾不知其稅駕矣・

脫離藝文週年宣言

吳震

去年五卅慘案發生・凡屬國民・同深慨憤・所以各地罷市罷工罷課及遊行請願講演等事・相繼而起・以爲外交後援・彼抱帝國主義者・尚不覺悟・尤逞殘酷手段・來屠殺我國民・當此荆天棘地之時。上海教會學校。如聖約翰大學校長卜訪濟壓迫學生愛國運動・又且撕碎我大中華國旗・以致激起全校學生公憤・於六月三日・全體同學一致脫離・轉瞬而溫州藝文學校亦受影響・遂於六月八日上午八時・全體同學一律出校・尤可恨者・藝校監學章賊文誄・素托藝文校長洋鬼子蔡賊博敏之威勢・屢次禁止學生救國運動・各同學久在蔡章二賊雙重壓迫之下・忍無可忍・早有脫離之心・苦無機會可乘・適五卅慘案發生・我們同學遂脫離外人麻醉式教育・我們脫離後・暫時寄居本城四明銀行、幸有谷寅侯先生憐惜我們脫離藝校之同學無求學之處・乃邀集熱心教育者・創設甌海公學・實行吾溫收回教育權之舉・伏祈各界了解甌海公學創設之原因・并希望加以援助・使甌公根本日益堅固・前途有所發展・不獨吾甌十六邑之幸・抑亦吾國之榮也・特此宣言・諸希亮察・

甌海公學學生自治會六八特刊

十七

英牧師在溫州宣傳亡中國

甌海公學學生自治會六八特刊

今日之中國

戚兆光

自歐爭以後・思想激變・各國之學術道德以及風俗習慣・咸煥然一新，獨我國今日四萬萬人民・猶在沈沈夢境之中・豈不痛哉・由是異種强於外・軍閥横於內・營私舞弊・禍國殃民・假借外人・爭奪政權・朝秦暮楚・寡廉鮮恥・而地方人民・遂不勝其魚肉矣・以此等蠹國種子・不早驅除・任其蔓延・國將若之何・民將奈之何，夫侵略政策・不外武力經費文化三端而已・今日英人以武力侵略・繼之以經濟侵畧・法人以宗教侵略・繼之以文化侵略・於是不惜工本・就各地開設學校・以誘我民・吾民乎・宜以國家觀念・印入腦中・首當掃除國賊・次則對外示威・方可免其無形侵略也・蓋無形侵略・非第制我生命也・直欲亡我之國粹・欲保存之・首在關稅收回・以護貿易・調劑生產・奬勵商人・如是始可得商業上競爭・不至我國市場・外貨山積・金錢外溢・歲數萬萬・使膏血竭盡・至破產之期也・次則收回文化教育之權・吾國以儒爲本・無所謂宗教也・今外人以宗教拘束人之思想・麻醉人之腦筋・更利用政治勢力以擴張之・吾民乎・倘不發揚文化・力圖自强・任耶教之勢日益擴張・於以誘惑青年・摧殘國性・直欲盡舉中國之民・爲外國順民・其居心何其險也・吾國民誠一致同心・無論何教傳入國內・一律反抗之・如歐洲十八世紀前之法國然・收回教會教育權・嚴定各種教育標準・國內任何公立私立學校・皆不得違犯・否則・飭令停閉・如此則教育歸於一統・而媚外之奴性・不除而自除矣・嗚呼・吾人惟知聲討軍閥爲摧殘教育・不知軍閥之摧殘・其禍猶淺・教會之摧殘・其害實深・今無知之徒・但謂外人設學校於國中・免收學費・近於博愛平等・不知未來之苦痛・

關係焉，我國教育，自昔稱盛，自軍閥專橫，教育腐敗，教者不得自由教授，學者不得自由發表，其所授之事，所表之物，悉聽軍人之許可，於是志氣活潑之人民，身體强健之男兒，上不能與國家之政事，下不能化無識之愚民，庇護外人，殘賊同種，而武人遂儼然干預教育之新制，外人知我國有此缺點，不覺野心勃勃，起而發難，初則租借我地，逼我政府，戮我同胞，以武力爲先鋒，以教育爲後盾，放肆無忌，令人難忍，愛國青年，奮身反抗，痛哭流涕，奔走於鎗林彈雨之中，而客歲五卅，竟演成一大慘劇，尸積黃浦，血流街衢，天地爲之變色，鬼神爲之悲號，而我政府反漠然忘國家之危，禁愛國運動派兵各處，外施保護之虛名，陰作外人之鷹犬，我愛國同胞，受此極大之刺激，熱血益發至湧矣，外人知以力勝人，終不足以靖人心，於是出其新巧之技，以教育相侵略，不煩一兵，不費一艦，而安然制我國之生命，其初藉口中國人民，智識卑下，不明大勢，我國念累世之夙好，棄近日之小嫌，取平等之地位，以普遍爲目的，整飭其學問，疏通其智識，入我內地，設立學校，引誘良民，授其書籍，滅我國粹，增其制度，變我民性，使愛國之子，皆化爲賣國之民，自强之夫，盡易依賴之質，久而久之勢必陷於印度朝鮮之狀況，豈不痛哉，言念及至，則今日對於收回教育權，固須臾所難緩者也，我甌海公學之成立，實開收回教育權之先聲，蓋客歲五卅慘案之後，藝文學校諸同人，於六月八日脫離英人壓制，組織而成公學，誠吾甌之大紀念也，所望同學諸君，共奮壯志，誓雪國仇，無始勤而終懈，覺今是而昨非，庶幾塵露之微，可以補益山海，螢燭末曜，然日月增輝，則我中華民國從此金甌永固矣，做一二件勞而無功的社會事業；像這種詭計陰謀，毫無價値的舉動，怎値得識者一笑呢？此外如別種教會，宣講所，青年會，更是專門做他們亂七八糟的事體，也用不着再說了。

由上面的結果，我們可以知道，基督教的立說，不能成立；流毒的危險，是誰也不能反抗的。可憐呵！我中華政治腐敗，內亂不靜，竟有一般無識國民，仍蹈其處，眞眞是痛心疾首、待亡無日了。誰知今年三一八的哀悼未了，去年五卅周期的慘劇又快要到了。我們回想去年那班爲國犠牲忠心赤胆的健兒，不顧自已的生命，轟轟烈烈不惜幾許沸騰的熱血，把一條光滑無塵的南京路，染得像血盤一樣。人們呵！你們明瞭他慘死的目的麽？他們無非爲國際地位，互爭平等；爲人民幸福，力主自由；然而竟遭這自命慈善宗教家心腸的碧眼洋鬼，無端慘殺。人們呵！你知道耶穌博愛的主義，是不是殺人？基督救世的色彩，是不是侵掠？由這樣看來，宗教儼然是一種軟化中國的工具了。他如果不是這種政策，爲什麽基督教徒，完全定在外人保護之下呢？怎麽不受我國政府之取締，却受治外法權的保障呢？人們呵！你快快起來反對宗教，收回教育權，從那條純潔光明，自由幸福的路上走去，庶幾使令這狂瀾一葉的中華，得到撥開雲霧，重見天日的一天。那時候，這黃泉路上，死難烈士的忠魂義魄，難道不無小慰麽？同胞呵！努力！努力！奮鬥！奮鬥！

六八感言

張　明

今夫文化爲先王經國之方，而教育實易俗移風之具，文化隨教育爲變遷，人民藉教育而進步，教育善則世治，庸夫高枕而有餘，教育劣則世亂，聖哲驅騖而不足，故教育之與國家，實有連帶之

159

我們已經有點明白；再進一步說，就是基督教流毒的危險了。他們的流毒，就是假託傳教兩名目，實際上調查我國的民情風化，做他們一種侵掠的參考書罷了；那裡有眞正拯救我國民的好意思麼？我現在把他侵掠的步驟，分做教育，慈善，二種。約略寫在下面：

(1)教育方面的侵掠：基督教辦學的目的，是在欺騙人們做他的教徒，受他的同化罷了。他還那裡管什麼學生的心理，學校的教學法麼？他們的學科，完全不適合中國社會的需要；他們的教師，又完全不懂得中國教育的原理；他們唯一的職務，就是引誘中國一般天眞爛漫的青年，天天做禮拜做禱告，把天性完全消滅掉，把愛國的觀念，移作愛上帝了；於是乎又予以一種籠絡的手段，使其永遠貼伏，就是要把人家介紹到什麼教會學校，或教堂裡，安神位置；有時把人家介紹到稽核所，郵政局，或者洋船裏吃洋飯；又要色庇人們，在社會上鼓弄是非，擾亂秩序；於是乎就造成買國的行尸，滅種的走肉，公然自命一種外國系的庇護派，始終不敢說一句反對外國人的話。這正是外人用教育侵掠的手段，豢養這班教徒的好功勞也；是他一種教育侵掠的好成績。

(2)慈善方面的侵掠：基督教創辦慈善機關如醫院等等，他的目的，就是戴起假慈善的面具，做他們一種侵掠的帮助罷了；那裏是眞正爲慈善動機而設立的麼？至於他們醫院的醫生，個個是虛擺門面，那裏能够管到病人的死活麼？他們只天天誇耀自己所舉辦的慈善事業多，以期博得無識者的贊許；其實他們所舉辦的事業，至多只好比閻錫山的小學，張季直的地方事業，有名無實罷了。但是有時也要學中國土財主的模樣，在那裏施點冬米寒衣；有時靠着假仁假義的架子，奮發，單單靠着什麼救主耶穌的能力罷了；此外的其他事情，一概與他無關什麼緊要了。現在把他荒謬的理由，略述如下：

（一）基督教的立說，有什麼耶和瓦無始無終，無所不備，等等的名詞。至於無始無終的定義，就是超出時間以外的意思，既然超出時間以外，那末他創造天地的七日中間，用那一天做開始的日子那一天做終止的日子，那一天做末日審判的日子呢？如果有什麼開始，停止，末日審判，等等的日子，也不得說無始無終了。無所不備的意思，就說是不需求外面的東西；既然不需求也，無費他們創造；若說有需求。必定說「所需求者是善，」然而既有求善的來源，那末當然有不善與之相對，但既然自命爲無所不備，也用着求什麼善；若說「善有不足的地方必定要人類的善，拿來彌補他的缺陷」，爲什麼又要說無所不備呢？所以他上面的什麼無始無終，無所不備的見解，實在多自相矛盾了。

（2）基督教的立說，又有什麼全知全能，絕對無二，等等的名詞；全知全能的意思，就是用他很大的力量，拿來創造一種純善無缺的人類，於是乎惡性亦無從而起；但是惡性既起，不得已只得歸罪於天魔，但是這天魔，是不是耶和瓦所造的呢？若說「是，耶和瓦所造，」當然這天魔，與耶和瓦是並立的，若是這樣，耶和瓦亦不得稱絕對無二了；若說「天魔違背命令，陷於不善」，耶和瓦既已全能，爲什麼不造一個服從命令的人呢？若說「耶和瓦是特造天魔，用以偵探人心之善惡，」耶和瓦既已全知，爲什麼也要偵探呢？由這等看來，他們的全知全能，絕對無二的荒說，簡直自已和自已相衝突了。

（三）基督教流毒的危險：基督教立說不極成，

機關，須受國家之監督，並隨時憑考查與檢驗・」所以我們應公認教育事業，即是公衆事業，教育機關，即是公衆機關・那末，現在教會學校，須一律經我中華教育部或教育廳認可後，方准招生開學・否則由該校所在地長官封閉之・

至於注册時，所應注意者，必具有下列條件：

（一）教育方針，不准以基督教主義爲其教育目標；且須與我國現在教育目標相符合的・

（二）教會學校之校長須爲中國人，萬一正校長不能時，副校長亦須爲中國人・教師之資格，應爲有注册學校之畢業生；凡已從事於基督教者，不得爲教師・

（三）校內不許置禮拜堂・且星期日爲學生休息日，不得強迫學生去聽那教士無稽的鬼話、

（四）校內課程編製，須一律照中國新學制辦理，・以上幾點，即我國教育部最近頒布取締私立學校令裏面也曾論及，不過法令，仍是紙上空談，還要希望我們研究教育者，速起而實行之・以光榮四千餘年史傳的中華，使我四萬萬民族自由的光明，永遠照耀在大地之上才好！

◎基督教立說的荒謬和流毒的危險

錢昭明

基督教迷信的一派鬼話，雖然那些稍爲學得一點科學的人們，極端反對；但是還有沒智識的同胞，仍然天天在那裏受他們的欺騙，什麼上帝於七天之內，造成天地，耶穌用五塊麪包，二條魚，喂飽五千人的一篇混話・所以我現在無論如何，總要把他拿來作一番辯論的根據，可以分做兩層說：

（一）基督教立說的荒謬：基督教的立說，無論什麼事情，總以上帝做目標，揭出什麼博愛救世主義，做他的護身符，使人類的志氣衰頹，無所

境內，拿起教會學校的旗幟，要使這些國度都成為基督化了。口口聲聲說：耶穌基督，要使我們無量數富有革命性的青年，都變做無抵抗的奴隸了！

我們於此，再推論宗教與教育是絕對不能混合為一的。何以故？

(一)性質不同　教育得了民衆的命令，為大家的公僕；而宗教則利用一種職權，宣傳自己的信仰。

(二)職務不同　教育促進社會之文化，求自然界中的眞理；而宗教則敵發文化之理智麻木，宣揚文化之陰氣消沈，且以種種無稽之說，來蒙蔽一切眞理。

(三)目的不同　教育是養成建全人格，發展共和精神；而宗教從基督教與感情生活觀察起來，確是利用情意之弱點，而助長其矛盾。

以上三項，足以證明宗教混入教育之中，無一可恕之處；且其眞義，相去甚遠。是故洋鬼子之設教會學校，不是學校，反是很完全的傳教機關，以繼續其帝國主義的工作。要之我們將上面略一想像其設計之不良，而不驚心動魄者，不是麻木不仁，就是甘心媚外。青年人們！我們是理性的動物，並是軒轅的後裔，切勿作無意識的動作，及帝國主義的走狗。應該奮起精神，想出良策，來對付那宗教主義的學校。

茲就我個人的管見，略寫在下面：

教會學校，須向我國教育部或教育廳，呈請注冊。何以故？教育為國家性命生死的機關，教育權喪失，則國家主權喪失。故一七九四年普魯士宣佈：「學校為國家機關，其職責在教授青年以有益的見聞，與科學的智識。」「一切學校與教育護傳教教士之生命。所以，那時候一教士足跡所到的地方，卽帝國主義者千萬顆子彈所到之處，現在呢？國內教會學校多設一個，卽帝國主義者之大本營多設一個。你們倘不相信，請回憶去年五卅慘案發生時候，上海聖約翰大學，絕對禁止學生愛國運動，甚至把我們很神聖很莊嚴的中華國旗撕了。這種極野蠻的舉動，不是那班聲聲口口說上帝說公道的教會學校校長所做出的嗎？南京路流血成渠，橫尸山積，他們眞沒有看見嗎？那時候爲什麼不說上帝愛人？爲什麼不責備本國的政府？非但沒有責備，而且替本國政府辯護文過，這也是眞正辦教育者—基督教徒自稱—所應該做的嗎？這樣看來，那些教會學校校長，沒有一個不是狼心狗肺，借慈善家的假面具，暗中作帝國主義的工作，侵佔我土地，使我中華民族無形滅亡！

我現在不妨把教會學校的內容，略述一述：教會學校裏的課程，以聖經爲最主要必修科；談到訓育罷！無非根據那本很卑賤的聖經上耶穌的種種鬼話，所以天天朝會的時候，做訓育主任的，就對你說：「你們當信仰那無所不能無所不知無始終的天父，那末，上帝就保護你們，憐愛你們。」這種狗屁不値的鬼話，全是傳道師在講台上常談的套語。還有可聽的價値嗎？至於他們聘請教師，不問學問怎樣，資格怎樣，祇要是宗教家的門徒；不管他是猪是鬼是人，便叫他來教我們。從這幾點歸納起來，可以得到一個很明晰的結論。教會教育，確是將中國成一個耶教化的國家，滅絕我文字，奴隸我人民。換言之，帝國主義者，欲滅亡中國，或壓迫世界弱小民族，則以教會教育之無形的侵畧，爲其最奧妙的工具。所以他們戴人道和平之假面具，奔走世界弱小國度的麼力量封閉他強制他呢？這種治本方法，只有得諸異日罷！最好的治標法子「只有請大家覺悟」自動的不入他們學校裡念書，不受他們什麼免費，什麼畢業後即有位置的欺騙「要知道天生我才必有用」「豈昂藏七尺的身軀，不進外人學校，將來就沒有噉飯的去處麼？並且更應當知道我國社會這樣地混亂，無非受外人不平等條約層層束縛着，我們應當極力運動取消一切不平等條約，那麼人民自然有快樂的日子；一進了他們學校，仰洋大人的鼻息，還敢膽反對他們政府已得的權利麼？

大家快快地覺悟罷！不要進教會學校裏念書，無論那學校是英人辦的，是日人辦的，是法人辦的，是美人辦的……都不要進去．如已在他們校裡，請快些退學，另入我們自辦的學校裏去．不然，我們不得不以甘當洋奴西崽看待他，不把他當作中國的公民，簡直是將來的漢奸罷！」這話未免過激些，祈閱者原諒．

教會教育問題

卓鳴嶽

帝國主義之壓迫我民族，初用巨大的兵艦，和狠利害的機關鎗，綠氣砲，來恐嚇我們；次則自由投資中國，借興辦實業開礦築路為名，利用少數中國資本家及軍閥，為他們的走狗，實行他們經濟侵略的政策。那末，現在我民族大半智識較前增進，能看破他們的政策，而且狠勇敢的反對他們，如各種罷教罷學罷工罷市等運動。帝國主義者，觀察我民族已經覺悟了，自已知道以武力經濟之侵略，終無效果；於是他們再三思維，想出一種很溫和，但是最利害的政策，來接續他們的事業．這種政策是什麼？就是文化侵略。—宗教主義的教育—此種侵略，非自今始，他的種子，早已潛伏於武力侵略之中；試觀拳匪之亂，雖因清廷之昏憒，我民之無知；究其遠因，在於保

105

們卻誠誠懇懇地用他國的教育方式，已是不合於我國的國情；况他們並非是教育專家，於教育學有研究的，不過是二十世紀在西方不能立足的牧師神父，除了念幾句新舊約全書以外，還有什麼事情曉得呢？兼出以教育為他侵略的工具、所以辦起學來，請了幾個已經被他們教義軟化過的教徒來主持．這種教徒，崇奉洋人大的奴性，早經養成了，於洋大人，只有唯命是聽「先意逢迎」．校內課程，由洋大人，或稟命洋大人隨便定一下，不管這種功課是否是對的；非僅僅不管牠，并且用種種方法，消滅我國固有的文化，麻醉青年們的腦筋，「如外國話鐘點非常的多，中文的鐘點很少很少，且不把愛國的文字給你們讀．」致養成無國民性的奴隸式的青年．這種青年，識了一大批洋字，寫起外國文字來，很是敏捷；叫他寫一段中文，反白字疊出，令看者莫名其妙．

上海公學[illegible]年自治會六八特刊

他們只知有外國文字，忘却祖國文字；畢業後又在外人洋行公司裏，替他們招生意，作漢奸，受了外人剩下來的利益——俸薪——就感激不盡，還胆敢道外人一個「不」字麼？還管祖國被外人侵凌麼？我國有一部分人是這樣子，豈不是這部分人成了外國化反來「助桀為虐」剝削同胞麼？所以外人辦的教育，影響於我國是很危險的．

總之外人所辦的教育，其目的是傳教，是侵略；其方法非僅不適合於我國國情，且有害于青年；其影響養成奴隸式的中國人，那麼他們教育可告成功了；而我國人的受煽毒，已沒有救藥的法子了．因以上種種的緣故，所以我們竭力反對他，不許他繼續存在我堂皇疆土上面．

至於對付的方法，大家都說收回教育權，外人辦的學校，須向我國教育部註册，有不對的地方，可隨時封閉他．但反觀我國現在的情勢，有什

七

146

官僚們的敲索，經濟界日呈窘促的現象，今天舉外債，明天發公債，終是日窮一日，沒有一點兒辦法，所以已創辦的各國立或省立的大學中學的經費，月月只收到幾成，致不能夠維持下去；還有什麼力量多設幾個學校，提高太多數人民的智識呢？那麼，外人拿他們的金錢，」其實並非他們自己的金錢，實間接向我們掠掠奪去的，現在姑且這樣說，……來替我們辦教育，應該特地歡迎他，感激他；爲什麼還要反對他呢？這句話，非先了解外人辦教育的目的所取的方法及我們所受的影響，不易明瞭的。

(一)外人辦教育的目的　他們在我們內地辦了許多學校，豈眞爲提高我國人們的智識及文化麽？否！否！他們以傳教爲目的，設了學校，好煽動許多半文明的人們，所以入他們的學校，一定要信教，讀聖經，并且把聖經當作主要的功課，

非讀不可；不僅這樣就够了，還有一種頂重大的目的，就是替他們政府作偵探，你們不信這句話，我找了一個好證據給你們看看，始信這句話是不錯的。前幾年燕京大學的學校長司徒雷登牧師在紐約宣稱：

『中國盜風日熾，列强遲早必干涉中國內政。中國時局日趨惡劣，其景象使人失望，…………但中國之前途，在道德上(基督教)革命，不在政治上革命。目前如無舉動，則美人旅行中國內地者，將有生命上之危險云。』(中國青年第二期)

司徒雷登是那班基督教徒式的中國文人所敬仰的；美國猶其是我同胞所認爲與我國最表同情的最親善的國家，也是這樣子，那麼，彼英日法……諸國只有過之無不及，可不用說了。

(二)外人。辦教育的方法及我們所受的影響　他

一到後來，因五卅的呼聲漸漸低下，他們也就仍他的舊貫了，返豈不是可憐極的嗎？嗚呼黃浦江邊之血跡未乾；而救國之呼聲已變為甘作外人走狗的默認了。

流水似的光陰，已是五卅的週年了。可是測看這一年裏的我們溫州收回教育權聲中的教育，實在不堪設想，雖說有幾個為脫離而辦的學校成立；但是外人的詭計百出，我們富於情感的中國教育者，怎能作他們的敵手呢？此人這一年裏外人的教育，並沒有委靡。茲略舉外人的詭計如左：

(一)甌海藝文中學—該校因脫離了沒有學生，所以就於去年下學期招生的時候，大揚一翻免費的話，到後來就有減費的舉動；且對於基督教徒，有格外優待的辦法。至於這學期以多請良師和減費的話來引誘一般貪利的學生

(二)法人辦的將要開幕的College.—該校用校舍的宏大美景，引誘一般物質的人們、又以兩性共同生活，來誘一般血氣未定的青年。

(三)崇真小學—此校極力聯絡基督教徒。又用半免費的辦法，使得學生增多且說辦此校者不是英人，乃是美國的人。

(四)育德女子學校—這個學校，亦用半免費聯絡基督信徒的手段。

啊！萬惡的外人，引誘我們的方法多極了。處于這種情形之下的同胞，實在難能保持心無搖動。所以我只希望我同胞勿為利誘，勿為色迷，並且心坎中的血是時時熱烈的，極力為國爭光，以期達到教育權完全收回的目的才可。

十五，五，二十三日。

我們為什麼反對外人辦的教育

池淲

我國受了各國條約的束縛，外債的負担，軍閥

想、只曉得他們狗屁不通的牧師的意見。換句話說，就是要消滅我們自由獨立的思想，奴隸我們的性情，摧殘我們的人格，完全變為一個「洋奴」「番狗」。

諸君呀！你們也羨慕那座高大的藝文學校的洋房子嗎？這無非是妓女的裝飾品，誘惑我們血氣未定的青年，而後施行他毒辣的手段，銷毀我們的國民性。想到這一步，眞可痛心啊！現在還有少數無知的青年，受他們的誘惑，受他們的侮辱；我親愛的少數青年呀！入迷途而速返，覺今是而昨非，你們快快醒來罷！快快回頭罷！

諸君既知道我們脫離藝文學校的原因，便曉得「六八」紀念日的價値了。但我們很盼望未脫離教會教校的學生，都叛逆起來罷！以爭回我中華教育權。使四千年史傳的中華，和軒轅後裔的民族，狠光榮地立於地球之上！請諸君最後還要記得兩句口號：

一、不入任何「妓女牌」的教會學校！

二、繼續「六八」的精神！

●溫州收回教育權聲中之外人的教育

朱特造

自從去年五月卅日，那蔑視公理的，英，日，人，逞其凶悍的手段，在上海南京路上屠殺我中華愛國的烈士以後，一般受外人所麻醉的中國青年，也猛地裏從沉沉大夢之中醒轉來，脫離了教育侵略的羅網，那眞眞是令人贊許，令人欽佩啊！可惜我們中國人，終是不能達了「三百秒熱度」之譏好像我們溫州去年脫離藝文學校英人辦的……學生正當脫離的時候，有幾個最喜歡出風頭的，眞是鬧得「不亦樂乎」。如露大講演咧，化裝講演咧，分發傳單咧，遊行示威咧，從他的外表看起來，好似願爲國盡悴的；熱烈的青年，但

149

難歟・諸君皆青年翹楚・夙分黑白・試思父兄之亂命・孰與同胞之慘死・經濟之壓迫・孰與祖國之淪胥・不待智者・而後明也・況二十世紀、正青年奮鬥之時也・具此七尺昂藏之軀・豈終無一術以謀生・而竟甘於出此也・諸君乎・倘能從此翻然覺悟・悔過自新・全體離校・步吾儕之後塵・仍不失爲良好之國民・吾輩亦不念舊惡・和衷共濟・爲學界發異彩・爲祖國爭光榮・使彼外人無所肆其技・微特甌之幸・亦吾國之幸也・若負固不悛・甘心媚外・非僅吾輩目爲國賊爲漢奸・抑亦四萬萬同胞之所不齒・將來諸君人格之如何・亦吾儕所不忍言矣・敢布腹心・望諸君其三省之・

甌公學生自治會公啟

「六八」紀念

卓鳴鑾

諸君呀！我們於六月八日，爲什麽開一個紀念會？因爲我們——曾受過「奴隸式」教育的學生—被五卅諸烈士那種很悲壯很可崇拜的精神提醒之後，不忍受藝文校長英國人的侮辱，和那班番狗郎拍「洋馬屁」的教員的唾罵；已於去年六月八日，高唱國歌，一致離校，擎起「反帝國主義」的旗幟，和那些洋鬼宣戰了。所以「六八」這一天，也可算我們溫州反帝國主義，及收回教育權空前運動的第一天。那紀念「六八」的範圍雖小，而其意義，與我們的關係，却比「五四」「五九」……紀念日，還要深切哩！

現在將我們脫離藝文教會學校的原因，告訴諸君：

藝文學校的教育，是要中國學生們，忘了求學的眞正目的，只曉得萬應靈膏的上帝；忘了我國社會政治經濟教育實業等等狀況，只曉得做「木偶式」的禮拜祈禱；忘了我中華偉人的思

甌海公學學生自治會六八特刊

忠告藝文諸同學

二

巍巍華夏・滿地腥羶・客歲滬上諸同胞・竟受帝國主義者之殘殺・流血漂杵・人道蔑有・公法淪亡・基督之博愛安在哉・英日之文明如是乎・吾輩憤強隣之壓迫・痛祖國之陵夷・遂於六月八日・全體簽字・脫離藝校・幸賴吾甌各界偉人・翠策羣力・幾經艱難・組織甌公・不受奴隸之教育・自謀文化之發展。此吾國學界未有之光榮也・諸君皆明智博達之士・何昧大義・忘國恥・貪兎費蠅頭之末利・甘屈伏外人胯腋之下・仰洋鬼之鼻息・是何心乎・諸君之在斯校・爲榮譽歟・抑爲恥辱歟・淸夜捫心・能不愧然汗下乎・夫五卅死難諸烈士・熱血未乾・含寃誰訴・兎死狐悲・物傷其類・况我同胞・能無哀慟乎・且斯校長・專制異常・學生略有小過・卽以拳足相加・昔美人之於黑奴・不是過也・眞正辦教育者・豈如是耶・乘之斯校・未經吾國教育部之註册・畢業後・欲升入國立大學・戛乎其難・其課程偏重英文・崇拜聖經・而吾國固有之學術・反唾棄而不顧・長此以往・智慧被其蒙蔽・思想受其束縛・國民性之剝奪・何堪設想・若夫中山週年之紀念・北京慘案之表示・五四五九之運動・五卅烈士之追悼・諸君俱不參與・不知身爲何國人・學爲何處用・對此種祖國人恥辱・同胞大痛苦・乃漠然不關痛癢・諸君豈中洋鬼子之鴆毒歟・抑別有用心歟・誠非吾輩之所能了解也・而英國許牧師之來甌・反淸道歡迎・何況寂於彼・而盛舉于此・諸君媚外之醜態・實昭昭然在人耳目・雖欲文飾・其可得乎・夫外人在吾國設立學校・陽爲傳教慈善之事業・陰行文化侵掠之詭計・固爲智識界新公認・抑亦諸君所明知也・而諸君猶眷戀不捨者・其或出於父兄之命令歟・其或迫於經濟之艱

151

Wenchow S/O No. 365 of 1926.

Enclosure.

(Published by the Students' Self-governing Society of the Wenchow College).

The June - 8th Special.

民國十五年六月八日印

六八特刊

甌海公學學生自治會編輯科出版

甌海公學學生自治會六八特刊

目次

每册售銅元四枚

一

定價每册銅元四枚

15

編輯者　學生自治會編輯科

發售處　本校消費合作社

印刷所　溫州美本印刷公司

碧，莫蹉跎，忘了我仇讎，刀如雪。報國志，皎似月；雪恥意，何時滅。拖長槍，電掃歐亞島國。封豕長蛇甯有厭？拚他一頸沙場血。不自由甯死，是男兒；錚錚鐵。

未必亡秦眞是汝。肯教擾亂付兒曹。問君欲展平生志。惟有屠奸借大刀。書生原不喜譚兵。觸目瘡痍淚欲傾。畢竟興亡憑果決。願從萬死繼先民。

滿江紅

沙家觧

荏苒時光容易過、又逢五月、猶記得去年今日、是紅羊刼、黃浦江頭漢沙地、漂流多少英雄血、恨胡兒碧眼肆侵陵、憂心惙、懷往事、增嗚咽、譚國恥、何曾雪、正楸枰殘局、一時難拾、烽火連年元氣竭、閑愁爲斛憑誰說、莽神州、孰把淚波平、陰霾撥、

▲五世紀念有感

鄭眞

已死英雄血未乾。紅羊疊劫最心酸。可憐社鼠藏身固。忍作諸侯壁上觀。伏波已死班生老。世亂滔滔孰品評。大好江山供玩具　吁嗟胡馬任縱橫。

謀祖。兵糧齎寇敵。吾校應時生。仁智相組織。篳路啓山林。百事待匡翼。痛癢既相關、興亡繫喜戚。本此救國衷。願傳到遐逖。但愧南飛雁。稻粱杞忝稷。生活討蠹魚。青燈動四壁。世變日紛紛。杞憂安有極。

●哭五世諸烈士

錢昭明

江山無恙、
風景依然！
去年今天、
不是紅羊慘劫？
猶記得黃浦血痕未乾、
沙漠血肉又飛濺！
莫恨胡兒心兇險、
只怕我團體不堅、
哀鳴一聲、
黃沙萬里、
大家奮起、
來殺碧眼紅髯、

❀ ❀ ❀ ❀ ❀ ❀ ❀ ❀

榴火飛紅、
申江流恨！
一望平原，
蔓草縈骨，
夕陽返照荒坟，
愈顯出烈士的自由血！
飛鳥悲鳴天空，
夏虫哀訴殘月，
茫茫宇宙，
吾來何處哭英魂？

●滿江紅

池灝

咄咄驚人；南京路，彈聲轟烈；江漢畔，伏尸如簀、又翻舊轍。五月榴花染鋒火，一腔熱血千秋法權呀！償金呀！聯絡軍閥，壓倒我民，使屈膝於帝國之下這種壓迫的熱度，可以說已經達到攝氏表百度左右，吾是怎能再受過一些呢？但是多數暮氣沉沉的國民，以爲這種不關痛癢的要求，國自國，我自我、祇要把金錢財帛積得厚些，就可以享用無窮，管什麽國家興亡的事情呢？但是那些有知識階級的人們，想作一番宣傳運動，希望喚醒同胞們大家努力。與這不共戴天的帝國主義爭生死；反被他冷一聲熱一聲，中國衰弱的民氣，不能一致的緣故；所以吾們中國一天黑暗一天，一天擾亂一天、正是是沉沉着獅子熟睡了，任他們殘殺和宰割，像這樣的情形、是不是可憐可痛嗎？回想去年今日、一般死難的烈士們。難消受這種帝國赧殺、不忍作壁上觀、犧牲一己的充分精力、爲我們爭光榮爭自由、盡至到了血肉橫飛、頭顱粉碎不顧自己的死活、竟把那條南京路上染成殷紅，在那時候，我們的國民、纔從那裏昏沉沉中醒起來，感覺到自己身上的危險、和帝國主義的害。唉！五卅不是可恨可怨的麽？當在五卅之先後天天黑暗中被帝國主義侵掠，沒有不甚於這個五卅慘劇；但是這次五卅慘劇、不過他生命的痛苦直接表演罷了、至於他們去年的死，即所以給吾們今日的生；然而吾們不曉得保護生存的道理、那就同死一樣，豈不是很可憐嗎？

△五卅週年有感

馬翊耕

天步何艱難。風塵久未息。舊事憶去年。申江演慘劇。厄運値紅羊。華工被壓迫。愛國類青年。一腔灑熱血。所事雖不成。亦足懾殘賊。爭得治外權。恃此一綫力。吁嗟國無人。媚外同鬼蜮。甘作亡國奴。遑論斯民溺。荏苒換年華。聲嘶力已竭。京滬日色黯。鄒魯絃歌熄。陰霾慘不舒、腥羶誰蕩滌。敎育乃國魂。民性賴挻植數典偷忘其中英輪佔四十五艘。由此可見帝國主義在五卅運動中的損失的一斑。因此，他們在此次運動中不僅覺得中國民族運動，對於他們在中國的侵畧，有莫大的阻礙；并且也明白知道能引起他們國內的衝突！所以他們對於中國民族運動的鎮壓，便不得不加緊！一方面竭力利用中國軍閥，政客，以冷酷殘忍之手段，向工人學生及一切覺悟民衆，加以猛烈的進攻—另一方面鈎接一些反動大學教授，反動智識階級—如研究系，醒獅派等—以反赤化，反蘇聯之名義，以擴展反動之勢力！這些事實都是常常發現的，如封閉工會上海大學，九七屠殺，搜查北京各學校赤化分子，同濟風潮……等等，而於三月十八日的北京慘案，，更表現得明顯了！至於帝國主義與帝國主義之鬭，雖於五卅運動初發動時表現其利益的互相衝突，然因他們也有一致的地方，所以不得不有一致的險狠，來撲滅中國的民族運動！這在三月十八日北京慘案，也容易看得出來的。總之，五卅運動已使「被支配階級」與『帝國主義及一切支配階級』的雙方陣勢加緊了！五卅運動已使「被支配階級「與帝國主義及一切被支配階級的兩个陣勢加緊了、我們處在五卅後的支配階級」應當怎樣？難道也像三月十八日向帝國主義工具用叩頭請願的妙法嗎？呵！可憐的可搭尾巴中國人！

△不是五卅一回的痛苦

鄭眞

我們中國的衰弱、不僅只一天：被帝國主義的蹂躪，又非僅僅一天，想大家都知道了，就是的什麼「甲午」啊！「庚子」—呵！每次戰敗以後，我國在外交地位，就因之墮落，到了現在，無日不被帝國主義的壓迫和魚肉，吾儕無日不在痛哭和悲慘的中間，就是種種不入道的要求，什麼土地呀

——土耳其，埃及，波斯，爪哇等等，又漸漸地塞住了，於是他們的侵略，愈趨於東方來；而經濟落後的老大民族—中國，便成爲他們最所垂涎的地方了。他們覺得中國人，最散漫，最沒有反抗的力量，便以全力來經營。所以他們最近能從崩潰的狀態，變爲穩定的狀態；中國便是其中最大的原因。然而中國的「亞洲式的生產方法」，因帝國主義侵入而解體，便惹起勞動界的不安，而於五卅運動中，表現其深切地覺悟了！覺悟了來領導民族運動去反抗國際帝國主義了！，落後的中國也，來世界革命了！第一，因爲中國勞動階級的地位好，不會像歐洲勞動階級中間有不少的帝國主義的流毒，—如英國—所以能一點妥協地領導全國民衆去反抗外國的資本家，而發生空前的五卅運動故列甯有「落後的歐洲先於惡洲」之謂。第二，中國的人口，佔了全世界四分之一，是佔東方殖民地半殖民地國家的第一位置，的確不失睡獅之稱！所以這個睡獅一旦驚醒，自然是帝國主義的致命傷！—以上述這兩點，故五卅運動。自然能惹起西方的紛亂。因此我們可以曉得，五卅運動不僅引起西方無產階級的援助，而且能反促他們的無產階級革命！故將來世界革命的中心，或能由西方移到東方來！

五卅運動，既含有如是重大的意義自然他發生的影響，比歷來的民衆運動更要大了！已使個個帝國主義不寒而慄了！已使他們在穩定的。時期中又要感到崩潰的恐怖了！在這五卅運動中，帝國主義不獨在中國受了不少的損失；至於他的內部，損失也很大。香港一處，在一九二四年每日出入輪船平均二千另九十艘，共十五萬六千百六十餘噸，因去年七月一日爲滬案而起的罷工，每日出入輪船約只三十艘共五萬五千八百十九噸；同時每日停航之輪船（省河船在內）約七十三艘，我們中國人不過是害了一次癮疾，只有五分鐘！「只有五分鐘！」同帝國主義者只能說這一句了！他們怎知道在民七以後這運勢力，已慢慢地轉入大部分最有革命性的，最有力量的，最有繼續能力的下層羣衆—勞動階級去了！已經使他們—勞動階級—一旦驚醒，大吼其獅子之聲了！他們始而由於階級的經濟鬥爭繼而變爲國內的政治鬥爭，終之，都歸結於反抗國際帝國主義的民族解放運動；并且因爲在經濟落後的弱小民族的狀態之下，他們既然受了國際帝國主義壓迫最烈害；所以這三個階段便混成一氣，幾乎一點不能辨別了！自一九二三年二月九日京漢路工會，經了吳佩孚，蕭耀南摧殘屠殺之後，他們已完全感到與帝國主義及其工具軍閥利益之衝突，自不能同日並立；同時也深深覺悟了他們底歷史的使命，來領導中國民族運動；所以不惜以鮮紅的血，去換勞動階級與民族的自由！在五卅這一次運動，正是他們由醞釀而爆發的時期了！在上海爆發了一次，牽及學生及其他覺悟分子數十人而死；同時或稍後，又在漢口，青島，廣州，香港以及各處，都繼續爆發出來，他們的奮鬪，非常有組織，不稍一點妥協的！守着他們的紀律，一點不怕死！這是處處都可以表現他們的階級的精神！所以這次的運動；假使沒有軍閥的摧殘，而能盡量的發展出來，則不難結合全國平民的革命實力，以達到國民革命的目的！總之，中國的民族運動，已由引導的勢力，形成真的勢力來；而於五卅運動中，表現其空前的擴大了。

第二，我們要曉得，五卅運動是表現世界革命傾向東方的趨勢，國際帝國主義這些野獸，既給國內無產階級的打擊，便想發展於殖民地，半殖民地，以做他們的出路；然而近東的一些出路，強呢？

最後我敬告同胞：救國是羣衆的事情，反帝國主義的旗正向你們招搖，你還是繼續諸烈士的工作呢？還是縮身偸生呢？

▲五卅運動之意義及其影響

楊悅禮

在這個反革命惡勢力奔騰澎湃的狀態之下，當我們各盡了一徵粒的努力，拚命地來作奮鬬的工作的時候，便自然而然的而且必要的回憶到過去的經歷上面來。

五卅事件已是過去一週了！到底這會運動在時間空間上有什麼波瀾？怎樣振動？啊啊！一些商人老板說：「吶喊，遊行終於等於零零；罷市、罷工也不過自棄其業罷了！」這話在一方面，固然表示他們戰鬬力的薄弱；他一方面，對於這話的內容而言，也未始全是瞎說。請你想想，去年工人不是空罷了三個月的工嗎？帝國主義所雇辦的中國政府，一點不能利用，致有什麼司法調查、什麼增加附加稅，這樣慢慢地把這件宣告結束了！你要認識盧山的眞面目，請你跑到廬山外面去！你對於「五卅」的觀察，當是一樣的。你要從遠處。來着這會運動，才知道他是含有重大的意義！并且在當時、大家都還料不到有必然的絕大應響，可是時間到了現在，已由客觀的事實完全證明了。

五卅運動究竟有什麼意義呢？

第一，我們要曉得五卅運動、算是中國民族運動、眞勢力擴大之空前的一次表現。中國自辛亥革命以還、國內的民衆、先後都得了覺悟。其初。是一部分的知識階級，資產階級，從事於羣衆的運動。其發生的應響，雖已使帝國主義者心內戰慄，可是他們仍敢站在峨岩之巔，不顧死活地說

(一)教育—凡是稍有智識的人，都知道一國之能夠成立，和開通智識，最神聖的，最有自主權的，是政治與教育；猶以後者爲重要。因爲教育能夠變移風俗，左右文化，一國的民氣，志趣，態度，都跟他爲轉移。如德英日的教育重武，所以日人以武功名於世界；古時雅典尙文，國人以治文顯於天下。帝國主義者，欲消滅我們同胞的民氣，退化我們的智識；所以不惜重資，在我們設立學校，使救國者—學生都被他收伏，至於學校的內容，眞是不可說了！終日是聖經和外國文，中國文到棄而不重，這樣學生對於本國有什麼益處呢？

(二)傳敎—至於傳敎，則更其可怕而顯明了！他們所說的，無非是根據聖經上所說的愛敵的無反抗主義，使我們都成了無抵抗主義的信徒，那末，他們帝國主義，就可以任意宰割我們的同胞了，不信，可以從歷史上證明：如英國，法國，西班牙，葡萄牙，荷蘭，等國，在十九世紀之末之殖民地，那一處不是以敎士做先鋒呢？卽我國外交史上的交涉差不多什九都是與敎士有關的，不然，他們如果眞實是耶穌信徒，要傳他的道，爲什麼南京路流血，大買賣爆尸呢？而且無一句罪話及到信徒愛活生等呢？這都是傳敎的「亞彌陀佛四個字，只念別人不念自」的態度，總之，敎育與傳敎不但是損害主權。并且還要滅人國哩！

除以上說的二件運動外，我們平時還要培養國力，因爲國力是一國强弱之背景，并且成正比例的，譬如我們要中國强應該充足經濟力；我們就要努力工作生產，我們遇必要時可用武力與外國開戰要取消國際間種種不平等，我們應該先提高自己的智力，再用道德心做後盾，則我國何患不

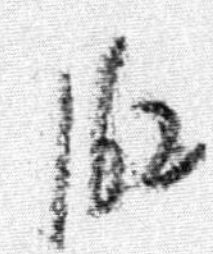

們對於愛國諸烈士所最慚愧的！現在五卅周年到了，我們為喚起民眾的腦海裏去年今日的悽慘，印象起見，所以開了這次的紀念會。我們在這次紀念會中，除報先烈以相當的狠誠摯的敬禮外，不但是要游行講演，分發傳單，開市民大會，并且還要從積極方面做去！振作我們的勇氣，堅固我們的戰陣，去做一次大規模的運動、以慰先烈在天之靈！我們的唯一目標，是繼續去年諸烈士所未竟的工作，去打倒帝國主義。剷除强盜的軍閥，使我中華民族解放、獨立，自由，的光明永遠照耀，第一點，我們認清宣傳是反帝國主義所必需的，因為勢力是民眾的。拿破崙道：『世上民心所傾向的地方，任何人也不能禁止！』所以我們做事最緊要的，是要得到民眾的了解和扶助；尤其是要宣傳及指導無產階級，因為無產階級的勢力、在民眾中最大，并且最有愛國心的、最能夠耐苦的，最受帝國主義所壓迫的，也是他們。他們因為知識缺乏的緣故。雖然受苦，却都歸之於天命！畢竟不知道苦的原因！我們如果告訴他們的痛苦；間接是帝國主義，直接是軍閥所造成？，則他們自然覺悟、會有一種反抗帝國主義的心生出來！如此，多宣傳一個人、就增多一份反帝國主義的力量減小一份世界上那些被壓迫民族解放獨立運動的阻礙！力推之、一國人民都是如此，那末，帝國主義不怕他不消滅於中國了！其次、我們要我們的戰線整齊，軍備充足，反抗帝國主義的最要條件，是要反對文化侵略、（因為帝國主義、從十九世紀到現在，所用的侵略工具很狡鬼；自武力侵略，一變為經濟侵略，更從經濟侵略，變出一個狠溫和的，但是最利害的工具來，以謀最後的勝利就是「文化侵略！」所謂文化侵畧，便是教育與傳教。現在把他分開說罷；

進步。而社會中熱心教育者。亦莫不同心贊助。為祖國爭榮譽。嗚呼。此真吾學界中良好之機會。奮鬥之精神也。彼媚外亡國奴。沈迷于帝國主義者。入其宗教。甘為利誘。受其豢養。甘為西崽。痛何如乎。夫人非涼血動物。冥頑不靈也。生處今日。而猶不悟外人領土擴張之政策。改為經濟文化之政策。揣其居心。直玩視吾國青年。不達其目的必不止。而無識人民。反一律歡迎之。迨至生計日迫。種族日蹙。各國羣爭。瓜分豆剖。於此始歎宗教之學校。不啻是外人殖民之學校。斯時縱有血氣義烈之士。鬬爭祖國光榮。收回教育權力。豈可得哉。豈可得哉。或者謂我國孔墨諸家。亦以博愛為主義。今之基督教。意亦類是。予何絕之深乎。不知滬上五卅慘案發現。至無人道。基督教真相。豈如是乎。試觀波蘭之為俄滅。言語文化。俄人無不過絕之也。朝鮮之為日滅。政治教育。日人無不干涉之也。吾輩青年。不肯自强。甘為波蘭朝鮮之覆轍。則亦已耳。如果發憤為雄。擴張學術。必自力拒外教。勿使蔓延於內地、吾中國庶幾其有瘳乎。有志之士。盍興乎來。

怎樣紀念五卅

趙景熙

時間真快，去年轟動全世界的五卅慘案的紀念日又到了！在過去的一年中，麻木不仁的中國國民，因受了這樣的興奮劑，一個個都從睡夢中醒來，做他們的奮鬥生活；各地的救國運動，也如風起雲湧，一呼百應，這不可不算是中國的民氣激昂的表示！如果全國人民都不斷地向前繼續做去，也許能夠發揚國魂，洗雪國恥！但是一面因為受了帝國主義所卵翼的軍閥所壓迫；一面因為我們太怯弱自餒和戰綫不齊的緣故，所以不久便如雲散煙消，熱度也漸漸地降到冰點點了！這是我的反帝國主義者的運動潮流也照了正比例的擴大高漲到攝氏表一百度了我們中國近年來國民運動的發展已爲不可掩的事實；帝國主義者對於這種切身利害的國民運動，自然要視爲目中之釘，勢非撲滅不可所以去年五卅的慘案、乃是帝國主義者無公理壓迫，無人道的蹂躪，而無疑的。可憐啊！我們中國被帝國主義者的侵掠和壓迫；已非僅僅一天了。所以我的被壓迫民族的積憤和忍痛，到現在始普遍的共同發現，一發而不可再遏的現象，並且能的地變爲熱烈的，堅持到的，團結的、去做耐久而犧牲的浩大反抗運動了。同胞呵！你們現在已經是在蜜甜的睡鄉中驚醒了，快快從那條有希望的路上走去，同那班惡魔奮鬪，勿怕前途荊棘和虎狠，拿着大刀闊斧從人類的血跡裏面闢出一條自由光明的道路來，那時候，可以食帝國主義者肉飲帝國主義者血，何等快意啊

●時局感言

戚兆光

嗚呼。我國自滿清初葉。政府抱鎖國主義。不與外人交通。至道光沒年。爲鴉片戰爭。國勢漸挫。五口通商。至光緒中午。中日失和。庚子之年。拳匪啓釁。聯軍入京。兩宮出走。歸國講和。賠款億萬。而國際外交。遂墮落不可收拾矣。辛亥以還。有志之士。推翻滿人。光復漢族。震我雄威。冀雪國恥。不料系統之組織未成。外蒙之交涉又起。此實爲我國開國史上之汚點。嗚呼痛哉。迄今內黨分爭外侮日甚。遂演出舊歲五月間之慘案。此實我國未有之恥辱也。夫英日之帝國主義。一日不除。則吾同胞之苦痛。因之日烈。試觀由滬上而廣東。由廣東而漢口武昌。相繼對外。迭受壓制。於是外人建設之學校。吾國學生。皆發憤而反抗。而我溫藝文學校。亦全體脫離。另組甌海公學。不受外人之支配。自謀文化之

165

十餘人，醫治無效而死者七人。傷者無數。其中以學生爲最多。傷心慘目。有如是耶。

五結果。

自慘案發生以後。全國民衆。羣起抵抗。各界即成停罷之風潮。并要求政府嚴重抗議。懲兇。賠償。各教會學校學生。亦一致運動。罷課永遠脫離。如滬上約翰大學、甯波斐迪大學．武昌博文大學、天津新學書院、温州藝文中學等、或自創學校、或轉入他校、收回教育權、爲祖國爭光、乃五卅後之佳果、旋政府向六國委員會公共談判、而英日二國、故意延宕僅有七萬五千元、以慰諸死者之家屬、五卅交涉、如是而已、

六尾言

當禍機之初發也、舉國興悲、各界人士、奔走呼號、聲滿天地、而媚外軍閥、爲英日帝國主義、表裏作奸、竟以苛辣手段，封閉救國机關、禁止民衆運動、交涉竟成泡影、烈士有知、亦當怒髮衝冠、抱恨黃泉矣嗚呼，

五卅慘劇的感想

陳希良
錢昭明

同胞呵！去年的五卅，是不是我國有史以來空前未有的慘劇麼？兎死狐悲，物傷其類；況且人類爲萬物之靈，怎樣不會表同情呢？此次慘案的始末，想人家早已明白了。但是我們現在對於帝國主義者的野心，再略說一說；五卅慘殺的行爲，一般人多以爲禍從天來，是偶然發生的事情；其實履霜堅冰，由來者漸，並非一朝一夕的禍患，乃是應有的事情；而且可以說是必然的事情，爲什麼呢？因爲帝國主義者；一方面要維持其生產過剩的恐慌，一方面要延長其國內，被壓迫階級所要推翻的壽命，所以不得不向這半殖民地的中華，一天甚一天的剝奪侵掠，以滿足他們慾壑。可是帝國主義者而殖民地的進攻愈甚，　殖民地

國人民。得以僑居吾國幷准其租賃土地。我國於是始有　界之名。由是。列强相率效尤。外人租界日多租界之內。司法權力。華洋共操。辛亥革命以後。不但華洋互訟事件。華官失却判斷權。卽華人互控案件。亦由領事宣判。且會審公廨。絕對不受中國司法機關管轄。中國租界。已化爲列强殖民地。彼等肆行無忌。故有釀成客歲五卅未有之慘殺，此爲遠因。

三近因。

慘殺一案。肇自上海。日本所設之內外紗廠。殘殺工人顧正紅。以致全國罷工，罷學，罷市。釀成莫大之風潮。然此次之動機。以日人苛待工人。使效牛馬之勞役。無相當之報酬。致起衝突。凡受壓迫於日人勢力之下者　類皆罷工。當時失業者。不能以千萬計。日復一日。風潮逐漸擴大。而日人不設法以解决之。直至五月十五日。內外棉織會社。第七分廠工人。因要求改良待遇。發生衝突。而日人于離亂之時。開槍擊斃工人顧正紅。受傷者不少。一時滬上人民。悲憤莫名。遂造成五卅慘案之導火綫。此其近因。

四慘殺情形

五月卅日。愛國學生。爲無辜工人鳴不平。赤身空拳。分隊入租界講演。痛告此次工人正紅被殺之眞相。以及租界內中國主權之喪失。引起各界注意。當時。只分發傳單。絕無出軌之行爲。此時。英國巡捕以學生與工人表同情。於是遷怒學生。遂拘捕多名。當日下午三時。學生及其他羣衆共三百餘人。向南京路進行。至老閘捕房門首。忽有一西捕名曰斯梯温。出而與涉。拘捕學生二名。向老閘英捕房進去。一時人山人海。目擊心傷。憤無可洩。而捕頭愛伏孫猶爲未足。召集多數巡捕。站立門口。開槍轟擊。飲彈死者計四可謂不專。其責任不可謂不重。而吾輩負此重大責任。使仍怠惰自甘。不力循正大軌道以行。何以免前途之危險。彼政客也。官僚也。軍閥也。大多數以欺騙爲能。搗亂爲事陷我人於亡國奴地步者。宜一律掃除之。否則傳所謂慶父不死。魯難未已者也。近日北京國務院前之流血。山東濟南學生之呼聲。刺激於吾人耳目者。可謂極烈矣。而收效果何如耶。然而失敗爲成功之母。大業非一蹴可幾彼弱小民族之呼號奔走。以謀恢復祖國者。不一而足。況我國有二千餘萬方里之土地。四千餘年璀璨之歷史。而竟消沉寂靜。坐視東狄之侵陵。恥孰甚焉。我青年學生乎。非今日創造新生命之主人翁乎。同具圓顱方趾。各有耳目心思。或爲愛國而讀書。或因讀書而救國。抱定宗旨。實爲昌言。須知吾校與慘案。有連帶之關係。吾校在甌東。有新興之紀念。自覺覺人。自強強國。庶幾本刊出現。或能受社會歡迎。空氣更新。定可蘇國人耳目。世有同志。企予望之。

五卅慘案略史

郭樞
張鏡驄

一導言；

五卅慘案。舉世所忿！英日二國。逞強陵弱。蔑視吾國體。蹂躪吾種族。野蠻殘暴。莫甚於此。夫以吾國同胞。竟受異種之任意屠戮。吾國之領土。乃容外人之耀武揚威。竊以國勢不同。公理則一。天日猶存。黑暗至此。吾民生命等於螻蟻。國際公法已成芻狗。而彼二國。不知悔過。隱滅眞相。虛造事實。反誣我以暴徒。誣我以赤化。是可忍孰不可忍。茲將經過情形。略述其一二於下。

二遠因。

鴉片戰爭。爲中國外交失敗之嚆矢。西曆一八四二年。中英江甯條約訂定後。五口通商。於是英

弁言

馬毓驊

青皇返駕。赤帝司權。九十韶光。忽焉已過。有心人當此。能不倍增悵觸耶。曾文正有言曰。時乎安樂。雖賢者不能作無事之饗饜。時乎困苦。雖達者不能作達衆之懽忻。今日時勢。爲樂觀耶爲悲觀耶。稍留意國事者。當能下一斷語焉。且夫前事之不忘。後事之師也。憶客歲榴火飛紅之日。正申江學林慘變之時。一般愛國諸青年。憤帝國主義之殘殺勞工首領也。大聲疾呼。羣起赴救。卒至飲彈血槍。演成驚天動地之慘劇。猶幸國魂不死。繼起有人。如漢口重慶南京廣州等處。屢仆屢起。再接再厲。與碧眼胡兒相奮鬭。此誠全國同胞。所飲泣吞聲。痛定思痛者也。而我學生界一種爲國犧牲之精神。已永永不滅矣。雖然。天下事理之發生。有近因必有遠果。欲策善後。貴審先機。彼外人侵略我國之工具。豈止一端而已哉。試觀滿清末造。如大東溝之戰。如八國聯軍之入京。猶祇武力侵略已耳。旣而逼我租借。擾我路礦。據我商港。則進而爲經濟侵略矣。其方法愈演而愈新。其手段愈試而愈辣。而其用意最深。不煩一兵。不費一艦。直可以制我中華人生命者。厥惟文化之侵略。比來教會學堂。到處設立。大興土木。豁免學資。誘我莘莘學子。入其彀中而勿脫。自表面觀之。儼若利於吾國。而窺其設心。直欲消吾民愛國之心。移而愛彼國耳。據近日調查。外人設立中國學校。全數達三千以上。生徒都二十餘萬人。校中教科。只以讀聖經習英語爲重。其餘則多不注意。長此以往。國民性之受其剝削摧殘者。何堪設想。言念及此。則收回教育權一事豈容須臾緩哉。今我甌海公學。即根據去年五卅慘案而發生。當時我儕同學。脫離英人專制勢力之下。組織斯校。其毅力不

Wenchow S/O No. 365 of 1926.

Enclosure.

(Published by the Students' Self-governing Society of the Wenchow College.)

The May-30th Special.

五卅特刊

甌海公學學生自治會編輯科出版

目次

中華民國十五年五月三十日

.—42]

170

INSPECTORATE GENERAL OF CUSTOMS.

PEKING. 20th July 1926.

ear Sir,

I am directed by the Inspector General

nform you that your S/O letter No. 365 ,

d 3rd July , has been duly

ved.

Yours truly,

F. W. Lyons

Personal Secretary.

~~Private Secretary~~.

nadsky, Esquire,

WENCHOW.

CUSTOM HOUSE,

No. 366.

Wenchow, 12th July 1926.

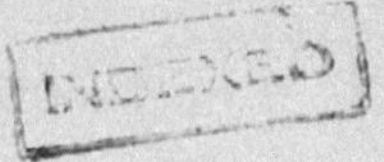

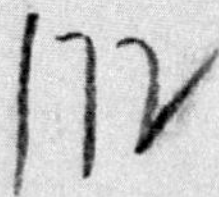

Dear Mr. Edwardes,

nese Factory
ducts. I.G.
cular No. 3681.

On the 7th instant Mr. C. A. Butland, the Agent here of the Asiatic Petroleum Company interviewed me in connection with the new procedure by which -

factory products when shipped coastwise or to interior on or after 14th August are to bear a stamp showing clearly the brand and name of the factory either on the article itself, or on the label or on the actual packing of the article itself.

He stated that the Company has a large stock here of such products already packed and that they cannot send this cargo to

interior

H. F. EDWARDES, ESQUIRE,

Officiating Inspector General, ad interim,

PEKING.

2.

173

interior before the 14th August - the date from which the new procedure will be introduced here -, therefore he asked me to allow them to extend the old procedure for the cargo in stock as well as for the cargo which will arrive here from Shanghai under special arrangement. He told me that the Company had already obtained permission from the Shanghai Office to ship their cargo now in stock coastwise or to the interior after the 7th of August under the following special label. "The ~~cargo~~ cases covered by this application, having ~~packed~~ been packed before the introduction of the rule that the immediate packing of factory products shipped coastwise or to the interior must be marked with the brand and name of the factory, special permission has been granted to mark the cases in lieu thereof."

I told Mr. Butland that if the Shanghai Office to meet the special circumstances

agreed

3.

174

agreed to modify temporarily the procedure for factory products shipped coastwise or to the interior, then there would be no objection on the part of this office to release such cargo on its arrival here and to issue Yün-tan for it. And I agreed also to issue Yün-tan on cargo in stock here the amount of which will be checked by us just before the 14th August if it will bear the same label as that of the Shanghai Office. But I explained to him that the Chinese Authorities have notified the inland offices of the new procedure and therefore if it (the procedure) is modified even temporarily then the Company must be prepared to meet certain difficulties in the interior for which the Customs cannot take responsibility. If they want to avoid such trouble in the interior then they must apply to the Chinese Authorities concerned.

Yours truly,

E. Bernatzky.

.—42]

175

INSPECTORATE GENERAL OF CUSTOMS,

PEKING, 22nd July 19 26

ear Sir,

I am directed by the Inspector General

nform you that your S/O Letter No. 366,

d 12th July, 1926, has been duly

ived.

Yours truly,

F. W. Lyons

Personal ~~Post~~ Secretary.

ernadsky, Esquire,

WENCHOW.

186

INSPECTORATE GENERAL OF CUSTOMS,

S/O

PEKING, 19th July, 1926.

Dear Mr.Bernadsky,

I am directed by the O.I.G.to send you the enclosed newspaper cutting,in which an Assistant - presumably Mr Cholmondeley is meant - is accused of obstructing business.

I am to request you to enquire into the charges made,and to report semi-officially,returning the cutting.

Yours truly,

G.C.J.Holland

Monsieur Bernadsky,

W E N C H O W .

INSPECTORATE GENERAL OF CUSTOMS,

PEKING, 15th July 1926

171

My dear Bernadsky,

I was very sorry not to be able to grant you the short leave you have asked for, but I am unable to make the arrangements I considered necessary for your replacement, and there are various reasons why Cholmondeley is too junior to be placed temporarily in charge at present. I hope that your wife will be able to make the necessary arrangements with regard to placing your children at school.

Yours sincerely,

[signature]

176

CUSTOM HOUSE,

No. 367. Wenchow, 24th July 1926.

INDEXED

Dear Mr. Edwardes,

ndard Oil
pany's Case.

The Standard Oil Company on my request to pay the fine and duty according to the instructions contained in your Despatch No. 1394/108,120, informed me that the question of the fine will be laid before you through the usual diplomatic channels, but the duty will be paid by them if I advise the Company showing on what basis the amounts have been determined.

In my reply of July 23rd 1926 I advised them to pay the duty and fine now, indiscriminately whether they will protest against the payment of the fine or not, otherwise through the non-compliance with the obligations of the Bond and Licence

the

. F. EDWARDES, ESQUIRE,
Officiating Inspector General, ad interim,
PEKING.

2.

117

the latter becomes invalid and the tank will become a non-bonded Tank without transit privileges.

As the Company is going to make a protest against the payment of the fine the question will be referred to you officially after receiving their reply to my letter of July 23rd, 1926.

Yours truly,

E. Bernadzy.

179

CUSTOM HOUSE,

No. 368.

Wenchow, 2nd August 1926.

INDEXED

Dear Mr. Edwardes,

sation against Cholmondeley Assistant, A.

In reply to your S/O letter of July 19th 1926,

forwarding me "Wenchow Newspaper" cutting of June 29th, 1926, in which Mr. Cholmondeley, 4th Assistant, A, is accused of obstructing business,

I beg to state that my investigation proved that there were no grounds for this accusation.

1. I asked the editor of the Wenchow Newspaper to give me for investigation, a case of an application being delayed by the General Office for several days, but he declined to do so and advised me to get the case from the Customs brokers.

2. For import cargo here are three brokers: Chi Chi Hsin (吉記新), Lu Yung Fa (盧榮發), and Wang Min Chih (王敏之) through

I. F. EDWARDES, ESQUIRE,

Officiating Inspector General, ad interim,

P E K I N G .

2.

180

through whose hands practically all the cargo is produced to the Customs. They stated:

a. there was no case known to them of an import application being detained by the General Office for several days for cheking purposes and that

b. All applications pass the General Office at present as quickly as before.

3. Mr. Cholmondeley does not know of any such cases of delay as stated in the Newspaper.

4. No complaints about delays in the General Office were brought before me, except by the note under consideration, which was investigated by me semi-officially in due time.

5. To keep strict control over the speed of the General Office work, I have instructed Mr. Cholmondeley, the Assistant in charge of the General Office to send me at the end of the day a special record of outstanding applications for that day if there are such,

giving

5.

181

giving reason why they could not be passed through the General Office on that day.

The newspaper cutting accusing Mr. Cholmondeley, 4th Assistant, A, is returned herewith.

Yours truly,

E. Bernadsky

ł.—42]

INSPECTORATE GENERAL OF CUSTOMS,

)

PEKING, 16th August 1926.

ᐧear Sir,

I am directed by the Inspector General

ınform you that your S/O Letter No. 368,

d 2nd August, has been duly

ıived.

Yours truly,

F. W. Lyons

Personal Secretary.

~~Private Secretary~~.

ᐧernadsky, Esquire,

WENCHOW.

錄六月二十九日溫州民報

關員辦事不甚敏捷

甌海關幫辦任事以來辦事不甚敏捷以致進口報單每於投報後越三四日尚未見核對簽字交驗貨員檢驗故一般商人極感不便云

TRANSLATION

<u>The Customs Employee not quick in his works.</u>

Since his appointment, the Wenchow Customs Assistant has been not very quick in his works. Consequently, import applications which are sent in to the General Office for his checking can scarcely be delivered to the Examiner for examination until 3 or 4 days afterwards. Hence the merchants feel inconvenient.

甌海関税務司台鑒 謹啟者前
承 劉君来社問及関員辦事不
甚敏捷並囑調查事寔云云但此
事事寔完全在於報関行手中
而報関行又在該幫辦之下焉
肯將此事寔告人 鄙意擬請
税務司將進出口報驗單調閲即
可知其有無稽延情事無庸局

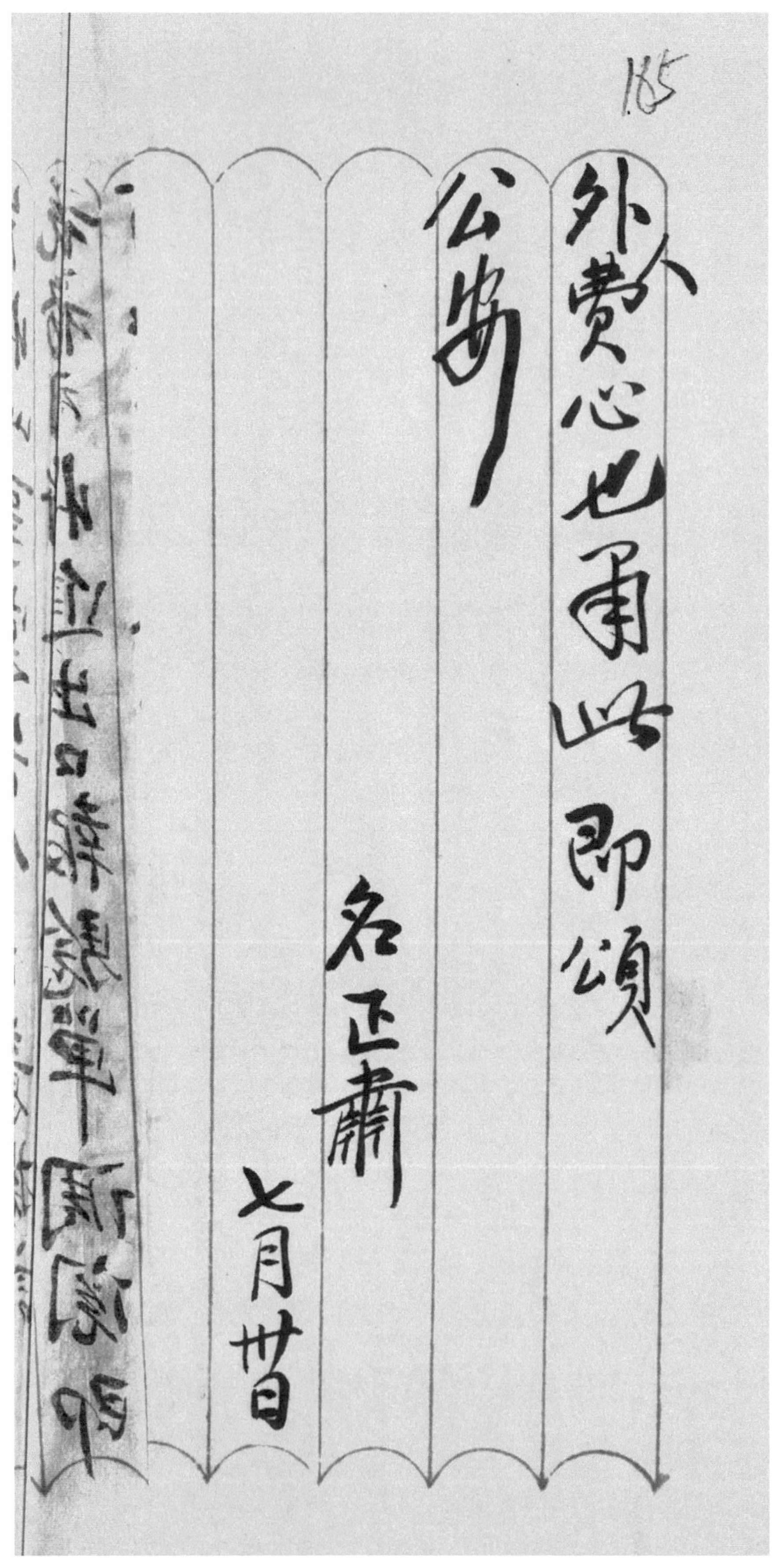
185

外费心也。耑此，即颂

公安！

名正肃

七月廿四

INSPECTORATE GENERAL OF CUSTOMS, 178

S/O PEKING, 5th August 1926

Dear Mr. Bernadsky,

I have duly received your S/O letter No. 367 of 24th July:

Standard Oil Company's Case.

This matter has been dealt with officially.

Yours truly,

E. Bernadsky, Esquire,

WENCHOW.

CUSTOM HOUSE,

No. 369. Wenchow 9th August 1926. 187

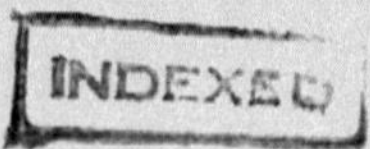
INDEXED

Dear Mr. Edwardes,

era.

On the 22nd of July last I received a telegram from the Shanghai Commissioner "cholera epidemic Shanghai". The Ningpo Commissioner advised me by Despatch of 30th July, 1926, that the Customs Medical Officer states that an epidemic of cholera exists at that port. The Superintendent of Customs and the Medical Officer were notified at once, and the Sanitary Regulations are being applied to vessels arriving from Shanghai and Ningpo. According to local newspapers statements the cholera is spreading here also and I have asked the Superintendent and the Customs doctor to keep me informed of the course of the disease and probably during

I. F. EDWARDES, ESQUIRE,

Officiating Inspector General, ad interim,

P E K I N G .

188

during the next few days I shall be obliged to inform the neighbouring ports that there is cholera epidemic in Wenchow.

and quarters.

In view of the approach of the season for movements and promotions, I beg to bring to your notice a few words about certain members of the Wenchow foreign Outdoor Staff and about the Customs quarters.

Mr. G. E. Cross, Acting Tidesurveyor, is a very energetic Tidesurveyor and Harbour Master and is always glad in addition to his ordinary routine work to do something more. I believe that a bigger port than Wenchow will suit him.

Mr. C. Finch, Assistant Examiner, A, is a very quiet, punctual and diligent employee with a good knowledge of examination work, which he likes and which interests him.

Mr. B. S. Abramoff, 3rd Class Tidewaiter, although a very young employee, works quite satisfactorily. He is detached for Native Customs work and the Assistant in

charge

139

charge of that office has many times highly recommended him. I am sorry to say that the Southern climate does not suit to him. He is now looking very poorly and though he is not sick in the strict meaning of this word, yet he is getting run down quickly and I recommend his transfer to a Northern port as soon as possible.

All these three employees deserve promotion to higher ranks.

There is an Assistant Examiner's House on Conquest Island, leased to the Asiatic Petroleum Company. According to the lease agreement a month's notice is to be given to the Company if the Customs wants to terminate this agreement. At present this house is not required for Customs employee, but if an appointment of a married Out-door employee for Native Customs is going to be made, then this accommodation will be required, and I shall be obliged if you let

me

4.

190

me know in time of the proposed appointment, if it is in the view.

Yours truly,

E. Bernadotg.

1.—42]

191

INSPECTORATE GENERAL OF CUSTOMS,

PEKING, 19th August 1926.

Dear Sir,

I am directed by the Inspector General to inform you that your S/O Letter No. 369, dated 9th August, has been duly received.

Yours truly,

F. W. Lyons

Personal Secretary.

Bernadsky, Esquire,

WENCHOW.

192

CUSTOM HOUSE,

No. 370.

Wenchow , 20th August 1926.

Dear Mr. Edwardes,

lera epidemic
Wenchow.

On the 10th instant all neighbouring ports were informed by me that the Customs Medical Officer states that an epidemic of cholera exists at this port. According to the Customs Doctor's opinion the number of daily fresh patients is about 40 at present. The local merchants, gentry and officials have opened three cholera hospitals in the city, but no latest treatment of curing the sickness has been applied there and the result is about 40- 50 % of mortality. There is a rumour that people are going to send a petition to higher authorities requesting them to close these hospitals. At the very appearance of the cholera here there

H. F. EDWARDES, ESQUIRE,

Officiating Inspector General, ad interim,

P E K I N G .

2.

193

there was a very dry weather and majority of wells were dried. Beggars of the city utilised the situation for their own benefit and took charge of the public wells where some water was still in existence and sold the water @ 5 cents per bucket. The poorest population could not stand such a price and used the water out of dirty creeks and that was probably also the reason of the quick spreading of cholera at Wenchow. There are two Customs employees on cholera sick list:

Hu Nien-chao (胡念招), Boatman since 16th instant.

Shih Chiu-hsing (史久姓), Lushih since 20th instant.

Typhoon. On the 15th instant a fairly severe typhoon passed through Wenchow and caused considerable damage in the place. A full report of it together with the estimate for damages to Customs property will be sent to you officially in a few days time.

Yours truly,

E. Bernadsky

[.—42]

199

INSPECTORATE GENERAL OF CUSTOMS,

PEKING, 3rd September 19 26

Dear Sir,

I am directed by the Inspector General

inform you that your S/O Letter No. 370,

d 20th August, has been duly

ived.

Yours truly,

F. W. Lyons

Personal Secretary.

~~Private Secretary.~~

madsky, Esquire,

WENCHOW.

CUSTOM HOUSE, 195

/0 No. 371. Wenchow, 2nd September 19 26.

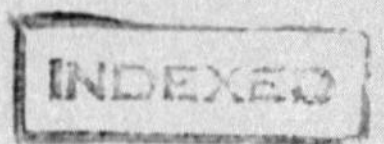

)

mplaints regarding
:amination and
ading of cargo.
G. Despatch No.
'88.

Dear Mr. Edwardes,

After correspondence and personal consultation with me the Superintendent seconded my efforts to make the merchants concerned understand that the payment of special permit fees Hk. Tls. 3.00 for Sunday permit cannot be waived without the entire revision of the Wenchow Native Customs Sunday working procedure. At present all cargo is examined before loading and under this system there can be no dispute about weights and quantities; but if any change is to be made in this system and shipment of cargo allowed before examination by the Customs, then if disputes arise about weights of such cargo as timber, paper and charcoal and more thorough examination is required,

the

H. F. EDWARDES, ESQUIRE,

Officiating Inspector General, ad interim,

P E K I N G .

2.

196

the merchants must be prepared to stand the extra expenses and delays entailed, which will probably be greater than under the present system.

The merchants have some inkling of this, and accordingly they and the leaders of this petition cannot come to a mutual agreement. They promised the Superintendent to inform him of their wishes later on, but he feels almost certain that no one will come to discuss the matter further with him. The Superintendent proposed to me that I should postpone my reply to the end of the year, because then it would be possible to tell with greater certainty what real foundation there was to this petition, and whether the merchants would continue to support it, when they fully understood the situation.

olera.

I am glad to state that the Customs doctor expects that in a week or a fortnight the cholera will probably fall below

3.

197

below its epidemic stage.

Temporary Cholera Hospitals in the city were closed on the 1st September and all patients who want to go to a hospital will be sent to the Blyth Hospital, which is under the Customs doctor's supervision.

Our boatman Hu Nien-chao (胡念裕) died from cholera on the 22nd of August.

ents in connection
th Shanghai
ouble, etc.

Enclosed with translation is the copy of a note which appeared in the local newspaper "Wenchow Min Pao" (温州民報) of the 1st instant showing that there is now a strong agitation amongst students against missionaries schools.

Yours truly

E. Bernadotg.

198

Wenchow S/O No. 371 of 1926.

ENCLOSURE.

Copy of a note which appeared in the local newspaper "Wenchow Min Pao" (温州民報) of the 1st instant showing that there is now a strong agitation amongst students against missionaries schools.

錄温州民報 九月一日

洋人學校招攷消息

温州自往年五卅運動以來各界對收回教育權運動頗具熱力本年由學聯會發起召集各界組織收回教育權大同盟對勸告通知尤不憚再三盡力法國人所辦增爵學校於前日開攷各校學生即在該校門口對投攷學生苦口勸導卒至應攷寥寥所取人數不足該校於昨日又續招新生由收回教育權大同盟及各校學生仍在該處勸告當勸告時有該校聘員二人入校出題經學生勸告不聽反出口罵人學生大憤即將兩教員痛斥一番始已同時有兩個學生新從鄉間來亦將入該校即經各生阻止極力勸告聞此兩生頗有覺悟立誓不入此校以保國民人格云

2.

199

Wenchow S/O No. 371 of 1926

ENCLOSURE.

Translation of a note which appeared in the local newspaper "Wenchow Min Pao" (温州民報) of the 1st instant showing that there is now a strong agitation amongst students against missionaries schools.

ENTRANCE EXAMINATION IN FOREIGN SCHOOL HERE.

Since the May-30th affairs the public has taken much interest in reclaiming students from the foreign schools. This year the Educational Union Association (學聯會) has organised with the public an Educational Rights-claiming Alliance (教育權大同盟) to start a campaign to persuade the public not to send their children to the foreign schools in the city. The French Missionary school held its entrance examination a few days ago but owing to persuasion by students from the other schools very few candidates came to take the entrance examination. As so few came the school held its entrance examination again yesterday. But members of the Educational Rights-claiming Alliance and students from other schools went there to persuade the candidates not to sit for the examination. There were two Chinese teachers going

3.

700

going to examine the candidates; the students tried to persuade them not to go but the teachers refused to listen to this advice and scolded them instead. This made the students very excited and they blamed these teachers severely. There were also two candidates who had come from the country intending to enter this school; but these two were won over by the students with the result that they swore an oath that they would maintain their Chinese personality by going to a Chinese and not a foreign school.

CUSTOM HOUSE, 202

No. 372. Wenchow, 15th Sept. 1926.

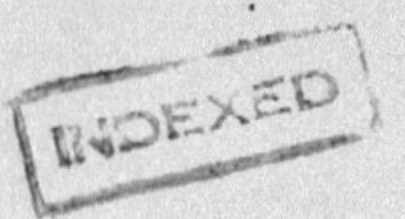

Dear Mr. Edwardes,

arture of erintendent of toms, Wenchow.

In accordance with Marshal Sun Ch'uan-fan's (孫傳芳) instructions Mr. Ch'êng Hsi-wên (程希文), Superintendent of Customs, left Wenchow for Hangchow and Nanking on the 8th instant and does not expect to be back soon.

ive Customs: lection of duty goods passing nt'ou: system of trol to prevent ud, approved. I.G. patch No. 1397/ ,292.

After receiving your Despatch No. 1397/108,292 I consulted the Superintendent and the Joint Notification re establishing a system of control for junks trading between Kuant'ou and Wenchow was issued on the 16th of August 1926. The Superintendent wanted in addition to the four rules approved by the Shui-wu Ch'u to state in the Notification that a duty on goods

H. F. EDWARDES, ESQUIRE,

Officiating Inspector General, ad interim,

P E K I N G

2.

204

goods exported from Kuant'ou outside 50 li radius is to be collected by the Kuant'ou office. Though I know that there is such a practice in existence I objected to recognise it officially on the ground that this question is a new one which was never discussed before and that I have no authority to make any arrangement with him in this respect. According to the Joint Notification bonded vessels only are allowed to trade between Kuant'ou and stations within 50 li radius. The junkmen carrying this trade came to me and stated that their trade is too small and that they cannot produce the required guarantee as there is no shop which is ready to chop the guarantees for them and proposed to give us their mutual guarantee. I told them that there is no objection on my part in accepting it if the Superintendent agrees. They petitioned the Superintendent, but the latter strongly objected to guarantee of such a

kind

204

kind and insisted on their producing guarantees signed by two reliable firms. Owing to this the whole traffic and trade between Wenchow and Kuant'ou was stopped for several days beginning from 1st September. Then the Superintendent in view of the impossibility of the junkmen obtaining proper guarantees proposed to me to find out another system of control on goods exported from Kuant'ou within 50 li radius for referring of it to the Shui-wu Ch'u. Evidently the system approved by the Shui-wu Ch'u does not satisfy the Superintendent and he is trying every means of doing away with it, therefore im my reply I explained to him that in view of the special circumstances the junkmen's mutual guarantees as proposed by them may be accepted as temporary guarantees. Privately I expressed my opinion to him that the Shui-wu Ch'u will be surprised if we are not able to settle such a small question locally. Eventually he agreed to this

4.

this temporary measure.

lera. I am glad to state that there were very few cases of cholera at Wenchow during the last week and the Customs doctor informed me that the disease had fallen below the epidemic stage. All ports having direct intercourse with Wenchow have been notified that the Quarantine Regulations in force against this port may be removed from 14th instant.

Please find herewith enclosed an interesting account taken from the local newspapers, of the religious ceremonies held by the people of Wenchow in connection with the cholera epidemic.

acy. Few days ago a Fukien junk was looted by pirates near Ping-yang (平陽). The laodah and 3 boatmen were wounded and brought here to Blyth Hospital for treatment. They gave information about the pirates to the Water Police and the Water Police gunboat "Hai-ping" left Wenchow for a cruise

on

3.

206

on the 11th instant. She came in touch with three junks with about 80 pirates near at San P'an (三 盤) and fought them for about a day. One of these junks with about a half the pirates escaped but the other two were eventually captured and taken in tow. A guard being placed on one of the junks only, while towing the junks one of them sank - the one without a guard on board. It was presumed that the pirates themselves sank her and they were all supposed to have been drowned. So the "Haiping" brought in the one junk and 14 pirates prisoners who were put on board the gunboat and were handed here over to the local authorities on the 13th instant.

Yours truly,

E. Bernadsky

207

AN ACCOUNT OF THE RELIGIOUS CEREMONIES HELD BY THE PEOPLE OF WENCHOW IN CONNECTION WITH THE CHOLERA EPIDEMIC.

In view of the seriousness of the cholera epidemic in Wenchow the local gentry carried out their proposal that Gods from the various temples should be taken in procession through the streets to drive away the Plague Demons. There was also held the ceremony called the Lo Tien Ta Chiao (羅天大醮) or "grand sacrifice to the spirits of the upper sky" at Tung-yo Miao (東嶽廟), where a shrine had been built to accomodate those Gods who had been taken through the city and others who had also been invited to attend. The object of this grand sacrifice to Gods was to beg them to drive the Plague Demons back to their homes, as it supposed that they had sent these Demons to destroy the people by cholera and other diseases.

To help the Gods to drive the Demons away, a paper ship with a wooden hull was also built, the intention being that this ship should be towed outside the harbour by a sampan and there burnt.

In

2.

In the ship were models of thirty-six of the city's shops and each shop was provided with a full complement of goods and furniture on a corresponding scale.

At the shrine dramas were held in honour of the Gods and the requisite ceremonies lasting seven days and nights from September 2nd - 8th were performed by the priests.

At midnight on the last night (September 8th) the ship was carried from the shrine to the Customs jetty by eight men followed by several hundred people. The crowd which followed kept up a fusillade of shouts to frighten and drive away the Plague Demons, supposed to have been confined in the ship by the Gods, who formed part of the escort.

When the ship reached the North Gate of the city, all lights except the one in the ship were extinguished. A sampan had already been ordered to hold itself in readiness at the jetty to tow the ship outside the harbour and burn it. To make that the ship reached its destination, a temple banner had been placed at the appointed place, and the sampan men had to produce this proof of service rendered,

before

3.

209

before they could claim their reward. A God was left on guard at the jetty till daybreak to prevent the return of the Demons.

All noises from firecrackers, musical instruments, gongs, etc., were forbidden for the day following. The ricksha pullers also were not allowed to ring their bells.

-42]

710

INSPECTORATE GENERAL OF CUSTOMS,

PEKING, 29th Sept. 1926.

ar Sir,

I am directed by the Inspector General orm you that your S/O Letter No. 372, 15th September, has been duly ed.

Yours truly,

Assistant Secretary.

ernadsky, Esquire,

WENCHOW.

INSPECTORATE GENERAL OF CUSTOMS,

201

S/O

PEKING, 23rd September 1926

Dear Mr. Bernadsky,

I have duly received your S/O letter No. 371 of 2nd September:

Complaints regarding examination and loading of cargo: Superintendent's proposal that reply to the petition from the merchants should be postponed till end of year.

Yes, wait till the end of the year.

Yours truly,

E. Bernadsky, Esquire,

WENCHOW.

CUSTOM HOUSE,

No. 373. Wenchow, 25th September 1926.

INDEXED

Dear Mr. Edwardes,

dsky's application ong leave.

To-day I have forwarded to you an application for one year of leave of absence. The financial difficulties owing to which I was not going to apply for this leave, as stated in my S/O letter No. 358 of the 8th May 1926, are not yet solved. But if I am not mistaken it is my duty to send this application for leave of absence to meet the Service requirements.

sion of lorcha s, I.G. Desp. 410/109 203.

The owners of lorchas have complained many times that their lorcha trade is very poor, and therefore I expect that they will take advantage of the permission to

F. EDWARDES, ESQUIRE,

Officiating Inspector General, ad interim,

P E K I N G .

2.

216

to trade as junks from Wenchow. But the typhoon of the 15th of August badly damaged here 8 of the local lorchas and till the present repairs have been completed, i. e. nearly up to the end of this year we cannot expect to see them trading as lorchas or junks.

Yours truly,

E. Bernadsky.

INSPECTORATE GENERAL OF CUSTOMS. 211

S/O

PEKING, 5th October 1926

Dear Mr. Bernadsky,

I have duly received your S/O letter No.373 of the 25th September:

Commissioner's application for long leave.

The reply to your S/O letter No.358 instructed you to let the I.G. know how much of your leave you wished to spend in the East. It would appear, however, from this letter under reply that you really do not want to apply for leave at all. I think you must have misunderstood the Circulars. Nobody is compelled to apply for leave. If you do not want your leave, you can apply officially to withdraw your application. If, however, you do want to go on leave and spend part of the

adsky, Esquire,

WENCHOW.

218

the leave in the East, you must give the information asked for in the I.G.'s letter of 27th May.

Yours truly,

CUSTOM HOUSE,

No. 374. Wenchow, 7th October 1926.

249

INDEXED

Dear Mr. Edwardes,

to Yang Kuang applied for.

On the 29th September Mr. Chang Kuei-jung (張桂榮) who is in temporary charge of the Superintendent's Office called upon me and asked me to help the Yang Kuang Chü (洋廣局) - the office collecting a local taxation on all goods which are brought to Wenchow by steamers. Up to now all the required information was obtained by them through one of the Customs brokers; but they found that such a system was not accurate and not very reliable, therefore the Head of Yang Kuang Chü applied to the Superintendent and asked him to make an arrangement with the Customs,

so

I. F. EDWARDES ESQUIRE,

Officiating Inspector General, ad interim,

PEKING.

2.

VW

so that the import and export figures which they required could be supplied by the Customs. I explained to Mr. Chang that I could not do this.

ts in connection Wanhsien affair.

Please find herewith enclosed, a copy of an article published in Sin Ngao Chao (新甌潮) of 26th September 1926 and the translation re Inauguration of the Association for strengthening the diplomatic situation in Wanhsien.

Yours truly,

E. Bernadsky

411

Wenchow S/O No. 374 of 1926.

Enclosure I.

News Published in "Sin Ngau Chao" (新甌潮) on 26th September 1926.

●組織萬案後援會開會紀

溫州學生聯合會、爲萬縣英人慘殺事件、昨晚(二十四日)假座永嘉縣商會召集各界開代表大會、討論組織溫州各界萬案後援及各種對付方法，到會團體、有十中學校教職員、十中第一院，十中小學部，甌海公學，女子師範、溫州中學、縣立女高、增爵各校學生代表、及溫州青年協進會，永嘉縣議會、溫州婦女協會、溫州女界國民會議促成會、中華基督自立會等，議決事項，(甲)組織溫州各界萬案後援會，(乙)對付方法、一、講演、二發表宣言、丙、通電、四、A、聲援四川同胞電、B，電四川楊森嚴重交涉、C、電北京外交部嚴重交涉，D、電國民政府外交部嚴重交涉、E電上海各報館轉電全國各界同胞等，關於第一次講演由各學校及各團體自行組織講演、時間至少十日、最後推舉金榮軒王亦文蔡雄林枚卲錦榮朱超等六人、組織幹事會云，送

222

Wenchow S/O No. 374 of 1926.

Enclosure II.

A translation of a news published in "Sin Ngao Chao" (新甌潮) dated 26th September 1926.

INAUGURATION OF THE ASSOCIATION FOR STRENGTHENING THE DIPLOMATIC SITUATION IN WANHSIEN.

In view of the slaughter at Wanhsien by the British Gunboats, the Wenchow Students' Union Association (溫州學生聯合會) held a meeting on the 24th September 1926 at the Wenchow Chamber of Commerce, in which delegates of the various circles were present. They discussed how to form an Association which will include all the grades of Wenchow people to back up the Wanhsien case and also what measures should be taken. Among those present were the teachers and students of the Wenchow 10th Middle School (十中學校) with their preparatory school students (十中小學部) and representatives of the Wenchow College (甌海公學), Wenchow Girl Normal School (女子師範), Wenchow Middle School (溫州中學), District Girl High School (縣立女高), French Missionary School (增爵學校) and many other schools,

and

223

and the Wenchow Young Men's Mutual Help-Giving Society (温州青年协进会), the Wenchow District Assembly (永嘉县议会), the Wenchow Women's Mutual Assistance Society (温州妇女协会), the Women's Society for urging the establishment of the People's Rehabilitation Conference (温州女界国民会议促成会) and the Independent Christianity Association of China (中华基督自立会), etc.

At the meeting they passed the following resolutions :

(a) to organise a Wenchow Public Association for backing up the Wanhsien case.

(b) Measures to be taken :

(1) speeches and orations.

(2) announcements of their attitude.

(c) Telegrams to be despatched to :

(1) backing up brethren at Szechuan.

(2) General Yang Sen (杨森) to urge him to deal with the question severely.

(3) the Ministry of Foreign Affairs at Peking to lodge a strong protest against the matter.

(4) the Canton People Government to take up the

3.

224

the question seriously.

(5) the various Shanghai newspapers Offices for conveying their decisions to all brethren of various grades of China.

Speeches and orations will be delivered voluntarily by the various schools and organisations at Wenchow for at least 10 days. Six members of those who were present at the meeting were elected to form a committee.

42]

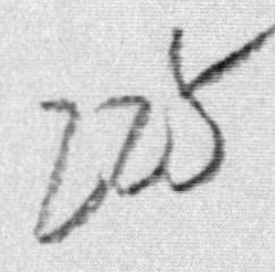

INSPECTORATE GENERAL OF CUSTOMS,

PEKING, 19th October 19 26

Sir,

I am directed by the Inspector General

rm you that your S/O Letter No. 374,

7th October, has been duly

d.

Yours truly,

Stanley F. Wright

Personal/Secretary.

~~Private Secretary.~~

adsky, Esquire,

WENCHOW.

CUSTOM HOUSE, 229

Wenchow, 11th October 1926.

INDEXED

Dear Mr. L. de Luca,

With reference to your Memorandum of the 1st October 1926, under which a list No. 9 of additions to the Customs "Private Telegraphic Code" was forwarded to Wenchow, I beg to state that on the page 6 of the list stated :

opposite YFXO .... Ebey, H. D,

but in the Private Telegraphic Code of this office the above place has been occupied by "Ehara, K." If no mistake has been made in the list No. 9, then kindly inform me of the place that is to be given to Ehara, K.

Yours truly,

E. Bernadsky

e Luca, Esquire,

Statistical Secretary, I. G.,

Inspectorate General of Customs,

S H A N G H A I .

S/O

INSPECTORATE GENERAL OF CUSTOMS,
STATISTICAL DEPARTMENT,

226

SHANGHAI, 14 October 1926.

My dear Bernadsky,

List no. 9 is correct!

Opposite:

YFXO .... Ebey H.D

YFZO .... Ehara, K.

is the right version. Someone must have made a wrong

in your copy code.

Yours sincerely,

[illegible]

CUSTOM HOUSE,

No. 375. Wenchow, 16th October 1926.

Dear Mr. Edwardes

ssioner's long
. I.G. S/O
r of 5th October.

I am very glad to know that I was wrong in my interpretation of the previous queries about taking long leave by me as well as of the spirit of the Circulars Nos. 3677 and 3678, and therefore to-day I am sending an application for a withdrawal of that one for long leave.

The reply to I.G. S/O letter of 27th of June was given by me in S/O letter No. 362, in which I stated that I was going to stay with my family two months' time in the East to help them to make arrangements for housing accommodation, etc.

Yours truly

E. Bernadsky

F. EDWARDES, ESQUIRE,

fficiating Inspector General, ad interim,

PEKING.

[42]

729

INSPECTORATE GENERAL OF CUSTOMS,

PEKING, 28th October 1926.

Dear Sir,

I am directed by the Inspector General to inform you that your S/O Letter No. 375, of 16th October, has been duly received.

Yours truly,

Stanley F. Wright

Personal Secretary.
~~Private Secretary.~~

...dsky, Esquire,

WENCHOW.

CUSTOM HOUSE, 250

No. 376. Wenchow, 20th October 1926.

Dear Mr. Edwardes,

-ture of Marshal
troops from
-ow.

On the 16th instant at about 10 p. m. the Commander of the local garrison (駐温警備隊統帶) received telegraphic instructions from the Governor of Chekiang province to disarm non-Chekiang troops at Wenchow and to send them out of this province. On receiving this telegram the Commander sent a message to the Officer in charge of Marshal Sun Ch'uan-fang's troops and invited him with the fully armed soldiers to come to the compound of the local garrison wherefrom they all jointly would go to the South gate of the city to keep there order, as it was expected to be a certain action at that place

F. EDWARDES, ESQUIRE,
Officiating Inspector General, ad interim,
PEKING.

2

231

place that night. The Officer to whom this message was addressed took 18 out of his 20 men and immediately proceeded to the place requested where they were surrounded by the local garrison and disarmed. They were informed of the telegram received and were equipped with $ 10 each, including those two soldiers who were left on duty and could not come to the compound and sent to Shanghai by S. S. "Haean" on the 17th instant in the morning.

On the morning of the 17th instant Mr. Chang, who is in temporary charge of the Superintendent's Office, whose Office was guarded by Sun Ch'uan-fang's troops, called upon the Taoyin and Commander of the garrison to find out the situation. He was informed that there was no news except the telegram in question. He telegraphed to the Superintendent - who is Marshal Sun's man - and asked him to return to Wenchow. The Superintendent replied

that

3

252

that the political situation was changed now and that he was temporarily living in Shanghai. Evidently he is not coming back to Wenchow as he asked Mr. Cheng to send him at Shanghai all his belongings and to continue to work as before.

Yours truly,

E. Bernadbug

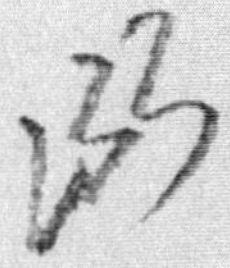

[42]

INSPECTORATE GENERAL OF CUSTOMS,

PEKING, 29th October 1926.

D[ear] Sir,

I am directed by the Inspector General [to] in[fo]rm you that your S/O Letter No. 376, [da]te[d] 20th October, has been duly [rec]eiv[e]d.

Yours truly,

Stanley F. Wright
Personal Secretary.

[...]adsky, Esquire,

WENCHOW.

CUSTOM HOUSE,

239

No. 377. Wenchow, 25th October 1926.

Dear Mr. Edwardes,

in connection
the political
nt at Hangchow.

On the 23rd instant Mr. Chang Kuei-jung (張桂榮) who is in temporary charge of the Superintendent's office notified me privately that on the 22nd instant he received a telegram from the Superintendent in which the latter stated that the Governor of Chekiang Hsia (夏) had fled, that everything was normal again and that he would be back at Wenchow soon.

In connection with this political movement, please find, enclosed herewith, (i) a copy of the translation of the joint proclamation issued by the Wenchow Taoyin and the Commander of the Precautionary Force and

(2)

F. EDWARDES, ESQUIRE,

Officiating Inspector General, ad interim,

P E K I N G .

2.

240

(2) a copy of a proposal by the local missionaries for information of their Consuls.

Yours truly,

E. Bernadsky

Wenchow S/O No. 377.

241

ENCLOSURE NO. 1.

The following is the translation of the joint proclamation issued by the Wenchow Taoyin and the Commander of the Precautionary Force.

A small change took place in the political situation in Hangchow but the situation has now been restored to its former condition. Peace and order are maintained as usual. On the 22nd instant, a telegram was received from the Commander of the First Chekiang Division, Ch'en I (陳儀) to the effect that he has been appointed Acting Civil Governor of Chekiang by Marshal Sun. As soon as he hands over charge of the Division, he will proceed to Chekiang from the front. From this point of view, it is evident that the situation is now in normal, as a responsible man has been appointed to take over the Administration. Consequently rumours will automatically have ceased to spread. As Wenchow is far away from the provincial capital, news received here is comparatively rather out of date. It is feared that many people in Wenchow do not know that Marshal Sun's government has been definitely restored

in

2.

742

in Hangchow, and it is to these people, who might be wrongly informed that this proclamation is specially addressed. All the merchants and people are expected to respect peace and order and to carry on their daily life as usual. They should pay their taxes and dues as usual and not pay the slightest attention to remours, which attention might result in their punishment.

Wenchow S/O No. 377.

ENCLOSURE NO. 2.

Wenchow, Oct. 25th 1926.

The recent Declaration of the Independence of Chekiang by Hsia Chao revealed a state of things in Wenchow which we think should be brought to your notice.

As soon as the news came to Wenchow the local section of the Kuomingtang, which up to that time had held its sessions in secret, began to hold them in public, and for the first time the thoroughness of the preparations of the organisation for taking control of the city and district was revealed to the people generally. The Student Association, the chief supporter of the Kuamingtang, wished to proceed to extreme measures which included in regard to foreigners the following;-

1. Britishers to be given to the end of the month to leave Wenchow.
2. No British goods to be bought.
3. No British ships to be travelled in.
4. No British cheque or banknotes to be used.
5. No politeness to be shown to British Commissioners of Customs.
6. No food to be supplied to Britishers.

7.

2.

264

7. No service to be given to Britishers.

The Kuomingtang and Students Association asked the the local officials for confirmation of the news of the Declaration of Independence before proceeding to carry their programme into effect and were advised to wait a little. When the news of Hsia Chao's flight and the reassumption of control by Sun Chuan Fang was received the Kuomingtang retired into obscurity again.

Sufficient information has however come to light since the event to make it evident that in case of Sun Chuan Fang meeting with a reverse, Wenchow would, for a time at any rate, be in the hand of the local Kuomingtang, the Students' Association and a band of the most unruly elements of the city and that foreigners would be cut off from all communication with outside.

The local officials have not the means to keep the Students' Association and all the unruly elements that will be attached to it in check, and before responsible officials could take charge much damage might be done.

42]

14-5

INSPECTORATE GENERAL OF CUSTOMS,

PEKING, 8th November 1926

Dear Sir,

I am directed by the Inspector General to inform you that your S/O Letter No. 377, dated 25th October, has been duly received.

Yours truly,

Stanley F. Wright

Personal Secretary.

~~Private Secretary.~~

Madsky, Esquire,

WENCHOW.

CUSTOM HOUSE,

No. 378

Wenchow, 8th November 1926.

INDEXED

Dear Mr. Edwardes,

ts in connection
political
ment at Wenchow.

The Commander of the local Garrison Lü Ho-yin (吕和音) in accordance with the Hangchow authorities' instructions surrendered charge on the 6th of November 1926 to his successor Liu Po-p'ing (刘伯屏) and on the same day Mr. Lü started with his family for Chüchow (處州), his native place. This replacement was the result of the disarmament by Mr. Lü of Marshal Sun's troops and their despatch to Shanghai.

f. (a) 19 days' leave of absence has been granted by me to Mr. C. Finch, Assistant Examiner, A, from 3rd to 21st November to proceed to Shanghai to meet his wife, who is

. F. EDWARDES, ESQUIRE,

Officiating Inspector General ad interim,

P E K I N G .

2.

247

is expected from England next week. Mr. Finch told me that he would be glad to return to Wenchow as soon as he could get a passage back after Mrs. Finch's arrival at Shanghai. During his absence Mr. G. E. Cross, Acting Tidesurveyor, will look after the Examination Office.

(b) Mr. B. S. Abramoff, 3rd Class Tidewaiter, who is transferred to Tientsin has been detained here up to the middle of November, as it is desirable that the Native Customs here should be left without a foreign officer for as short a time as possible.

Bureau opened functions at how

Please find, herewith enclosed, a copy of Provisional Regulations for a Consumor's Tax - and its translation - of Wine Bureau on Foreign Wine, established here from the middle of October. A copy of the translations of these regulations will be attached to the Trade Report for the December Quarter of this port, but as it may

3.

may be of some interest to you I forward them to you now.

Yours truly,

E. Bernadsky

Wenchow S/O No. 378.

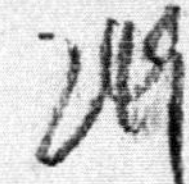

Enclosure.

TRANSLATIONS OF PROVISIONAL REGULATIONS FOR A CONSUMER'S TAX ON FOREIGN WINES.

(1) All merchants trading in Foreign wines within the province of Chekiang are hereby notified of the imposition of a tax on imported foreign wines to be levied according to a fixed tariff of a similar manner to those on cigarettes and native wines.

This tax is an indirect tax on the consumer, who will be to a certain extent restricted in his use of these luxuries.

(2) This tax will be collected by the various Heads of the Wine and Tobacco Bureaus, assisted by their subordinates.

(3) The Tariff for this Tax is being drawn up separately.

(4) Wines, which pay a tax according to this Tariff, must have wine revenue stamps affixed to all bottles containing them irrespective of the size of same. The stamps are being issued by the Head Bureau in 9 denominations, viz. \$0.50, \$0.40, \$0.30,

\$0.20

2.

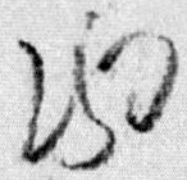

$0.20, $0.10, $0.05 $0.01, $0.02, $0.03.

(5) All merchants within the province of Chekiang trading wholesale or retail in foreign wines, whether or not they already possess a license must obtain from their local Bureau a license to sell foreign wine. No fee will be charged for this license, but $0.20 will be charged for a supplementary issue in case of loss.

(6) Those who forge wine Revenue Stamps, or use stamps, which have already been used, will be punished according to the law dealing with the forging of valuable documents.

(7) Infringement of these rules and regulations will entail a fine. A list of these regulations and the penalties for breaking them is given below.

(8) The office allowance for collecting this tax shall not exceed 20% of the proceeds.

(9) These rules and regulations will be enforced, as soon as they have been sanctioned by the Commander-in-Chief of the five provinces, Tupan and Sheng Chang of Chekiang.*

(10)

---

*The regulations were duly approved by the provincial authorities and enforced in Wenchow from October 15th 1926.

24

(10) These rules and regulations are subject to modification and amendment.

RULES AND REGULATIONS FOR COLLECTION.

(1) When foreign wines are imported, each package will be examined by representatives of the local Bureau who will keep a record of the various kinds imported, and their quality and quantity. Taxes will be levied on these according to the Tariff. When the tax has been paid, the corresponding stamps will be issued to the merchants and must be affixed to all bottles exposed for sale, including even the smallest, so that it can be easily discovered whether or not the proper tax has been paid.

(2) The stamps must be pasted over the mouths of the bottles, and on them the vendors must stamp a chop bearing their name, so that half the chop is on the stamp and half on the bottle.

(3) Bottles of wine imported before the introduction of this tax must have stamps affixed to them before they can be sold.

(4) Both vendors and buyers of foreign wines must give free access to all officers sent by the

Bureau

252

Bureau to make sure that the tax has not been evaded; but the officers will not be allowed to extort money through excessive hindrance of trade, or they themselves will be punished.

(5) Information concerning an evasion or false declaration may be given by any one.

(6) When a seizure is made of foreign wines uncovered by stamps, the owners will be dealt with as is laid down in the "Fines Regulations", and a Certificate giving particulars of the fine will be issued to them.

The proceeds of the fines will be allocated as follows: 50% will be paid to the informant, 25% to the Revenue, and 25% as office allowance to the office in which the case is tried.

If the seizure is made without information received, 50% will be paid to the Revenue, 25% to the office in which the case is tried, and 25% to seizing officers.

(7) Magistrate and police authorities are required to render their utmost assistance, when called upon, and they are equally responsible with the Bureau in preventive work and in attending to the investigations resulting from seizures.

(8)

253

(8) The above rules, if found unsatisfactory are liable to any changes or additions that the authorities may see fit to make.

FINES REGULATIONS.

(1) Offenders convicted of breaking § 1 of the "Provisional Regulations for a Consumer's Tax on Foreign Wines" by not paying the required tax, shall besides paying a full tax be dealt with as follows:

(a) for first offence, 1-5 times tax.
(b) for second offence 5-10 " "
(c) for each additional offence. 10-15 " "

(2) Offenders convicted of breaking § 1 by resisting examination shall besides complying with the procedure as laid down in § 1 be fined as follows:-

(a) for first offence $ 50-500
(b) for second offence $100-700
(c) for each additional offence $200-1,000.

(3) Offenders convicted of breaking § VII by not affixing to the bottles the requisite value of stamps, shall pay a full tax, and in addition a fine of three times the tax.

(4)

254

(4) Offenders convicted of breaking § IV by resisting the officers of the Bureau shall be punished twice as heavily as is laid down in § 2 of the Fines Regulations.

(5) Officers on duty having cognisance of an offence against the four rules mentioned in the "Fines Regulations" and failing to report it, shall, if the offence is not serious, be dismissed and reprimanded, but if the offence is a serious one, shall be brought before a judicial court.

(6) Offenders convicted of simultaneous offences against 2 rules shall be punished for both such offences.

TARIFF.

Name.	Value per dozen.	Value per bottle.	Tax per bottle.
Brandy	$ 21.00	$ 1.75	$ 0.35
Brandy	$ 22.50	$ 1.87	$ 0.37
Brandy	$ 18.60	$ 1.55	$ 0.30

Claret

7.

255

TARIFF (continued).

Name.	Value per dozen	Value per bottle	Tax per bottle.
Claret or Hock	$ 6.60	$ 0.55	$ 0.11
Claret or Hock	$10.00	$ 0.84	$ 0.17
Curacoa	$21.00	$ 1.75	$ 0.35
Champagne	$21.00	$ 1.75	$ 0.35
Peppermint Wine	$18.00	$ 1.50	$ 0.30
Beer Tsingtao	$ 3.00	$ 0.25	$ 0.05
Beer, Japanese	$ 3.00	$ 0.25	$ 0.05
Beer, Peking	$ 3.00	$ 0.25	$ 0.05
Whisky	-	$ 2.90	$ 0.58
Whisky	-	$ 2.60	$ 0.52
Vermouth	-	$ 1.15	$ 0.25
Vermouth	-	$ 1.25	$ 0.25
Port Wine	-	$ 1.50	$ 0.30
Port Wine	-	$ 1.00	$ 0.20
Sherry	-	$ 1.50	$ 0.30
Gin	-	$ 1.40	$ 0.28
Claret or Red Wine	-	$ 1.20	$ 0.24

Note: There are very many kinds of wines. In future taxes on any new kinds of foreign wines will be levied on them in proportion to their values. Alcohol and spirits of wine are not mentioned in the above table, as they have been already taxed according to a fixed tariff, which was approved by the authorities last year.

浙江菸酒事務局徵收洋酒稅價格稅率一覽表

牌名	西文	每打價格	每瓶價格	稅率
三星白蘭地	BRANDV	二十一元	一元七角五分	三角五分
象頭白蘭地	BRANDV	二十二元五角	一元八角七分	三角七分
廣東三星象頭白蘭地	BRANDV	十八元六角	一元五角五分	三角一分
廣東葡萄酒	CLARET Or HOCK	六元六角	五角五分	一角一分
葡萄酒	CLARET Or HOCK	十元	八角四分	一角七分
口利沙	CURACOA	二十一元	一元七角五分	三角五分
香賓酒	CHAMPAGNE	二十一元	一元七角五分	三角五分
薄荷酒	PEPPER—MINT WINE	十八元	一元五角	三角
青島啤酒	BEER	三元	二角五分	五分
太陽啤酒	BEER	三元	二角五分	五分
五星北京牌啤酒	BEER	三元	二角五分	五分
紅為四開	WHISKEV		二元九角	五角八分
哈末為四開	WHISKEV		二元六角	五角二分
法凡姆酒	VERWOUTH		一元一角五分	二角三分
意凡姆酒	YERMOUTH		一元二角五分	二角五分
元芳波德文	PORT WINE		一元五角	三角
[illegible]	[illegible]		[illegible]	[illegible]

257

浙江菸酒事務局徵收洋酒稅罰金條例

第一條　違犯本章程第一條之規定不依則納稅者除責令照章納稅或補稅外處罰如左

（一）初犯者照正稅處以一倍以上五倍以下之罰金

（二）再犯者照正稅處以五倍以上十倍以下之罰金

（三）所犯在二次以上者照正稅處以十倍以上十五倍以下之罰金

第二條　違犯稽征規則第一條之規定不服檢查者除責令補照規定手續辦理外處罰如左

（一）初犯者處以五十元以上五百元以下之罰金

（二）再犯者處以一百元以上七百元以下之罰金

（三）所犯在二次以上者處以二百元以上一千元以下之罰金

第三條　違犯本章程第七條之規定不依法寔貼印照及貼不足數者除責令補納正稅外照三倍處罰

第四條　違犯稽征規則第四條之規定有抗拒情形者比照本條例第二條第一二三項加倍處罰

第五條　稽征人員當執行職務時遇有前四條之違犯行為知情故縱者輕則撤懲重則交法庭究辦

第六條　一人而犯本條例二條以上者各依本條併科處罰

258

浙江菸酒事務局徵收洋酒稅稽徵規則

第一條　凡洋酒入境時應由各該地所設之征收機關逐件檢驗記明品名數量按照稅則表之規定征稅發給印照粘貼於最小容量之賣罌上以為納稅之識別並發給查驗單備考

第二條　印照應寔貼於封口開合處並於容器及印照上騎蓋本店之圖章

第三條　凡各商店原有存貨應補購印照一律粘貼方准發售

第四條　各地征收機關所派稽征人員執行職務時商人買户不得反抗稽征人員亦不得有需索留難情弊致干懲處

第五條　遇有漏稅或報稅不足私行發售者無論何人皆得告發

第六條　凡經人告發及稽征員查獲之無印照洋酒查照罰則分別辦理並掣給受罰人罰單一聯

此項罰金分為十成有告發人者以五成獎之二成半歸公二成半歸處罰機關為津貼辦公之用經稽征員查獲者以五成歸公二成半歸處罰機關二成半給查獲之人

第七條　稽查偷漏暨執行處罰及其他一切事務有需縣知事警察協助時各縣知事警察應極力協助同負責任

第八條　本規則如有未盡事宜得隨時呈請改正之

259

浙江菸酒事務局徵收洋酒稅暫行章程

定於民國十五年九月實行

第一條　凡在浙江境內營銷洋酒之商人應仿照捲菸特稅暨酒類門銷捐例一律照稅則表征稅此稅間接取諸買戶寓禁于征之意

第二條　此項洋酒稅收暫由各區分局長督率稽征員辦理

第三條　此項洋酒稅則表另定之

第四條　凡依稅則納稅之洋酒須于最小之容器上實貼印照其印照分為五角四角三角二角一角五分一分二分三分九種由省局製造發行

第五條　凡在浙江境內營銷洋酒之整賣商及零賣商不論有無門銷牌照均須向所在地徵收機關領洋酒營業執照

前項執照不收費但遺失毀損補換時每執照一紙應繳印刷費二角

第六條　偽造印照或曾經貼用揭下再貼者應查照刑律偽造有價証券條例論罪

第七條　違犯本章程及各種規則者處以罰金

前項罰金條例另定之

第八條　辦理此項洋酒稅之征收機關應需各項辦公經費共計不得超過稅收銀百分之二十

第九條　本章程及各項規則條例俟呈准總司令聯帥省長核定後公布施行

第十條　本章程及各項規則條例如有未盡事宜得隨時提出修改

Wenchow S/O No. 378.

Enclosure.

PROVISIONAL REGULATIONS FOR A CONSUMER'S TAX ON FOREIGN WINES.

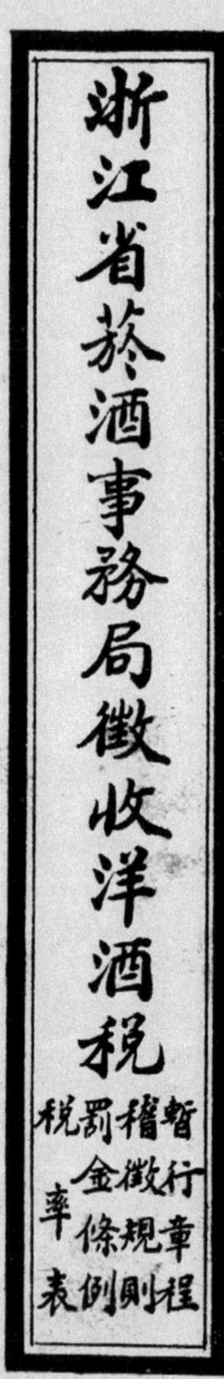
浙江省菸酒事務局徵收洋酒稅

暫行章程
稽徵規則
罰金條例
稅率表

[2]

261

INSPECTORATE GENERAL OF CUSTOMS,

PEKING, 26th November 1926.

Dear Sir,

I am directed by the Inspector General to inform you that your S/O Letter No. 378, dated 8th November, has been duly received.

Yours truly,

Stanley F. Wright

Personal Secretary.

~~Private Secretary.~~

...sky, Esquire,

WENCHOW.

CUSTOM HOUSE,

262

No. 379

Wenchow, 20th November 1926

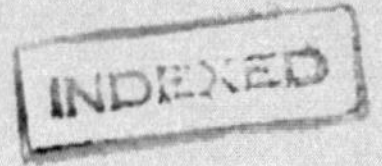

Dear Mr. Edwardes,

...e Customs
...sed petition
...ise scale of

In the second part of October last a joint petition from the Lushih, Examiners and Watchers of the Native Customs was presented to me with a request that I would ask you to consider a general revision of pay to cope with the ever increasing cost of living. The reasons given in the petition were

(1) They have been carrying on their dities faithfully and efficiently at all times even in times of anxiety for which they have reveived the Inspector General's recognition;

(2) The treatment accorded to the Maritime Customs employees such as the general

increase

F. EDWARDES, ESQUIRE,

fficiating Inspector General *ad interim*,

PEKING.

263

increase in pay in July should be similarly extended to them as both Maritime Customs and Native Customs employees are under the Inspector General;

(3) The work in the Native Customs is more complicated and the hours longer than in the Maritime Customs, while their pay has long been lower than the Maritime Customs employees'; and

(4) In view of the general increase in pay lately effected all round in the Postal, Telegraph and Maritime Customs Administrations their case should meet with sympathetic consideration.

They informed me also that similar applications have been forwarded to Peking by the Wuhu, Shanghai and Santuao Native Customs and asked me to support their petition. I took their petition the item by item and explained to them that all the reasons given by them were not sound enough for

forwarding

3.

264

forwarding this petition to you with my favourable support and taking in consideration that the revision of Native Customs scales took place from 1st June 1925 I am of opinion that the petition is the product of some agitation only. I gave them time to reconsider their application and to inform me if they wanted their application to be sent to you. Now the Assistant-in-charge of the Native Customs has informed me that the petitioners want to withdraw the case.

Yours truly,

E. Bernadsky.

270

INSPECTORATE GENERAL OF CUSTOMS,

PEKING, 9th Dec. 1926.

ir,

I am directed by the Inspector General

you that your S/O Letter No. 379 ,

20th November , has been duly

Yours truly,

Stanley F. Wright

Personal ~~Private~~ Secretary.

adsky, Esquire,

WENCHOW.

CUSTOM HOUSE,

o. 380 Wenchow 29th November 1926.

271

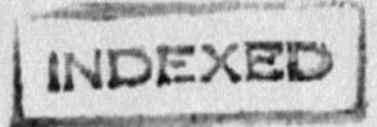

Dear Sir Francis,

l Law at
w.

According to Marshal Sun Ch'uan-fang's (孫傳芳) instructions the Commander of the local Garrison declared Wenchow to be under martial law from the 17th instant.

In examining the regulations to be imposed under Martial Law as sent to me by the local Military Authorities I have found that Officers in Command

(a) have the right to prohibit export of any cargo required for military use at any time when it may be necessary and that

(b) they are ordered to station soldiers and police at the wharves for searching purposes,

therefore

RANCI AGLEN, K. B. E.,
Inspector General of Customs,
PEKING.

2.

272

therefore I have instructed the Customs staff to take all possible precautions to avoid any friction with the military and to report to me any unusual steps taken by them at the wharves.

ches containing low phosphorus, cases of: re-ortation of to ce of original pment authorised G. Despatch No. 8/104,761) but not take place.

On the 19th instant I and Mr. Chang Kuei-jung (張桂榮) who is in temporary charge of the Superintendent's Office discussed the question of the non-re-exportation of the 80 cases (three shipments = 8,000 gross, value Hk.Tls. 1,600) of those phosphorus matches which were imported here just after the 1st of July 1925, and which, though permitted to be re-exported to Shanghai - the place of original shipment (I.G. Despatch No. 1348/104,761 of the 17th September 1925), were not re-exported there despite our urging. Now as I was going to enforce the bonds - under which the cargo was allowed to be discharged into godown - equal to Hk.Tls. 1,600, the owners of this cargo petitioned the Superintendent and me

requesting

3.

273

requesting the return of the bonds without enforcement, as the cargo was damaged and rendered valueless by the Wenchow climate. I told Mr. Chang that I cannot accept the explanation stated because the applicants had had enough time to re-export the matches before they became damaged and also because I cannot be certain that the cargo is damaged as the applicants did not inform me at the proper time. But the Superintendent requested me to postpone enforcing the bonds as he is going to write to the Shui-wu Ch'u and ask them to treat this case leniently. Of course I agreed.

Yours truly,

E. Bernadsky

265

Phosphorus Matches imported into Wenchow from Shanghai after 30th June 1925.

Date of importation	Name of Vessel	Applicant	No. of Tins	(Nominal Boxes)	No. of Gross	Value, HK.Tls.
1925 July 3	Lorcha Chin Tung Fa	Chi Chi Hsin	240	(20)	2,000	400.00
" 27	" Chin Yung Li	" " "	240	(20)	2,000	400.00
" 15	[illegible]		"		"	

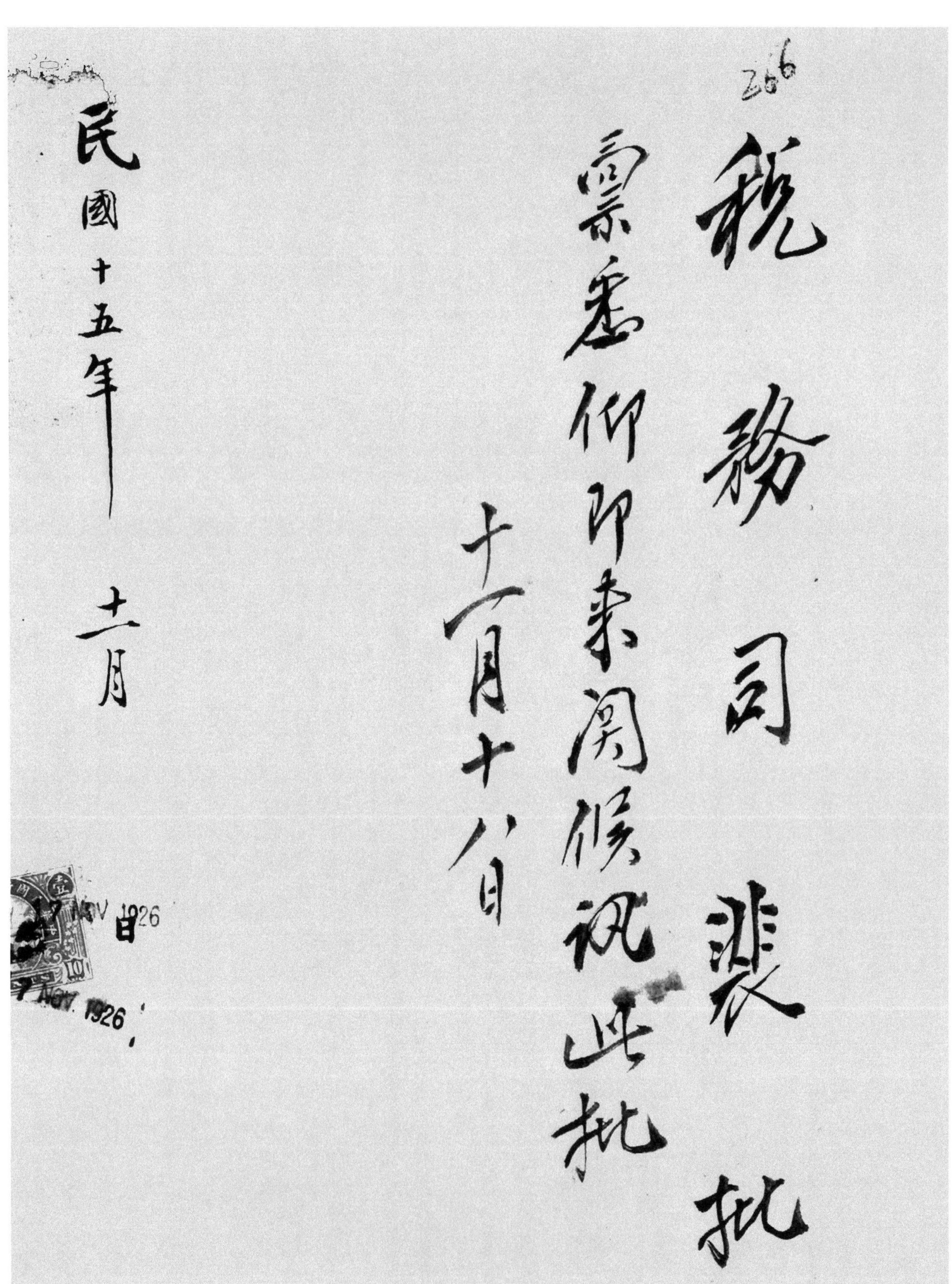
266

税務司 裴 批

禀悉仰即录闵候视此批

十一月十八日

民國十五年 十一月 日

17 NOV 1926

變通办法、奉諭將大柴暫停存放西門外炭棧內、不料去
秋七月間颶風大雨、所存大柴被濕、加重霉爛、當即稟報
本關監督在案、續將稍好之大柴揀取轉存南門外益泰源
棧內、因斯時天熱炎蒸、所存大柴發熱燒燬、無留確可查
察、況所剩霉爛火柴已成廢物、尚可試驗、伏查商等對于所
办火柴、奉諭存棧、迭遭風雨霉爛、又被燒燬、損失鉅大、事
隔年餘、苦況不可言狀、不得已瀝乞
稅務司大人察核、恩准垂憐、曲體商艱、懇請給還、俾結、誠為鄉商、
感德無涯矣、謹稟

7 NOV. 1926

具禀商民孫萼卿、胡瀛甫 協豐號 王薈芝

為奉諭暫留之火柴，除遭風雨霉爛及被燬外所剩殘物，確可試驗，瀝乞恩准從寬給還，保結而卹商艱事。竊商曾於去年四月間向上海購辦砂火八十箱，于六月間分裝恒興、永利、同發三尾船運甌，但裝辦之時，未蒙鈞關嚴禁期間之內，其所有火柴均經遵章完納正稅出口，待開駛之後，因天時不佳，在途遲延，直待七月一日後方可抵甌，到埠時，據關員云火柴禁期已届，囑商退還申埠等情。彼時各船正在停秋修理之際，無船可裝，且此項火柴係由現銀辦來，再加在艙日久，概受霉爛，無法退還申，不得已請求甌海關

CUSTOM HOUSE,

275

/O No.381.

INDEXED

Wenchow, 11th December 1926.

Dear Sir Francis,

roposed stoppage
China Merchants
eam Navigation
mpany shipping.

It appears that on account of interference by military and sea-men's union the China Merchants Steam Navigation Company is going to stop running its ships "Haean" and "Kwangchi" between Shanghai and Wenchow. The local China Merchants Steam Navigation Company Agent and several of the Wenchow merchants left for Shanghai to try to charter these ships for themselves.

aff.

10 days' leave of absence from 10th to 19th instant has been granted by me to Mr. R. W. Cholmondeley, 4th Assistant, A, to proceed to Shanghai for dental treatment.

I and my family send you Christmas greetings and all good wishes for the New Year.

Yours truly,

E. Bernadsky

R FRANCIS AGLEN, K. B. E.,

Inspector General of Customs,

P E K I N G .

CUSTOM HOUSE,

277

No. 382.

Wenchow, 23rd. December 1926.

Dear Sir Francis,

uation at Wenchow.

The first news of the approach of 3,500 retreating soldiers from the Fukien province (Shangtung troops) reached Wenchow on the 12th instant. The local population accepted this news as that of the advance of enemy forces and panic spread throughout the city.

December 13th-15th. Several meetings were held by the officials, gentry and merchants to discuss how to divert these soldiers from Wenchow or how to deal with them if diversion proved impossible. A Protection and Peace Bureau (保安事務所) was organised and the owners of property and merchants were classed

FRANCIS AGLEN, K. B. E.,

Inspector General of Customs,

PEKING.

6.

278

classed into several grades for contributing to meet the expenses of feeding these soldiers and of forwarding them on their way.

The local students were afraid of coming into any friction with the soldiers and left their schools; and the result was that all the middle schools were closed.

In spite of some posters issued by the local authorities requesting the people not to be alarmed by the arrival of the soldiers from Fukien, the middle and upper classes began to desert Wenchow for Ningpo and Shanghai and the poorer classes, afraid of being conscripted by the soldiers as coolies to carry their luggage, rushed into the interior.

On the 15th instant Mr. Suzuki, the Agent of Mitsui Bussan Kaisha called upon me and asked if the foreigners were going to take any steps in connection

with

3.

271

with the expected arrival of the soldiers. I told him that as far as I knew no question of taking any precautionary measure had been discussed by foreigners at Wenchow. But if the Commissioner for foreign affairs should inform me that the foreigners here ought to take some steps to protect themselves, then all the foreign community including Japanese would be informed by me at once. Then Mr. Suzuki informed me that the local officials (Taoyin, Commander, and Magistrate, etc.) asked him very privately to allow them to take refuge in his house in case of trouble and that the Japanese community wanted to ask the Japanese Government to send here a gunboat for their protection.

16th December. The Acting (temporary) Superintendent of Customs informed me privately that the movement of soldiers is proceeding in perfect order and that he does not expect any trouble from them for

4.

280

for foreigners or Chinese. He also told me that he is going to discuss with the military authorities concerned the questions of issuing badges for the recognition and protection of the Customs employees.

18th December. Mr. Lü Ho-yin (吕和音), the former Commander, who recently was dismissed by Marshal Sun, arrived by the Ningpo steam launch and tried to take charge of the local garrison. It was explained to him by the local officials that it would be dangerous for him to do so in a view of the approaching soldiers from Fukien. Accordingly he together with his soldiers left Wenchow and went inland.

The first lot of the expected soldiers arrived at night and found quarters in one of the local temples.

The Acting (temporary) Superintendent of Customs called upon me and asked me to detain steamers in port for the transportation of the soldiers. I explained to him

that

5.

281

that I had no right to do so, if the ship's papers were in order. And in further conversation I expressed my opinion that if the two ships in port should be detained by force then the question of the transportation of the troops could not be settled satisfactorily, as these ships can take only a small part of the soldiers, but that if the Chamber of Commerce was ready to cover the transportation expenses then we could soon expect some more ships here to take away the remaining part of the soldiers Whether it was for this or for any other reason I am glad to state that the ships left Wenchow in due time without interference from anybody.

19th December Japanese destroyer "Aoi" arrived at Wenchow at 10.30 a. m.

20th December. The captain of the "Aoi" called upon me and stated that in case of emergency he is able to land 30-40 sailors to protect foreigners, provided they

282

they assembled in one place. I told him that at present there was no reason to expect any trouble, but that in a case of trouble the Custom House was the place where all the foreigners and the Customs staff would be assembled.

<u>23rd December</u>. (a) The French Gunboat "Alerte" arrived at 1 p. m.

(b) Mr. Suzuki, Agent of Mitsui Bussan Kaisha, told me this morning that the military authorities of the newly arrived troops had asked him if he would be able to supply them with a Japanese ship to transport the soldiers and that he had come to ask my advice about it. I referred him to his Consul.

(c) The Acting (temporary) Superintendent of Customs informed me privately that 20 thousand soldiers are expected to come to the Wenchow prefecture from Fukien province.

(d) Practically all business at

Wenchow

7.

283

Wenchow is at a standstill. About half the population have left Wenchow for the country.

Yours truly,

E. Bernadsky.

-42]

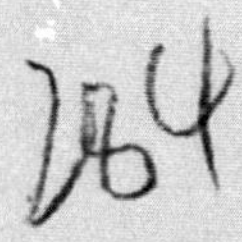

INSPECTORATE GENERAL OF CUSTOMS,

PEKING, 18th January 1927.

r Sir,

I am directed by the Inspector General

orm you that your S/O Letter No. 382,

23rd December, has been duly

ed.

Yours truly,

Stanley F. Wright

Personal Secretary.

Private Secretary.

dsky, Esquire,

WENCHOW.

INSPECTORATE GENERAL OF CUSTOMS, 214

S/O

PEKING, 24th December 1926

Dear Mr. Bernadsky,

I have duly received your S/O letter No.380 of the 29th November:

Phosphorus Matches, for whose re-exportation to Shanghai special permission had been granted, have not been exported: Commissioner intends to enforce bond but Superintendent states that he is writing to the Ch'u and requests postponement of the enforcement.

Nothing has been heard as yet from the Ch'u on this matter.

Yours truly,

[signature]

nadsky, Esquire,

WENCHOW.

CUSTOM HOUSE, 285

No. 383. Wenchow, 31st December 1926.

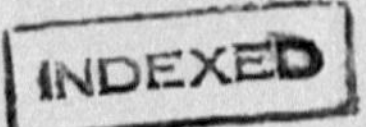

Dear Sir Francis,

uation at chow.

25th December. Japanese destroyer "Kiku" arrived from Formosa.

26th December. (a) Chinese gunboat "Chao-wu" arrived from Shanghai. The vessel brought foodstuff for the newly arrived troops here.

(b) The military authorities established patrols over the city. The former police disappeared from the streets.

(c) The gates of the city began to be shut from evening to daybreak.

27th December. (a) French gunboat "Alerte" and Japanese destroyer "Aoi" and "Kiku" left port for Shanghai.

(b) The soldiers started to conscript

coolies

FRANCIS AGLEN, K. B. E.,

Inspector General of Customs,

PEKING.

2.

286

coolies and ricksha-coolies to carry soldiers' luggage on the latters' way to Taichow (台州), Ch'ü-chow (處州) and Pingyang (平陽) - North, West and South of Wenchow respectively. Practically all the sailing boats have been commandeered by the military.

28th December. (a) Chinese gunboat "Chao-wu" left Wenchow for Shanghai with about 400 sick soldiers on board.

(b) Acting (temporary) Superintendent of Customs asked me privately to allow him and his family to take refuge in the Custom House in a case of trouble in the city. Certainly I agreed.

31st December. (a) Up to the end of the year about 10 thousand soldiers from Fukien passed Wenchow; and about 9 thousand of them left Wenchow for different places in the North, West and South.

(b) Japanese gunboat "Uji" arrived here at 10 a.m. The vessel on her

way

3.

287

way from Japan to Formosa had been aground near Snipe Island (about 21 li from Wenchow) since the night of the 29th instant. The Captain of the ship requested help from the Harbour Master to get the vessel off. The No. 1 Pilot went with the Captain and arranged for cargo boats, etc. to lighten the ship and then when the vessel was off brought her to Wenchow for fresh water.

Yours truly,

E. Bernadsky.

42]

INSPECTORATE GENERAL OF CUSTOMS,

PEKING, 12 Jan. 1927.

Sir,

I am directed by the Inspector General

rm you that your S/O Letter No. 383,

31st December, has been duly

d.

Yours truly,

Stanley F. Wright

Personal ~~Private~~ Secretary.

rnadsky, Esquire,

WENCHOW.

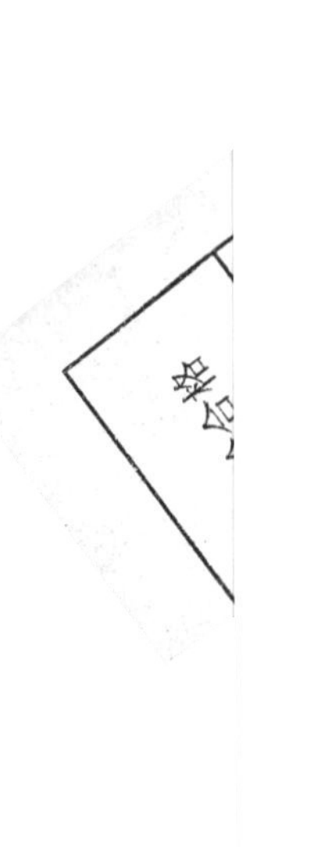